Comm...

"A wise and dear friend of mine once said the treatment of people with intellectual disabilities is the truest test of humanity in any society. Beth Porter's book is a beautiful and touching description of how L'Arche meets that test. She quotes Jean Vanier, the founder of L'Arche, throughout the book. In his doctoral dissertation on Aristotle, *Made for Happiness*, he described the elements which lead to happiness as friendship, pleasure, and the attempt to live justly and truthfully. This book brings this happiness to life in an eloquent and detailed description of several decades of community living in several L'Arche homes in southern Canada. To read it is to deeply feel the joy and belonging of these experiences and to realize a new meaning of humanity."

Right Honourable David Johnston, Governor-General of Canada, 2010–2017

"I was humbled and inspired by Beth Porter's account of her first encounter with L'Arche in 1980 and of her life with members of the organisation over the years. It is a book that will enrich the lives of all who read it."

James Bartleman, 27th Lieutenant Governor of Ontario

"Through engaging stories of life shared over nearly forty years in L'Arche, Beth reveals honestly the challenges of community and the grace of walking with others in daily life and even towards death. While this is Beth's unique story, others both in and outside L'Arche will surely find encouragement here to invest in authentic relationships and work with deep purpose."

Stacey Cates-Carney, Vice International Leader, L'Arche

"Beth writes with great simplicity and a deep love of the 'folks' in her L'Arche community who so 'comfortably folded her into their life'. She tells the stories of the small, repetitive events of everyday life in L'Arche which when entered into with a contemplative attitude, reveal the depth of love and relationships so many people in L'Arche are enriched by. Her stories are particular to Daybreak, yet any member of L'Arche anywhere will see the echoes in their own community lives: the humour, the fun, the faithfulness and deep trust."

Hazel Bradley, former International Events Coordinator, L'Arche, and member since 1989

"Beth is close at our side in this book, as she shares her story of the 'accidental friendships' that emerge through her L'Arche experience, leading her deeper into self-knowledge and selfless attention. What Beth discovers is no less than the transformative relationships that create true community. Beth's story is a model for us all in discovering the significance of our ordinary, imperfect humanity. Getting in touch with our real selves can hold the key to becoming more truly attentive to the other."

Mary Kelly Robison, Benedictine Oblate of the World Community for Christian Meditation

"In Beth Porter's stories of community living, relationships are both mundane and profound. Daily irritations can become moments of healing. Beyond our assumptions about persons with developmental challenges, we see spirited individuals of depth and humour. Each sacred story deepens the sense of God's presence, challenges beliefs, and ultimately enriches our life."

Rev Dr Abigail Johnson, United Church of Canada (retired minister)

"Growing up, my first home was shared with core members in L'Arche. I was born into community and remain connected in different ways. It was my radical formation in L'Arche that paved the way to my profession. From my youth I understood that we are all vulnerable and that we all have gifts, that impairment is a natural part of our world, and that those most pushed aside – those labeled as having intellectual disabilities – make our world a richer place. Our family lived these truths intimately.

"Beth captures this life in a real and laid-bare way: how the mutuality of life in L'Arche has formed and shaped so many in truthful and nourishing ways that allow us to live and simply "be" differently in our broken and difficult world. Her book is a rare mix of vulnerability and beauty that tells us about life lived in a full and complex way!"

Jessica Vorstermans, Professor, Critical Disability Studies, York University, Toronto

"Beth has a gift for empathic listening and close observation of people's everyday lives. Her book thus succeeds where so many attempts have fallen short, to capture the resplendent, enticing individuality of people living with an intellectual disability. Beth's stories paint us a colourful, emotionally vivid picture of human particularity so that we feel like we are right there at the dinner table with David, Peggy, Gus, and can easily imagine what it felt like to be laughing and sharing a meal with them.

"She also has a beautiful way of articulating how surprising this can be to people who haven't spent time with them before, because our cultural history and contemporary focus on economic productivity tend to devalue them and treat them as a group, not specific, unique persons. Yet she does not dwell on this as a problem but moves gracefully forward with how the surprise can become a naturalized skill of discovering each person's full humanity with time and experience within the embrace of a supportive community like L'Arche. Her engaging stories take up universal themes of every heart such as finding good friends, a sense of belonging and a meaningful life, as well as grappling honestly with changes life throws at us via loss, conflict and rejection."

Pamela Cushing, Disability Studies Chair, King's University College at Western University, Ontario

"Through the art of story-telling, *Accidental Friends* encapsulates the significance and discovery of community as the coming together of people under a strong, common purpose. Beth graciously reflects this idea through personal experiences and engaging accounts of her time with the L'Arche Daybreak community, and the people who deeply impacted her life. This book is a true testament to the power that support and acceptance has in breaking down barriers and valuing people for who they truly are."

Marc Kielburger, co-founder of the WE movement of young people wanting to make the world a better place

"I have been associated with L'Arche communities since my stay at Trosly with Jean Vanier. In the decades since then I have witnessed their communities of vulnerability celebrating living together with their joys and struggles. Beth Porter's stories capture the range and depth of such a life with an integrity and a sense of wonder at what is possible when we can recognize the brokenness in each of us and can commit ourselves to accompanying each other in that human spirit."

Monty Williams, S.J., author of *The Gift of Spiritual Intimacy* and *The Way of the Faithful*

"This book reflects the passion that I know Beth has from her years of work for L'Arche Canada. She has worked tirelessly to make accessible to all the social and spiritual vision that recognizes and values each person's gifts. Her faithful dedication to communicating this message led her to create a variety of means to share it with people of all ages. Her integrity and faithfulness to her friends is a model for all."

Hollee Card, National Leader, L'Arche Canada, 2009 to 2018

"For years Beth Porter's gift as a writer of exquisite insight was on display in 'A Human Future', a thought sheet which provided insight into the values and thinking associated with L'Arche. She has brought the same talents to *Accidental Friends* only this time through the lens of her own relationships within L'Arche.

"And what a feast she has produced – a feast that rivals the flavours, playfulness and pure joy associated with legendary L'Arche meals. *Accidental Friends* is history as it should be written. It's a tender chronicle of the precious interactions of so-called ordinary people. Their lives, loves, sorrows, wisdom, and vulnerabilities reveal our common humanity and the significance of each and every life. Our world is richer because of the wonderful people Beth introduces us to. Your life will be richer by reading her book."

Al Etmanski, author of *Impact: 6 Patterns to Spread your Social Innovation*

"L'Arche is an ongoing miracle of the age. An island of compassion in a sea of indifference, L'Arche is a refuge for society's intellectually disabled who are cared for, energized to their potential and loved. Beth Porter has seen the magic of L'Arche from the inside. She tells its story and hers with insight, great good humour and a loving understanding of our responsibility to one another."

Michael Enright, host of *The Sunday Edition*, CBC Radio

"I have long been proud that L'Arche Daybreak is located in Richmond Hill. I always enjoy attending events there and am inspired by their commitment to being part of the wider community. At their Art Show openings and gala evenings at our Richmond Hill Centre for the Performing Arts, I meet again my friend Darryl, who lives in one of the Daybreak homes. For their 40th anniversary gala they created an imaginary town. My second most favourite 'Town' continues to be 'C'est La Vie,' with its Mayor Darryl."

David Barrow, Mayor of the Town of Richmond Hill

Accidental Friends

Stories from My Life in Community

Beth Porter

DARTON·LONGMAN+TODD

First published in 2019 by
Darton, Longman and Todd Ltd
1 Spencer Court
140 – 142 Wandsworth High Street
London SW18 4JJ

"L'Arche" is a registered trademark.
Royalties from sales of this book will be donated to L'Arche.

ISBN: 978-0-232-53387-3

A catalogue record for this book is available from the British Library

Phototypeset by Kerrypress Ltd, St Albans, Herts. AL3 8JL
Printed and bound in Great Britain by Bell & Bain Ltd., Glasgow

For the people of L'Arche,
and for all who long for community and a place of belonging

And in memory of Joe Child,
beloved community member and friend.
July 1942 – February 2019

Contents

Author's Note

This is a work of creative non-fiction. Mainly, I have used actual first names and, sometimes, second initials or surnames, either for clarity or because this is the way others customarily refer to these people. A very few events, names, and details of identities are blended or changed. I have given or read the longer portions about named individuals who are alive to these people, and I have received the individuals' approval. If people are no longer living, sometimes I have been able to locate a family member and have given or described the relevant portions to them and incorporated any feedback they offered.

I hope this book will give the reader some sense both of our life together and of the uniqueness of the individuals about whom I have written. On the whole, the L'Arche assistants are minor characters here, but Henri Nouwen had such a significant impact on our community and on my own life during his ten years as our pastor that he seemed to require a separate chapter. In telling these stories I am trusting in a dictum I heard often from this famed priest, writer and Yale and Harvard professor, that what is most personal is often most universal.

I wrote this book because it was begging to be written. In some ways it is an expression of my gratitude for the many rich experiences during my life at L'Arche over nearly four decades, and a tribute to some of the wise and wonderful people I lived with or came to know well. They and our life together have changed me. I recount portions of my life in L'Arche, and especially in Daybreak, that were formative for me or stand out in my memory. Someone else would write a different book, but I hope what I have written conveys some of the joys and challenges and rewards of our life in community. I could have gone on for many more pages had I included all the people and all the aspects of daily life that have touched and shaped my life. Of those I have not named or whose contributions I have treated inadequately, I ask their understanding. I am grateful for them all.

A Note about Language

Within L'Arche, we sometimes refer to ourselves as "people of many different abilities sharing life together." At times, however, more precise language is needed. Terminology to identify people who have intellectual disabilities (in the United Kingdom, learning disabilities) has changed frequently in recent decades, as what had seemed respectful, or neutral, repeatedly became laden with negativity. The word "retarded" had largely been abandoned only a decade or so before I came to L'Arche, and the term "mentally handicapped" was still common. I use the "people first" language generally preferred today, so "*people with* intellectual disabilities" rather than "intellectually disabled people" or, worse, "the intellectually disabled." Internally, since the late-1980s, L'Arche in North America has most often described its members with intellectual disabilities as "core members," conveying that they are at the heart or core of the community. Those who help are "assistants."

L'Arche is French for "the Ark," referring to Noah's Ark. Early L'Arche communities such as Daybreak chose unique names, but today most take the name of the city or area where they are located and preface it with the word "L'Arche." In urban areas, L'Arche homes are often designated by their street names, thus "Church Street" for the house on Church Street. I use "Daybreak" and "L'Arche" and "L'Arche Daybreak" interchangeably. In places, "L'Arche" can also be understood as the international network of communities. Thus, when I refer to L'Arche values, I mean values embraced by all L'Arche communities.

Foreword

Accidental Friends will find its echo in the experiences of many families and friends of people who have an intellectual disability and among people in L'Arche communities around the world. Beth's experience in L'Arche stretches back to the beginning of the 1980s. She tells stories of community life – some humorous, some poignant, some containing surprises, others with lessons for us. All reveal in some way the gift of sharing life with someone who has an intellectual disability and the certainty that each person is precious. Many of her stories are about people whom I remember from my visits to L'Arche Daybreak over the years – Michael, Peggy, Francis, Annie, Roy, Gord, Helen, Big George.

As Beth notes, her stories are mainly from the time when she was daily engaged in Daybreak's community life, but she brings the book up to the present with the stories of Michael and Ellen, whom she continues to accompany today. The core members who have passed away have each left a wonderful legacy in their humour, courage, creativity, and deep love for those they lived with in L'Arche. Their stories will continue to be told and passed down.

I am touched also by the stories of the assistants, who come as young people seeking a direction for their lives and develop lasting bonds with certain core members. Sometimes the entire course of their lives is shaped by their experience in L'Arche. I am similarly touched by the faithful long-term friendships of former assistants and others from outside L'Arche, such as Steve, George's musician friend, who simply enjoyed being with George and introduced George to his hockey team. George enriched all of their lives because Steve could see his gift.

I am glad that Beth included Joe Egan's story of interviewing Greg while Greg was still living in the enormous institution where he spent his childhood and youth. I remember well visiting such institutions in the 1960s. What a fruitful life Greg has lived because he had the opportunity to find a home outside the institution!

I chuckled when I read the stories about Helen. And I recall the question that Thelus asked me, "Why do assistants leave?" and the pain I knew was behind this question, and the silence in the room after she asked it. She asked this on behalf of all those who have struggled to bless and send off the young people who come to share our life together for a time. It is difficult to say goodbye to people we have loved and have perhaps nurtured into fuller adulthood. Thelus grasped what I said about her vocation being to teach them about love and then to send them off to live what they have learned. She drew strength from this knowledge as the years continued to unfold. At the same time, it is so important that L'Arche has assistants who stay, and Beth's stories reveal this also.

When I am writing or speaking, I often include stories I have heard or witnessed. Some seem like parables. I sometimes tell the story of driving from the airport in Santiago, Chile, into the centre of the city. We took a road that separated two very different communities — on one side an enormous slum and on the other a neighbourhood of very expensive homes. The driver explained that no one from either side ever crosses this road. This little story captures for me the deep disconnect of our world, in which the poor and the rich rarely meet, and even more rarely come to know each other. It carries a challenge for all of us.

Poverty takes many forms, and those who live in L'Arche with people who have intellectual disabilities, especially those with deep emotional wounds, know this. It is not easy to be with a person in great anguish. We feel inadequate. Often for young people today the great fear is of being humiliated, of not being able to cope, of shame. Life in L'Arche teaches that it is okay not to have it together. It is the people who have disabilities who reveal this to us.

Beth has particular gifts in writing, and her love for L'Arche and its people shines through this book. These stories can invite us into reflection on our own interactions and experiences.

Jean Vanier
L'Arche, Trosly–Breuil
France, 2018

Daybreak Farm Property, by Jo Cork (1983)

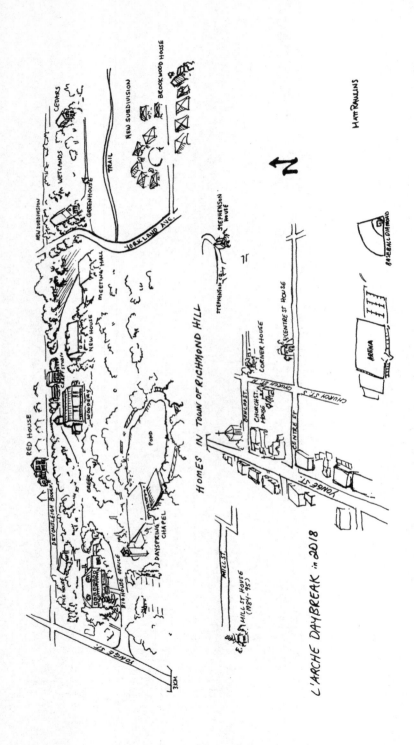

Homes in town of Richmond Hill and L'Arche Daybreak, by Matt Rawlins (2018)

Introduction: The Attraction of Community

*[Aristotle's] fundamental question is not "What ought we to do?" but
"What do we really want?" His ethics are not those of law. Rather they
look closely at humanity's deepest inclinations in order to bring them to their
ultimate fulfillment. Aristotle's ethics are not therefore based on an idea but
on the desire for fullness of life inscribed in every human being.* Jean Vanier

"When they scored, he would rap his cane on the glass. At the end of the game, win or lose, he would shake every team member's hand." As his bassoonist friend Steve Mosher recounted at George's funeral, the Gustav Mahlers hockey team (formed by a group of musicians who played hockey) had never met anyone like George. "They'd see him struggle to get out of the car and make it into the arena and they saw that he was there for them. To say that George was an inspiration would be an understatement. He got them in the heart." When George died, the team met at their favourite sports bar to reminisce about their friend and to thank Steve, their fellow player, for introducing them to George and bringing him, year after year, to their games.[1]

When I was thirty-five, I read a book that changed my life. The book was about community. This present book is also about community. More particularly, it is about some of my experiences over nearly forty years living in a L'Arche community with people such as George, who had an intellectual disability, and with other assistants and friends, such as Steve. In the 1990s, I helped out in our community's Seniors Club. There, each of the seniors was in the process of preparing a life story book. This was much more than a photo album. Each book was a large three-ringed binder containing letters from friends and family members describing special moments spent together, and also the seniors' own memories to the extent they were able to express these. The life story book provided a means of "life review" and a way for each person to savour and claim the goodness of his or her life. In a sense, this book is my own life story album of some of the moving and sometimes humorous moments I have experienced in L'Arche, and some of the remarkable people I have come to know and whose friendship I treasure.

Interest in community grew greatly in the 1960s, when many grassroots communities sprang up. Many communities of that era did not last, but L'Arche has endured and expanded around the world. Why? I think because the people who have intellectual disabilities, with their combination of needs and gifts of welcome and of living wholeheartedly in the present, call each person to engage with them, and thus they create an atmosphere in which community life can thrive. They have shaped one another's lives and the lives of countless others over the years. From them, I have learned much about myself and about what is really important in life.

For a community to be successful, its communal life must be good for all its members. No one would stay long if they did not discover themselves to be growing and receiving as well as giving. L'Arche has a process for both core members (those with disabilities) and assistants to discern whether the community is a good long-term fit for them. At the same time, many young assistants come just for a year or two before pursuing further studies or a career. They bring new life and they come to know themselves better and grow in confidence and competence. Of course, as in any community, there are antipathies, and mistakes are made. Decision making and communication may be poor at times. Those who stay find that the community's shortcomings are tempered by fulfilling relationships.

I belong to a particular L'Arche community, as does everyone in L'Arche, but L'Arche is also a movement, and, today, it is an international federation of many communities located in thirty-eight countries on five continents. All share a common vision and adhere to a common Identity and Mission statement. Communities are composed mainly or entirely of people from the geographic areas where they are located. They live according to the local culture, and they seek to be good neighbours, well integrated into the wider community.

∽○∾

Today in Western countries there is renewed interest in community.[2] Each person or family needs to discover for themselves the place of belonging that best suits them. Residential communities take various forms. Some, but not by any means all, have a faith base or shared ideology. The kibbutzim of Israel come to mind, as do co-housing groups or co-ops that have a shared financial interest and also a common commitment to the arts or to ecological practices or to social justice issues. Their members may pursue occupations outside their shared living environment. Some contemporary religious communities include married couples as well as celibate members. Some are closed traditional communities, such as the Hutterites, or cloistered communities of Christian or Buddhist contemplatives. Some traditional religious communities may have associate members or oblates, who live their spirituality "in the world." Some communities have a small, stable core of people and welcome many guests to live their spirituality and communal life on a temporary basis or in small groups in far off places. One might think of the Iona community in Scotland, which has a far-flung network of associate members, or Plum Village, the Buddhist community founded by Thich Nhat Hanh in France, or Bonnevaux, the new centre for the World Community for Christian Meditation inspired by Dom John Main's teaching. Those who offer a non-residential way of belonging require a less intense commitment. They may meet regularly to study or meditate or work on their particular concerns. Whatever form they take, the communities that last seem to be those where care for one another is a value, and where people are bound together by a strong common purpose.

Some residential communities that have a social justice focus also have a faith base, as do L'Arche communities, which are ecumenical or interfaith, and Camphill, which has communities similar to those of L'Arche but based on the philosophy of Rudolph Steiner. L'Arche communities have short- and longer-term assistants and confirmed

3

members with and without disabilities who do not plan to leave. Some members, but not all, live in community homes, and some may be married. Some may have a full-time engagement in a day program or in administration. Each L'Arche community also has friends (such as George's friend Steve), who may, over time, become associate members.

In the early days in France, most people in L'Arche were Roman Catholic. In Western countries where L'Arche is established, "faith-based" has long implied an ecumenical community based in the Christian faith, but from its beginnings in the 1970s L'Arche in India included people of the Hindu, Christian, and Muslim faiths. In other parts of Asia and in Africa and the Middle East where L'Arche exists today, it is likewise diverse, and now more and more in the West, people in L'Arche may come from a variety of religions or embrace no religion. Assistants' willingness to respect the faith life of the community and to support the faith of core members, whatever this may be, is key. Today, my community, L'Arche Daybreak, describes itself as "non-denominational and interfaith."

I hope that this book will be an enjoyable read in itself, that for some readers it will contribute to the discovery of community, and, for some, it will lead to the enrichment of new connections with people with intellectual disabilities. A healthy society needs and benefits from all of its members.

1. Labour Day[1]1980: A first encounter

Can we reasonably have a dream, like Martin Luther King, of a world where people, whatever their race, religion, culture, abilities or disabilities, whatever their education or economic situation, whatever their age or gender, can find a place and reveal their gift? Jean Vanier

I had arrived at the Green House (painted forest green) only minutes before, and I was seated in its homey living room on an orange wide-wale corduroy couch of the sort popular in the mid-1970s. To my right, halfway along the couch, was Peter, whom I thought to be about my age. He seemed a man of few words. Peter began shifting gradually closer to me as Joan, who was ensconced in an easy chair across the room, described their household and the plan for my visit – dinner and then a walk over to one of the other houses on the L'Arche Daybreak farm property. When Peter was close enough, he reached out his hand and touched my hair, which in those days fell over my shoulders. It was an interesting experience. I was certainly not afraid of or upset with him. It seemed clear that he was simply curious. I said something kind of dumb, like "Is it soft?" Peter complied with Joan's instruction to "give Beth some space," while to my left a young man entered the room with three or four large photo albums that tumbled out of his arms as he knelt on the floor in front of me.

This was Michael, I learned, and he wanted to show me pictures from his recent L'Arche vacation and photos of his family, particularly his brother, Adam. In spite of a speech impediment, Michael made me understand that Adam could neither walk nor talk and that he, Michael, was very keen that his brother should move to Daybreak. From Joan, I learned that Adam, who had grown too big for his parents to care for at home, now lived in a long-term-care hospital. There, a coterie of family and friends visited the young man to help him eat and get him out of bed so that he had some exercise each day.

Before dinner, I also met Francis, a voluble fifty-year-old who seemed speeded up in everything he did and consequently was continually dropping things – notebooks full of loose paper, magazine pages, pencils, markers. He talked so fast that I could not get what he was saying most of the time. I met Josie, who would soon be returning home to Australia to help with L'Arche there. And I met Lloyd and Phil, who cooked our dinner. I was told I would meet Peggy later. She would arrive home having already eaten, after spending the Labour Day weekend at her family's cottage.

We were eight when we all sat down at the large dinner table. The cooks were at the head of the table. Lloyd said grace (the familiar "For the food we are about to receive..."), and he and Phil served the meal – chicken and baked potatoes and squash from the large garden – designating the person for each plate as they were passed around. No one picked up their cutlery until everyone had their dinner. While we waited, I noticed certain features that Jean Vanier recommended in *Community and Growth*, the book that had led me to want to visit a L'Arche community. For example, care had been put into making the table attractive. At its centre was a bouquet of pink and mauve cosmos, doubtless from the flower bed outside the front door. Each person had her or his own cloth napkin in a different-coloured napkin ring. I had one labeled "Guest" in bold marker. A large bowl of green salad and a jug of water for refilling our glasses sat towards the end of the table. The seating, I soon grasped, was planned so that anyone who needed support to cut their food had an assistant beside them.

On the one-hour drive up to Richmond Hill from downtown Toronto, I had been wondering what people with intellectual disabilities liked to talk about. Would they have watched the news or read the weekend newspaper? Did they in fact read? I had never actually met anyone with an intellectual disability. As it turned out, there was no problem finding conversation topics, but the evening news certainly did not enter in! During the meal each person was invited to say something about how their day had been and what they had done. In addition, I heard, among other tales, the story of Michael's having gone missing during a wedding on the farm the previous summer and how, during a panicky search of the property by all present, Francis had proudly discovered him in the chicken coop that occupied one end of the large barn. Mike, as he told me he liked to be called, had wandered off and then apparently had a "spell." The older man seemed to have a kind of fatherly regard for Mike, and Mike called him Cowboy, a nickname that pleased Francis, who loved watching Westerns, I learned. But at this moment Francis was preoccupied with something he wanted to purchase – film, it seemed – for his camera. I gathered he took many pictures but often in haste, so he tended to cut off people's heads or tilt the camera to odd effect. He had recently signed up with Phil for an evening course in photography to be offered at a local high school.

Dinner proceeded slowly as some people needed more time to eat and others kept pace with them. Lloyd was silent and seemed withdrawn or a little sad until Phil nudged him and said that the ice cream we were to eat for dessert probably came from the milk of Jersey cows, since they had the best milk. Lloyd suddenly sat up tall, his face reddening, and cried out, "Hey! That's not true! Holsteins have the best milk!" And he smiled. Sometimes it was difficult to catch what individuals were saying. So far, I had mainly listened, but now I felt I could risk asking Lloyd why Holstein milk was better. With a little help from Joan, he explained that he had lived all his life on his family's Holstein farm, working with his aged father until his mother and then his father died. The family farm had been sold and Lloyd had moved to Daybreak about five years earlier. It must have been a heartbreaking time, I thought to myself.

The dining room of the Green House was the largest room in the house – a common feature of homes that L'Arche itself designed, I later learned. Its size signified the importance of mealtimes. The front door opened almost directly into the dining room, with only a short, wide hallway with a closet to hang coats. Near the end of the meal, the door burst open and Peggy entered, accompanied by her nephew, a tall, red-haired young man who carried her suitcase into one of the main-floor bedrooms. They were warmly greeted, and I was introduced, though no one left the table. Peggy was well spoken and clearly a woman of some dignity. She was about fifty, it seemed to me.

After dessert and a big pot of tea, a candle was placed on the table and everyone sat in silence for what seemed quite a long time. Finally, one person and another expressed a wish or a prayer or thanksgiving for something. What seemed to me another interminable silence ensued, and then on some signal I did not catch, everyone took the hands of those next to them, Lloyd said in his raspy farmer's voice, "Our Father . . . ," and all more or less joined in the Lord's Prayer. Francis ran ahead, repeating many of the phrases twice or three times as he waited for others to catch up. Mike, who could not keep up with even the relatively slow pace, echoed the last word or sound of each line:.... heaven...name... come...done...bread...passes...others...-ation... evil...-dom... glory...-ver....-men."

As the table was being cleared, Phil suggested that Lloyd show me his recipe book, since, as cooks, he and Lloyd would not be doing the dishes. The three of us walked down to the small TV room on the lower level to look at it. It was a loose-leaf book with drawings and pictures clipped from magazines. Each recipe step was numbered, the small amount of printing was simple and bold, and arrows and large numbers were used to indicate the settings for the oven and timer. Lloyd had recipes for two major meals: chicken – the meal we had just eaten – and pork chops with applesauce. Each was accompanied by a salad, baked potatoes, and a vegetable, which might be fresh or frozen. (They froze many bags of vegetables from the garden, Phil explained.) Lloyd also had directions for one simple meal: meat pies with a vegetable. For this, he used frozen meat pies from the supermarket. This was a meal for days when preparation time was short. I had noted on the bulletin board near the telephone a list showing who was cooking with whom and who was doing laundry with whom each day of the week, always an assistant paired with one of the "folks," as I was hearing Joan and Phil call those with disabilities.

After the dishes, Joan walked me along the farm lane and answered my two pressing questions: what length of commitment was asked of assistants, and did they receive any pay or just room and board? I learned that new assistants came for a three-month trial period or *stage*, to use the French word often heard in earlier days for short stays in L'Arche. (I soon discovered there were a number of "French-isms" in L'Arche lingo.) Assistants took one twenty-four-hour day away each week and one weekend each month. After the three months, if they wanted to stay, they were asked to make a one-year commitment beginning the upcoming autumn; that is, assuming they seemed a good fit from the community's point of view. That arrangement would suit me well. Three months seemed a good amount of time, and the monthly pay – at that time about $250 after room and board was deducted – was more than I would need to maintain my car, cover my Ontario Health Insurance, and spend on my time away. (They preferred to speak of "time away" rather than "days off," I learned, because the latter was the language of employment, not of sharing life in community.)

Joan told me a bit about herself. She was a registered nurse and had come to the community soon after graduating. She would be leaving, as she was engaged to be married the following spring to an assistant named Robin, also a nurse, who lived in one of the houses for more independent people, located in downtown Toronto. He was presently completing an additional nursing qualification. Likely, Phil would be asked to become the next house leader. I estimated the age of both Joan and Phil to be no more than twenty-five.

The Green House was one of three homes on the L'Arche Daybreak farm on the northern fringe of the Town of Richmond Hill. When I had turned in to the farm property, a couple of hours earlier, I had stopped at the large old red-brick house near Yonge Street. There, Gus, who was the assistant community leader, had met me and given me a brief orientation to the property. This house, with its impressive two-storey, south-facing wooden porch, was known as the Big House. It housed offices, a meeting room, and a chapel on the first floor, and on the second and third floors, a household of a dozen people. When I commented that each of a row of what I assumed to be bedrooms on the second floor had a door onto the upper porch, Gus explained that years earlier the house had been used as a convalescent home for nuns who had contracted tuberculosis. The patients could readily be wheeled out to take the fresh air and sunlight. In 1969 the Big House and the farm buildings and several acres had been given by a small order of nuns[1] who were touched by the vision of Jean Vanier and wanted to see L'Arche established in Canada.

I knew very little about L'Arche apart from what Jean Vanier had written about community in a more general sense in the book I'd read. I had heard him speak several years earlier in a crowded university auditorium. I was touched by the simplicity and power of his message about the injustices suffered by those who were most easily marginalized in our society. At that time, his life with people with intellectual disabilities had seemed unimaginable to me. However, I had returned with friends to hear him a second night. As one of my friends commented, "He had eyes like vacuum cleaners!"

I called Gus to ask if I might visit, and he had set up my invitation to dinner. He had accompanied me down the farm lane as it curved past a pond and a woodlot, over a creek, which I later learned was a tributary of the Rouge River, then up a slight hill and past a large green barn and other farm buildings, a sizable vegetable garden, and a pasture where cows and sheep were grazing. On our right after the barn, we passed one other house, the New House, so named, Gus told me, because it was the first house built after the Big House became overcrowded. The Green House was in fact a newer house, but no one proposed changing the name of the New House. Beyond the Green House, Gus explained, was the farm manager's bungalow, hidden by some cedars, and then there stretched to the east, as far as the Canadian National main railway line, a hundred acres of leased farmland.

On our after-dinner walk along the farm lane, Joan and I met David strolling and smoking his pipe. He lived in the Big House, he said. His hand was a bit shaky, and even as we talked he was frequently striking matches and relighting his pipe. He asked me about myself and nodded knowingly when I mentioned that I was an English teacher. Then he segued to a story about when he was in the war. The story seemed plausible to me, and I wondered whether he had been in Vietnam and had been injured, but when I asked him which war, he responded, "The Boer War." "Oh," I said, trying to recover and meet him where he was, "one of my great-aunts was a nurse in the Boer War." But David had lost that focus and drifted dreamily on along the road. Much later I learned that David participated in military re-enactments with some men from his church and hanging in his closet he had a wearable replica of a uniform from the American Civil War.

When Joan and I came to the New House, almost everyone in the house gathered around wanting to shake my hand. Anne Marie plied me with questions – Did I have any kids? Did I have brothers or sisters? And Thelus told me she would be baking pies the next day. The front door of the New House led to a mud room lined with coats and farm boots and then, as in the Green House, to a large dining room with a big square table surrounded by a dozen chairs. The room reminded me of a Shakespearean set in that it had a second-floor balcony with a wrought-iron grille overlooking the dining room. It might invite anyone who was about to descend the stairs from the second-floor bedrooms to pause, look below, and perhaps utter some proclamation.

Jo, who was the house leader, mentioned that there was a member of their house whom I could not meet at present as a nurse was helping him. His name was Bill Rous and he was bedridden with Alzheimer's disease – in fact, he had been so for quite some time. I could tell by the way she and others spoke of him that Bill was someone important to them in spite of what, it seemed to me, must have been significant limitations. Jo suggested that if I made a return visit during the daytime I should come by and sit with him for a few minutes. This was evidently something that others in the community did regularly.

At the end of our walk, we returned to the Green House, where I said goodbye. Michael had the final word: "I w-want you to come *back*!" he declared, doubling his volume on the last word.

∽०∾

Thinking over the preceding few hours as I headed south along Yonge Street, I was struck by how relaxed I had felt during the entire visit. I normally like to know exactly what I am doing and

11

what is expected of me, but from the moment I walked into the Green House, I was charmed, enchanted almost in the magical sense, and I was content to go with the flow. I was profoundly moved by the people I met and the life they lived together. I think they themselves created the openness in me by the way they welcomed me. It was as though they were already comfortable folding me into their life. I had no feeling of being evaluated, such as one could expect on first visiting a community where one might be a prospective member.

Driving north a few hours earlier, I had thought of the people with disabilities as "they" or "them," assuming they were other and very different from me. Now I found it difficult to think of the "folks" in this way. They were Peter and Michael and Peggy and Lloyd and Francis, and they were not so different from me or anyone else at the Green House table, even if more limited in their life options. I recalled my conversation with Gus at the beginning of my visit. He was informative about the physical aspects of Daybreak, but when I asked him what attracted the assistants (as I knew the helpers were called), he remarked only that L'Arche is a mystery — hardly a satisfying response for my fact-oriented mind, but one that I would ponder.

As I drove, I reviewed some of the key moments that had brought me to that day. I was thirty-five and had taught for ten years. I had moved through a couple of romantic relationships, knowing that I could not marry anyone who did not share my desire to engage in some kind of social justice work, and I felt more and more that I wanted to do this from a faith base.

My outlook was deeply shaped by the idealism of the 1960s — the sense that our generation really could change the world for the better. I did not have much of a religious background. I had grown up in a liberal Protestant family who attended church sporadically while I was in school. But I think I had a kind of spiritual hunger from early on. At one point as a child I was quite touched by hearing the Twenty-third Psalm read aloud, and I decided to memorize it. If it was really true, I told my childhood self, I would be totally fine, whatever life held! Later, as I began liberal arts studies at university, I conceived a great desire to know more about what I called ultimate reality. Back then, in my late teens, it had seemed to me that I needed to figure out the meaning of life before I could decide on my life's direction. "Does God exist?" was my driving question for some of those years. While English literature was my main academic focus, I took courses in history, anthropology, and the psychology of religion and read William James and Aldous Huxley, Evelyn Underhill, Rudolf Otto, Pierre Teilhard de Chardin, C. S. Lewis, the Bhagavad Gita, the Upanishads, books on Buddhism and Hinduism, and James Frazer's anthropological study of the Adonis myth. (Was Christ a kind of fertility god who died and rose again each spring?)

As soon as I finished my undergraduate degree, I had headed overseas with the Canadian University Service Overseas (CUSO) for two years. (CUSO was the Canadian response to the Peace Corps in the USA and Voluntary Service Overseas in the United Kingdom.) CUSO seemed to me a wonderful opportunity to come to know an unfamiliar part of the world while presumably making some kind of contribution to a developing country. I was deeply touched by the earnest and eager young people in the new, rural Trinidadian secondary school to which I was assigned. Many were of the first generation in their families to receive a secondary education. Some were the children of poor sugar cane workers who could not read, yet who invited me into their homes. I would feel embarrassed as they sat me alone at their table and stood around watching me eat the special meal the mother had prepared, urging seconds upon me. Usually the meal included meat – goat or chicken. I knew that the family could not have afforded meat very often.

As I prepared to return to Canada, I was aware that I had received far more than I'd been able to give as a young, inexperienced teacher. I also knew that there would soon be enough Trinidadian teachers with university degrees to fill even rural positions such as I had held. However, I was deeply grateful for my experience there and the friends I had met.

I carried back to Canada a stronger awareness of the disparities in our world. I wanted to invest my life in a way that would help make the world a better place for at least some people. I had been accepted into a graduate school before I left Canada, and when I returned I completed a master's degree in English, writing a well-regarded thesis on the female characters in the plays of the Jacobean dramatist Thomas Middleton. All the same, I realized I would not feel fulfilled in the world of academe and I declined a doctoral fellowship.

I still felt rootless in terms of a religious identity. While I was in Trinidad I had attended Hindu pujas and Muslim festivals and had tried to learn more about these faiths, but my own cultural experiences were so different that I felt I could not truly come to belong to either. During my master's studies, I read right through the Hebrew and Christian scriptures, and I tried to pray, hoping to develop a felt relationship with God. (This came later, when I became involved in groups akin to the Jesus People.)

I decided I would opt for Christianity, not because I thought it had a monopoly on spiritual truth but because it was culturally the faith system of beliefs and practices that would likely best suit my Western temperament and be most readily livable in Western society. I asked to be confirmed in the Anglican church on campus. I saw this as somehow a vocational decision – whatever I decided to do with my life in the future would not in any fundamental way be inconsistent. (This remained true even when, many years later, I seriously dated a Jewish man, the widower of a dear friend. We shared a commitment to social justice and an appreciation for the writings of Rabbi Abraham Joshua Heschel, who had marched with Dr. Martin Luther King, Jr. If we married, I decided I would be open to converting to Judaism to be supportive of his grandchildren in their faith. Love and respect would govern my decision.)

I had taken teaching positions at community colleges and, more recently, as a sessional lecturer at the University of Guelph. Once earning a teacher's salary, I discovered that having certain things I had once coveted – a sporty car, a good stereo – quickly emptied of satisfaction. I liked teaching and was fairly good at it, at least according to my students' evaluations, but I found I had barely got to know a handful of the students when the semester would end and a new cohort arrive. For a while, I invested all my spare time and resources in groups much like the Jesus People who were reaching out to homeless youth or other marginalized people, but these informal communities lacked stability.

Now, I was taking stock and asking myself where I should be putting my energies. My life seemed too compartmentalized, and I wanted to live in a more integrated manner. I recognized myself as being in one of the "passages" that Gail Sheehy described in a popular book of that title. (The book identified typical turning points – passages – or key decision-making moments, in the trajectory of a contemporary North American life.)

Meanwhile, at the university, where I was part of the precariat, as the sessional lecturers are sometimes called, a happy circumstance had developed, at least from my perspective. I had taught the maximum number of consecutive semesters and was asked to take a year's break. This rule, I understood, was to avoid the university's being sued by discontented sessional lecturers who had not received tenure after several years. I was assured by our department head that my sessional job would be awaiting me; I had some savings, and I knew that if necessary I could pick up part-time teaching to make ends meet. That spring, I gave up my small furnished apartment near the university and agreed to house-sit for some Toronto friends who were on a mini-sabbatical. This year would give me time to think more about my future and even explore some options.

That summer, I had participated in an Anglican group who were reading Jean Vanier's *Community and Growth*, a book which was rapidly becoming a best-seller in parishes and in newer as well as established religious communities. By this time, Vanier had become known as the founder of L'Arche. He was a Roman Catholic, and I thought Catholics might know more about creating long-term, stable lay communities of service. (I could not imagine joining a traditional Anglican or Catholic religious community. While I wanted to live simply, permanent vows, especially of obedience, were not something I could embrace.) Someone in our reading group had mentioned that there was a L'Arche community called Daybreak a few kilometres north, in Richmond Hill, and I resolved to visit it.

All this had run through my mind by the time I arrived at the comfortable Toronto home that I was looking after. Yes, I thought, as I turned the door key, I would accept Michael's invitation and would "come back" to further check out L'Arche. So far, my year of exploration seemed to be falling into two convenient three-month experiences. I had made plans for the autumn to visit a Catholic contemplative community that served the poor. It was located a few hours north of Toronto. This plan was part of my intention to give some time to prayer and personal integration. On an earlier visit there, I had met a priest whom I trusted as a spiritual guide. At Christmas, I would visit my family, and then, assuming Daybreak had a space for me, I would return there for a three-month *stage* and get a better sense of L'Arche. Soon, my friends would come back from their sabbatical. Before that, I would finish an article about the Manitoba humorist Paul Hiebert, which I had promised to my department head at the university. (He edited *The Journal of Commonwealth Literature*.)

∞

In the community where I was a guest, I joined in their contemplative life and prayer, which I found suited me. Small talk was discouraged, and conversation at mealtimes was, as much as possible, meant to be substantive, even edifying. Guests, mainly people like me who had vocational questions, were given simple tasks such as cleaning up the gardens in preparation for the winter or ironing in the laundry. There was a good library, and during my early weeks there, I happily read *The Cloud of Unknowing* and *The Way of a Pilgrim*, and I learned more about Jean Vanier and L'Arche. In fact, the book that was being read aloud after the noon meal was Vanier's *Community and Growth*, the same book that had awakened my interest in L'Arche several weeks earlier.

My priest-director put me in touch with a neighbouring couple who had lived in L'Arche in Alberta and who invited me for dinner and answered some of my questions. As well, there was a steady stream of shorter-term visitors through the community, some of whom, I discovered, were familiar with L'Arche. One, a French-Canadian Capuchin priest, had founded the L'Arche community in Saint-Malachie, Quebec, in 1973. Marilyn, a friend I had made among the guests, and I plied him with questions. He pointed out that many of the tasks of L'Arche assistants are small and repetitive and invite a contemplative attitude. Marilyn decided she would go to that community.

I was interested to learn more about Vanier's personal journey. At twenty, he left a promising career as a naval officer, knowing this would not be his lifelong calling. Having completed a doctorate in philosophy in Paris, he took some time to discern his life direction. He decided against ordination to the priesthood and accepted a position teaching philosophy at St. Michael's College at the University of Toronto. His classes were far from dry and were crowded with students drawn to what he had to say about Aristotle's understanding of friendship and about the human heart. In 1963, at the suggestion of a priest-mentor, on one of Vanier's frequent trips back to France he visited a large and overcrowded asylum for the "mentally handicapped" on the outskirts of Paris. The men, abandoned and lonely, flocked around him, clearly asking for relationship: "Will you come back? Will you be my friend?" they said with their eyes and gestures, if they could not actually speak.

Appalled by their situation, Vanier gathered some funds, and, in 1964, he bought a small, rundown house in the village of Trosly-Breuil, an hour northeast of Paris. He invited two men from the institution to live in the house with him. Together with a few friends, they renovated the house and installed internal plumbing. Seeing it as a place of safe shelter and community, Vanier called the house L'Arche, after Noah's Ark. He thought he was simply doing a good thing – an act of justice. However, he discovered that he enjoyed living with these men, with whom he could share nothing of the intellectual life. He saw that they had become his friends. When he travelled, he spoke about the laughter and "tomfoolery" they often engaged in together, and how he found himself being opened up and changed by his housemates.

Vanier was soon asked to take over a small institution in the village, and L'Arche began to grow very quickly, but it could not grow without people who wanted to share in their life and to help. Some St. Mike's students and other young people came as assistants, eager to experience this new kind of community. More houses and creative workshops were added. The workshops and a large garden provided daytime employment for all. What was different about

L'Arche and what gave it stability from early on, I learned from my conversations, was that the people who had disabilities were, and needed to be, at the community's centre, and these individuals called the others to become their friends, not just to help them practically. On my brief visit to the Green House, I had noted this sense of easy friendship among those around the table and on our walk.

Jean Vanier returned to Canada regularly to teach and make speaking tours. It must have been on one such trip that I heard him in the early seventies. When addressing church people, he made reference to the Beatitudes in Matthew's Gospel: "the poor" were indeed "blessed" with many gifts – friendship and welcome, resilience and creativity and love – that they could share if only given the opportunity. But Vanier could also speak very well to the "unchurched," including students, business leaders, politicians, and even prisoners. Similarly, while he is a devout Catholic, there was no insistence that the people who came to L'Arche should embrace a religion.

The permanent members of the community I was visiting were Catholic lay men and women and priests, all of whom had made lifetime promises of poverty, chastity, and obedience. They lived a rich liturgical life, celebrating the saints and all the major and minor feasts of the Church. Before coming, I had begun thinking about entering the Catholic Church, and I knew that I would learn much about Catholicism there. Like many people raised Protestant in my day, I had reservations about Roman Catholicism, but all my Anglican friends who cared about social justice were married and leading busy lives. I more easily met other like-minded single people who were Catholic, and I was heartened by changes in the Catholic Church after the Second Vatican Council.

I read a contemporary catechism and also the writings of John Henry Newman and G. K. Chesterton, and I learned more about the rootedness of Catholic contemplative spirituality in the wisdom of the desert fathers and of mystics such as St. Teresa of Avila. I realized there were many different ways of living within the Roman Church. Some Catholics were notable scholars; Teilhard de Chardin, whom I had read as an undergraduate, was one, and some of the most progressive thought had come in the 1960s from a cloistered monk named Thomas Merton; some Catholics were prayerfully devoted to Mary and the saints; some, like Dorothy Day and Catherine Doherty, lived out the social gospel in radical ways. In November, I entered the Catholic Church, feeling I would be most at home there. A few weeks later I said my farewells and headed off west along the Trans-Canada Highway to spend Christmas with my family in Winnipeg.

2. The Crash Pad: An orientation

I believe that those we most often exclude from the normal life of society, people with disabilities, have profound lessons to teach us. When we do include them, they add richly to our lives and add immensely to our world.
Jean Vanier

In January of 1981, when I got back in touch with Gus, he invited me to begin my time at Daybreak by joining a "Crash Pad," a one-week introduction to L'Arche that he was to lead shortly. The Crash Pad was just that, as far as accommodation was concerned. The three of us women were invited to "crash" on mattresses in the New House basement. It was clear that L'Arche was about a simple lifestyle, but the welcome of visitors is a fundamental principle of L'Arche, and we certainly felt welcomed by everyone we met.

The Crash Pad consisted of breakfast in one of the three homes on the Daybreak farm followed with talks by Gus and tours in the mornings, helping out with practical tasks in the afternoons, and then joining a house for dinner and the evening, but not being involved in caregiving. Another Crash Padder and I were asked to paint Peggy's bedroom in the Green House, since it had had some drywall work recently. She had chosen a delicate yellow color. It was relaxing to turn to this physical activity after a full morning session.

One talk was about the pedagogy of L'Arche as lived out in daily life: basically, to do *with* and not *for* the person who has a disability, to live together the normal life of an adult family in our society, and to nurture friendships. "Normalization" was a key principle. Thus, the assistants were to encourage individuals in their homes to make their own choices and find their voices as adults, to grow in self-esteem, and, according to their ability, to participate like other citizens in the daily life of the wider community where they lived. This was made possible in part by doing activities in pairs, or threesomes. In our society, if five people enter a store or bank together, they stand out, but this is not the case if two people do. Ideally, an assistant would be with one other person, whether shopping, using recreational facilities, or taking in entertainment. If people were able to grasp the key issues and interested in elections, the assistants should ensure they could vote. When out together with core members, assistants were to dress and carry themselves in a way that conveyed the dignity and value of the relationship they shared, and thus to serve as a model for those who might otherwise dismiss or stare at an individual with a disability.

Another talk gave us some background on L'Arche and Daybreak, which was in its twelfth year. Daybreak was founded by Steve and Ann Newroth. Steve, a seminarian at the time, had come to know Jean Vanier while Jean was teaching at the University of Toronto. In 1965, Steve and Ann were among the earliest of many Canadian young people to travel to France and spend time in Jean's little community. They were a striking couple, tall and sophisticated, and they must have attracted attention in the small rural village of Trosly, where a dairy lady crept down the cobblestone street with warm milk in her camionette, portioning it out to the villagers who would appear with their milk jugs. Steve and Ann set to work opening a new home and welcoming three men from the village. Ann ran the household and helped with many other tasks in the community, and Steve headed a maintenance team that gave daytime employment to several of the men.

Before they returned home, Steve had put aside the idea of being ordained as an Anglican priest, and he and Ann were soon looking for a way to begin L'Arche in Canada. Jean Vanier gave a retreat in King City, not far from Richmond Hill, and this elicited the nuns' offer of property, making the founding of the community possible. On October 16, 1969, Steve and Ann welcomed Bill V., a man still in his teens and in great need of a home, and the first community of L'Arche outside France was founded. In the next few months, more people arrived – among them Peter R., whose mother had passed away and who was living in a small institution; David, a very active young man whose father had died and whose mother was getting older; John S., whose parents had died; and others. As was the case with L'Arche in France, young assistants heard about the new community and came to help.

One of the male assistants, inspired by the title of Joan Baez's autobiography, suggested Daybreak as the name for the new community. The Board of Directors, which Steve had formed, were Daybreak Friends of L'Arche, and their job was to raise funds for the community. [1] Meanwhile, Steve, with the support of Jean Vanier and the Board, persuaded the government to give Daybreak a little funding. (At that time, almost all provincial funding went to maintaining the province's large "institutions for the mentally handicapped.")

As Gus pointed out, Daybreak departed from any early idea that L'Arche would be a traditional Roman Catholic celibate community, since it was founded by a married Anglican couple and Bill, its first member, had no religious background. Most of its early members were not Catholic, and one was a Jew. And yet it was recognized that Daybreak, like other L'Arche communities soon to come, had a faith base and certainly, also, a sense of its need to rely on providence. Prayer after the evening meal was a universal L'Arche practice. It often included the silent or spoken petition that the community's needs for money and assistants would be met.

L'Arche was seen as a sign of hope by families of people who had intellectual disabilities. When Daybreak began, besides keeping their children at home for their entire lifetimes, there were virtually no options other than institutionalization for parents of children with disabilities. (In Canada, Community Living associations of families and friends began to form and establish sheltered workshops and group homes in the early seventies.) Although L'Arche, because of its dependence on assistants wanting to come and share life in community, was and will always be small, it broke new ground.

In the wider socio-political scene after the Second World War, awareness of universal human rights was emerging. Eugenics policies which took the form of forced sterilization had been practised in some Canadian provinces. These policies, associated with Nazism, were recognized not only as violations of individuals' rights but also as based on poor science, and they were gradually abandoned. [2] The great need for decent living situations for people with disabilities was finally becoming evident, both to ordinary citizens and to governments.

Other societal conditions also facilitated the spread of the L'Arche model. A multitude of communal living experiments were taking place in the 1960s and early '70s, and the idea of L'Arche appealed to young people. Students generally graduated from college or university without debt, and jobs were plentiful. North American young people began to backpack, and Europe was a favourite destination. L'Arche was a magnet for Canadians, as the Vanier name was well known and trusted. (Jean Vanier's parents, Georges and Pauline, were prominent Canadians. His father was Governor General of Canada from 1959 until early in 1967.) Others besides Steve and Ann took L'Arche back to their home countries or sowed communities in other places of need. In 1971, the first L'Arche community was founded in India, where L'Arche is known as Asha Niketan, translated as House of Hope. There, Hindus, Christians, and Muslims live together. Soon after, L'Arche was being founded in Honduras, in Haiti and in Côte d'Ivoire, and new communities opened in France. In countries where there was great poverty, L'Arche often welcomed people with disabilities who had been abandoned to live on the streets. Some were children. The first communities in the United Kingdom and in the United States were established in 1974. By 1980, there were L'Arche communities dotted from east to west across Canada, and, before long, across the USA.

∽∾

During the Crash Pad week, we had three tours. The first was of ARC Industries, the sheltered workshop in Richmond Hill, where several of the Daybreak folks who were not interested in or up to labour on the farm spent their days working on packaging contracts or on lunch preparation in the ARC kitchen or participated in a recreational program. (ARC was the Association for Retarded Citizens, but by the 1980s, only the acronym was used.) Another tour took us to Daybreak's two homes in downtown Toronto. At one, we had tea with the folks when they returned from work.

24

Among others, we met Greg, an articulate young man who told us he had grown up in an institution and had come to L'Arche a year or so earlier. He had the use of only one arm. The other, he explained, had not developed because he had had a stroke when he was a baby. His mother had told him that, although she loved him very much, because of his needs, she could not care for him along with her other children.

The final and most memorable tour was of a very large institution two hours' drive north of Richmond Hill. I had never thought much about where people who were born with intellectual disabilities lived, probably because I simply had not encountered them. Most lived in large, isolated institutions, which they rarely if ever left. If families kept them at home, they often hid them out of fear of the stigma associated with having a child with a disability or for fear that the child and the child's siblings would be targeted for ridicule and bullying. That week, it was becoming clear to me that, while people with intellectual disabilities differed from the mainstream in their ability to learn, they were much like everyone else in many ways and often seemed gifted in their capacity to welcome others.

Visiting the institution helped me begin to see the immense need to which L'Arche was trying to respond, even if in a small way. I had been drawn to L'Arche because of the spirituality and communal vision of Jean Vanier and because it was a work of social justice. As it happened, L'Arche's focus was to provide good homes for people with intellectual disabilities, but initially, from my perspective, it could as well have been a community providing for battered women or homeless youth. Now I could see that very many people with intellectual disabilities were disenfranchised at the most basic level. Vanier has called them the "poorest of the poor." They had no power, nor any capacity to lobby for themselves, and they could make few choices. This was especially true in a large institution, where virtually every aspect of life was dictated, from the food served and the clothing available to the kind of work or activities to which people were assigned. Choice is such a fundamental part of human dignity. I had noticed the emphasis that L'Arche assistants put on making choices, whether a small choice, such as what cereal someone wanted for breakfast, or a bigger choice, such as how to spend their vacations.

From the outside, the institution we visited in 1981 looked like some nineteenth-century hospitals – a large old building set on spacious, well-maintained grounds. Indeed, in earlier days institutions such as this one were called hospitals (but, of course, people born with an intellectual disability are not "sick") and, before that, asylums, because people with intellectual disabilities were regarded as not much different from people who were mentally ill, with whom they were often housed. In such settings, they were vulnerable to abuse. This institution had opened in 1876. (It was finally closed in 2009.) At its peak, in the 1970s, 2800 people lived there, and in total over 7000 people lived in institutions across Ontario. Similar huge institutions existed across Canada and in most other "developed" countries.

The institution was bleak inside in spite of efforts to brighten some rooms with artwork and paint. To some extent the bleakness of the building was inevitable given its age. Its high ceilings, old lighting, bare wide corridors that echoed, and very large rooms, must have made it nearly impossible to create any sense of intimacy. The smell of disinfectant wafted here and there. The dorm rooms consisted of rows of single beds. While each person had a locker, these seemed not to be locked, and it appeared unlikely that personal clothing and other effects could be protected from being mixed up with those of others or swiped by individuals who took a fancy to them.

The public relations person who greeted us was clearly caring and talked of the enrichment they sought to give their residents. There was a choir that sometimes travelled to local churches to sing. There were art classes. There was a sheltered workshop in the building. And some "cottages" had been set up on the grounds in which small groups of residents tried out living in self-contained households where they learned simple cooking and other homemaking skills. Even sitting at a table for meals in a family-like setting of six or eight, rather than eating in the huge institutional cafeteria, needed to be learned. The people in the cottages were deemed to have potential for living in group homes in their communities of origin, or perhaps even in a L'Arche community. However, few people at that time imagined that everyone in that institution could, with proper support, be accommodated in the towns and cities from which they had come.

One of the attendants took us on a tour of a ward. She spoke about some of the "cases" they had, and she pointed out an isolation room with padded walls, where a young woman who had hit a worker lay prone on a plastic-covered mat on the floor. I felt very uncomfortable being invited to peer into the room through the small window in the door – as though we were at a zoo. Then, our guide introduced us to a young man in a wheelchair. "This is an epileptic," she said, as she stood near him. She did not tell us his name until someone in our group asked. I could feel the indignation rising in myself and the others as we felt the hurt that the resident surely had experienced in being referred to in the third person and only by his medical diagnosis. Before we moved on we thanked the man for greeting us.

Of course, not by any means were all who worked in institutions insensitive in the manner of this attendant. In fact, two wonderful Daybreak assistants came from such an institution a few years later. Both were kind, sensitive, and highly competent people who were drawn to the vision of Vanier and L'Arche.

The last talk of our Crash Pad week was given by Joe Egan, Daybreak's community leader. (The formal title of "executive director" was used with government people.) He had by then been in the community for seven years. Joe told us two stories of encounters that had had a deep impact on him. One was about his decision to stay on in the community, and it was connected to David, the pipe-smoking acquaintance of my first visit. Joe had come to Daybreak in 1973. After two years, he had decided he should move on with his life. (He had previously worked for an insurance company for a little while.) During his years living in the Big House, he had become close to David, so he took David aside to tell him privately that he was leaving. David started to weep and then asked Joe to wait while he went to his room for something. He returned with a small photo of himself as a boy, saying, "I want you to have this so you will remember me." Now it was Joe's turn to cry. What Joe really *wanted*, he realized immediately, was to stay. Doing an about-face, he told David that he would not leave. To this day, Joe carries in his wallet the now much-worn little photo of David, and their friendship continues.

Joe's second story was about his first encounter with Greg, whom we had met in one of the downtown L'Arche homes. Daybreak had had an opening, and Joe, who had become community leader in 1980, had been invited to a case conference at the institution where Greg lived with a view to deciding whether Greg might be a candidate for it. Joe told us, "I found the case conference difficult because I felt that, in spite of the huge file on the table, the staff didn't know Greg very well." Afterwards, Joe met with Greg alone and shared with him what was said. Then, Joe asked him to explain in his own words why he wanted to come to L'Arche. He was quiet for a moment and then looked right at Joe and said, "I want to know what life is really all about and I know if I stay here I never will." The interview ended quickly as Joe simply replied, "You can come."

Joe continued, "Greg's words touched me deeply because that was my question too – along with all the related questions which make up our common humanity such as Where do I belong? Where is my home? Who loves me? Who are my friends? Can I have a dream for my life? What are my gifts? And so many more!" He summed up, "I have learned much from Greg and others as we share day-to-day life in community and live our way into discovering some answers to those basic human questions we all have."

&

Many years later I would accompany Greg when he gave a fireside talk to some medical students. Greg told me he wanted the students to understand what his life was like in Toronto and in a L'Arche home. He stressed that in L'Arche, in contrast to his former life in the institution, he makes his own choices, that he has friends and also that he can move about in his neighbourhood and on public transit on his own. "Living in the institution was hard," he said. "It felt like I didn't even have a life, and people made fun of me a lot.

I felt lonely even though I lived with a lot of people. We never had our own bedrooms either. We slept in a very big room. I had one good teacher there. Her name was Wendy and she taught art. She never judged people by what they did or made fun of them."

Asked by one of the students how it was for him to move from the institution, Greg responded: "Coming to L'Arche, I didn't know anybody and it felt overwhelming. But over time people wanted to get to know me and that felt good. This was the best part – getting to know one another. It felt like family. I helped John Guido [an assistant] when his sister died. I went with him to New York to visit his family. His dad was ill, and I could bring his dad his coffee. I learned a lot about life. You are never too old to learn."

I have seen Greg at work in the Toronto supermarket where he has been employed for over a quarter century. An assistant found him the job and helped him figure out how he could do the required tasks. He sweeps the aisles with remarkable dexterity, stocks shelves when asked, gathers the carts from the parking lot, and greets the customers cheerfully. After so many years he is well known and appreciated by both the customers and the staff. His work philosophy is simple: "I treat people the way I like to be treated – with love and care." One of Greg's important contributions has been to a grief support group at the L'Arche Toronto community. He was initially a participant and then provided artwork and comments to a manual that L'Arche prepared for such groups. Recently, Greg, who is into his sixties, has been cutting back on his hours of work and he tells me, "I am looking forward to doing some things I really want to do." In the summer of 2018, he visited his friend Alan Cook, a former assistant and Anglican priest who is now a chaplain in England.

∽∘∾

Back in 1981, I was grateful for the Crash Pad. It enabled me to meet Greg and some other people and to visit other L'Arche homes and so to situate myself in the larger community of Daybreak and, to some extent, in its history. Most importantly, it gave me a sense of the very significant needs to which L'Arche was trying to respond, and the importance of this response.[3]

3. "You and your husband can come in": Early experiences in the Green House

If we listen to [those who have an intellectual disability], they bring us back to the essential. . . . They nourish us and heal our wounds daily. . . . They call forth light and love within us. Jean Vanier

After the Crash Pad, I was happy to learn that I was being assigned to the Green House. The house was built on a slope, with most of the bedrooms downstairs and with east-facing windows onto the grassy backyard descending to a wetland and cedar grove that hid the bungalow from sight. I was offered a small bedroom on the lower level. Its west-facing window looked out under the front porch, but I didn't mind as it was cozy, being next to the furnace room. Phil was the house leader by this time, and Annette, a young woman of twenty, had come as an assistant. I had met all the "folks" except for Cynthia on my dinner visit the previous Labour Day. She was a quiet, middle-aged woman who had come quite recently. She had spent a trial period in a Daybreak house downtown, but she had been very anxious there and it was thought that a more structured house, such as the Green House, might work out for her.

When I came upstairs on the second or third morning after I had settled in, I was shocked to see Michael stretched out board-like and unconscious on the hardwood floor of the dining room. He had just had a grand mal seizure, I learned. I had had no idea that he had epilepsy.[1] After a minute or two, Mike regained consciousness and sat up groggily. Phil helped him into his bedroom to rest as we ate breakfast. Later, he had breakfast and someone drove him to ARC, where he worked. The others in the house all took Mike's seizures so much in stride that I learned to do so also, but it was not easy. The day of any big event, such as his birthday, needed to be kept from him until the last minute or he would become so excited that he would have a seizure and miss the event. In addition to epilepsy, Michael has a severe peanut allergy, and if he ingests even the smallest bit of a peanut or peanut butter, he could die of anaphylactic shock. Given these two circumstances, an assistant was never far from Michael when we were out and about.

Michael could be grumpy and often gave male assistants a hard time, especially in the morning, but he was predisposed towards women, and he would say to me with a big smile, "I like you," as I cut up his meat at dinner or helped him set out his clothes for the next day. Of course, I was pleased and responded similarly. I enjoyed spending time with him. I was sure that a lot of his grumpiness came from frustration. The medication that he had to take slowed him down and kept him from performing some of the tasks he would have enjoyed, and it seemed to negatively affect his mood.

In the early spring of 1981, while Phil was on a L'Arche retreat in France, and a few weeks after I had passed the driving test for Daybreak vehicles and been put on the community's insurance, Mike and I were asked to run up to Penetanguishene to pick up Cynthia, who had been visiting there for a week. We would leave right after lunch and should be back well before dinner.

There was still snow on the ground, and we wore winter clothes and boots. Just before we left, I went to the medication cupboard and grabbed Mike's pills. We used daily medication containers, and it was easier to bring the whole container than to take only his "four o'clocks." The weather was excellent, a mix of sun and clouds, and the roads were clear. We made good time up Highway 400. At Barrie, we headed northwest towards the Penetang Peninsula, which stretches up into Georgian Bay – the enormous bay that runs along the northeastern side of Lake Huron. The peninsula is subject to the brunt of the winds, which are westerlies in this part of North America. We were driving our house car – a low-slung Chevy station wagon of mid-seventies vintage.

When the clouds closed in and a light snow began to fall, I thought little of it, merely following the example of oncoming traffic by switching on our headlights. Initially there was a good bit of traffic moving in both directions, but a few minutes later, as the snow continued and the flakes became larger and heavier, it seemed nearly all the other cars had disappeared. As I drove, I worked the radio but got mostly static and could not bring in a weather report. I was becoming concerned and glanced over at Mike but made light of the situation to him. The snow continued to build, and visibility worsened. I slowed to a crawl, barely able to see the single track of a vehicle somewhere ahead of us but no longer visible through the wall of snow. I knew we could not be far from Penetanguishene. I continued to keep an eye on Mike. He was staring straight ahead into the blinding snow, but he still seemed nonplussed and made no comment. I was hoping he would not become overly excited or upset. A seizure was certainly something we could both do without!

After another few minutes, a flashing red light loomed ahead of us. It was attached to a large yellow and black roadblock with the message ROAD CLOSED. We had driven right into one of what I later learned are notorious Georgian Bay blizzards that can blow in from Lake Huron, especially in the early spring. I thought at first that we were totally alone. Then I saw we were actually at a crossroads where a local road intersected the highway, and to our right through the blowing snow I could see a gas station. We crept into its parking lot, and I ran through a foot or more of snow to find that it was about to close. The attendant was very anxious to get home, but he allowed me to make one collect long-distance phone call. (Of course, this was many years before the advent of cellphones.) Unfortunately, I could not get through to Daybreak.

Returning to the car, I cleared the snow from the exhaust pipe and noted gratefully that we had a fairly full tank of gas. What could I do but settle down in the car with Mike and wait, perhaps several hours, for the snow to stop or for some snowplow driver to spot us — though at that point we had seen no plows on the road. I hoped we would not become too miserably cold and hungry — or worse, whatever that might be.

Amazingly, within a minute or two, a woman emerged from across the road. Beyond her, in moments when the wind died down, I could just make out the form of a small house that I had not previously noticed. I lowered my window, and she called in, "You and your husband can come into my house." I blurted out a "Thank you!" and something about our being "just friends." At that moment I realized like a lightning bolt that this was exactly what we were. I was certainly not going to tell her, "Well, Mike is actually a man with an intellectual disability and he also has severe epilepsy and many needs, and I cannot imagine being married to him…and I am actually his residential counsellor" – or whatever officialdom called us assistants in those days.

Mike and I clambered out of the car and, holding on to each other, plunged off into the wind and snow towards the little house. We had nothing with us but my handbag with Mike's pills.

The woman, as it turned out, had two young children, and Mike, who loves children, connected immediately with them. As soon as he had shed his coat and boots, he was down on the floor shooting little cars back and forth with the boy and his younger sister. The woman's house was very basic – one large room with a bare floor, a tattered couch, a kitchenette at the end of the room, two bedrooms opening off this main room, and a small bathroom at the end of the kitchen. She did not have a telephone. I thought that she was quite possibly on welfare, but she was incredibly generous. Not only did she take us in but she opened her cupboard and fed us. I think she had only a few tins in the cupboard – baked beans, spaghetti, soup – and some bread.

After a while, we heard a roar outside and a knock. A tall man in a full snowmobile suit and boots entered. Mike was very impressed by his appearance and wanted to engage him in conversation. I thought maybe he was the woman's boyfriend and would not be pleased to see us, but if so, he did not let this on. He stayed only briefly, and before he left I wrote down the phone number of the Green House and asked him to call and reassure the people there that Mike and I were safe and well. (He did indeed call and left a voice message that we were fine, though from the point of view of people back home, who did not know our circumstances, the message seemed hardly adequate.) As night closed in, the snow continued and it was clear we were going nowhere. I thanked God we had Mike's evening meds. Our hostess told us to use the cots in her children's room and she would take the children to sleep with her. In spite of the unusual situation, I think we both slept not badly.

All through that experience I marveled at Mike's resilience and good humour. He took everything in stride, and his calmness made it possible for me to be calm and to simply live the moment with gratitude. Mike was able to take his 4:00 and 8:00 p.m. pills on time, and I anticipated rising early, praying that we could somehow reach a pharmacy in Penetanguishene and arrange to get his morning medication more or less on time.

Fortunately, the temperature had risen by morning. We headed off through slush and were in Penetanguishene within a half hour of thanking our hostess and her children profusely and assuring them we would come back for a visit in better weather. A quick call by the Penetanguishene pharmacist to our pharmacy in Richmond Hill, and he provided us with Mike's morning meds. We picked up Cynthia, and we were back home by noon. Others had been worried about us, but we had done our best to communicate our situation, and, having come out of the experience unscathed, Mike and I both felt rather triumphant. I had had no money to offer our generous hostess, but when we returned to visit her some weeks later, we took along as our thank-you gift a homemade card with some money, bags of groceries, and a couple of roasts of beef from our well-stocked freezer.

Until the blizzard, I had been enjoying relationships with the folks or core members but the sense of responsibility I felt for them created a considerable gulf between us. Our Arctic Adventure, as I came to call it, was a life-changing experience for me because I discovered Mike as a friend and a calm, resilient, and courageous partner in a potential crisis. He was still a person with a disability for whom I was responsible, but this was his secondary identity.

Long after our adventure, I asked Mike how he had felt, especially when night had fallen and we were going to bed in our clothes in the children's cots. Did he feel scared or relaxed? "Yes, scared," he admitted. And I told him that I had been scared too. But I had not wanted to tell him or even to think about being scared at the time. It had seemed better to both of us to pretend the situation was not so abnormal.

∽∾

Phil helped me understand the expectations for an assistant. At first, he often urged me to be a stronger reference for the folks. He used the word "reference" in the French sense of a benchmark or standard, and it took me a while to catch on. Being a reference might mean reminding people, if they were in their pyjamas, to wear a housecoat when outside their bedrooms, or not to leave their clothes on the floor but to hang them up or put them in the laundry hamper.

The most challenging lesson for me in the first months was to learn patience and not to "do for" core members who were slow or not so well coordinated, but to let each person do whatever tasks they were able to do themselves. Phil pointed out that even if the task at hand was small, a person could have a sense of achievement in doing it independently – providing we didn't step in. Indeed, there might be only a few tasks that someone could accomplish independently in the course of a day. I learned this lesson most strongly from Michael, who would tell me if I was rushing him. "Go slow!" he would say in a commanding voice. He knew the steps of various tasks, but he needed time to carry them out. Similarly, when the dinner table was set by certain core members, the cutlery and napkin might be only in the general vicinity of each intended place, but what was important was the fact these people had set the table and that we could all receive their gift.

I frequently accompanied Mike for his nighttime routine and when he was doing his laundry. Standing nearby in case he really needed help – such as on the rare occasions when his laundry basket fell over – I would struggle to restrain myself as he slowly lifted each item into and out of the washing machine and dryer. At night, he was tired, and he found it more difficult to stay with a task. He was fine with opening drawers and setting out his clothes for the next day, but he also needed to put his belt through the belt loops of the pants he had chosen. (L'Arche tries to ensure core members have clothes that reflect current styles and are likely to elicit greater respect from other citizens, not items that could look institutional, such as pull-on pants.) I would sit beside Michael on the edge of his bed and try with all my might not to reach over and help him with his belt, especially when he missed a loop and had to pull the belt back, then lost hold of the pants and had to start over. By that time of the evening, I was tired too and could not wait for the day to end!

Annette had more patience than I. She pointed out that this time with Michael could be special – a time when we could chat about the day and about his various interests. Phil liked to allude to Jean Vanier's description of L'Arche as characterized by "comfort and challenge." There were always the moments that touched us, and there were the challenging moments that usually came when we were tired.

Every three weeks it would be the turn of the Green House to provide soup (or in summer, a salad) to supplement lunch for the farm team. Our house team took turns making the soup. The workers would arrive sharp at noon – in the winter pulling off their heavy farm jackets and boots in the mud room – and pad up into our dining room in their work socks, carrying their lunch bags of sandwiches. There were usually four or five of them in the winter and as many as eight in the summer. I had no knowledge of farming, and the farm held a bit of a mystique for me. I admired these men who knew how to be around large animals and who did heavy work. They would crowd around the dining table together with whoever else was at home for lunch.

My first assignment to make the farm team soup came soon after I arrived. My only experience with preparing soup was opening a tin, but I knew the expectation was for a homemade soup. Eager to please the group, I dug out a recipe for corn chowder from one of the Green House cookbooks, and, taking the house food money, I headed to the local supermarket to buy the ingredients. These included several tins of creamed corn. The farm team didn't think much of my cream of corn soup. They liked soups containing meat. And the others on the Green House team gently let me know that I had used a disproportionate amount of our food money shopping for one farm team soup. After that, I learned to make soups from the plentiful supply of soup bones in our chest freezer (after all, we lived on a farm that raised beef) and added vegetables from the root cellar. I enjoyed these lunches. They gave me a stronger sense of the community.

Gradually, I came to know the people in our house better, and how to be with each one. Peter enjoyed teasing people – Michael above all, and then the assistants. Once he found a topic that "worked," he had fun with it and would not let it go, especially if we let on that he was annoying us. "Don't bug you, eh, Beth?" he would say playfully, hoping that I would continue to let him push my buttons. Michael could not grasp Peter's intent to tease him, or possibly he chose not to as he himself spoke slowly and could not come back with a quick response. He would become angry with Peter. To help avoid the rancour, we made certain they did not sit next to each other at meals.

Peggy was almost fully independent. She sometimes took on the role of an assistant, telling Francis to slow down or Peter to calm down, and they respected her. Her bedroom was on the main floor because she had a weak ankle and had difficulty with stairs and even with walking on the unpaved laneway. Peggy spoke clearly, and she was generally easy to relate to. She listened to her radio and read the newspaper, where the Cold War was often headlined. Her fear of Communism could make her very anxious, and sometimes she was even suspicious of assistants who dressed in a hippie manner. I could be helpful by directing her attention to other matters.

Francis was a challenge to get to know. He was talkative, but when I tried to get into a conversation with him, he would become shy. His answers were very short, and he often repeated them. He was almost always in a hurry, and his appearance was a bit dishevelled. He rarely looked people in the eye when he responded to questions. At the same time, he seemed to have a quite positive self-image. He once explained to me that he was not handicapped. He was like everyone else who could not do some things. "Annette can't swim; I can't drive a car," he said, to clarify what he meant. He was right, of course. In the evenings, Francis would often sit at the dining room table copying words from a magazine onto loose-leaf paper. He very much wanted to learn to read, and he thought this would help him. Once or twice, I sat down beside him, but his body language conveyed that he did not want my help. He and some others in the community took a weekly literacy class offered by a kind nun, but no one in the class, to my knowledge, succeeded in learning more than to print their name.

One day I had a different experience of Francis. I was asked to run him up to the village just north of us, where he was invited to have dinner with his girlfriend, Linda, and her family. Someone had helped him buy some flowers, which he was proudly taking as a gift. Francis was obviously pleased to have been invited, and he had dressed in his best pullover sweater and pants. I noticed as we drove that he had a subdued gentleness about him that was different from how I usually experienced him. That made me wonder if what he really needed was to feel special, and if being singled out for an invitation gave him this feeling. Is that not what each of us likes from time to time? I thought to myself. I'd heard that he was one of a family of a dozen children, almost all boys. I supposed that he did not have such an experience very often in his youth. This insight stayed with me and helped me to have more patience with Francis and find ways to affirm him.

After our blizzard experience, Mike and I shared a special bond. In spite of the continuing threat of grand mal seizures, which could come with little or no warning, Mike was well most of the time. He could walk easily and sometimes would run. On Wednesday evenings, a group of us from the Green House would head to the local swimming pool. I discovered that Mike was a very good swimmer. He could swim in the deep end and he could also dive. I was always on the lookout for him, concerned that he could have a seizure, but to my knowledge he has never had a seizure in the pool. Quite often Rex, Mike's father, would join us, and occasionally after our swim he would take us to a local donut shop for hot chocolate – a much appreciated treat.

Lloyd was a very quiet man who seemed a little lost. He would often trail after Francis, who would ask Lloyd to agree with him about this or that. "That's right, Lloyd, isn't it?" Francis might say several times in rapid succession until he got a response. But, on his own, Lloyd was easier to get to know. His speech came slowly, but I realized he knew a lot more than one might have thought. He could tell me where certain things were kept in the house, for example. I would always thank him, and I would ply him with questions about his family's farm. He seemed to enjoy telling me about it and showing me the ribbons his prize Holstein calves had won.

However, a problem arose. Before very long Lloyd became quite fixated on me and would watch me constantly. I learned from Phil that he had told people we were going to get married, and also that this was not the first time Lloyd had fallen in love with a female assistant. In wanting to show him my appreciation for who he was, I had touched more deeply into his longing for relationship than I had ever intended, and now I was going to cause him hurt and embarrassment by confronting him. Phil and I met with him together. I explained to Lloyd that I liked him but in the same way that I liked the others in the house. I was not thinking at all of getting married, and I did not want him to spread rumours.

Afterwards, I worried about Lloyd's having been humiliated, but he seemed to take the conversation we had had in stride. It occurred to me that this was not the first time he had experienced humiliation. I felt awkward with him for a few days, and then our relationship seemed to settle into a new normal pattern. I paid less one-on-one attention to him, and he did not seem to fixate on me or look for my attention.

Everyone in the house was still getting to know Cynthia. She did not talk much, but she had a sense of humour and would laugh when Peter teased us, and she seemed to be starting to feel at home. We all liked her. Then things started going off the rails. She seemed confused, as though in a dream. To help her move about in the house, we needed to take her hand. She began to wander, and one night someone found her on the farm lane in her nightgown and slippers. We did not have locked doors, and, in any case, she was able to leave the house through the fire door near her bedroom on the lower level, not a location where anyone was likely to see her. As a team, we were at a loss. We had meetings with professionals who were adjusting Cynthia's meds and meeting with her. Everyone hoped that she could settle in, but her confusion and wandering persisted. Phil decided he would sleep on the floor outside her door, and he did that for a few nights. When he awoke to find her about to leave, he had difficulty stopping her as she would wrestle with him. Phil was becoming exhausted, and we were all at our wit's end. When the professional team learned that things had come to this, they declared that it was not good for Phil and the team or for Cynthia, and one of them arranged for her to be assessed at a hospital for people with intellectual disabilities who also had a significant mental illness, with a view to her being admitted long term.

This was a blow to all of us. We had a brief house meeting in which Phil explained that he was going to take Cynthia to a hospital where she would stay. I think there was not a person in the house whose heart did not go out to Cynthia, and to Phil, who had tried so hard. We said goodbye and waved the car off. Phil was driving, with Gus sitting beside Cynthia in the backseat for fear she would bolt. Annette and I and the remaining five core members ate together mostly in silence that evening. Peter repeated over and over, "Cynthia gone?" A couple of the Green House core members worked with a therapist. Whether they realized Cynthia was seeing a therapist too, we were not sure, but in the days to come they seemed the most uneasy about her illness and departure. I suppose they wondered if such disorientation could happen to them and whether they could end up having to leave.

After Annette and I helped with the evening routines of those who needed assistance, we lit a candle and sat in the living room awaiting Phil's return. Finally, after midnight, he arrived home looking totally drained. The hospital had admitted Cynthia. The chapter of her life with us was closed. The three of us clung together and wept, and then someone started the Our Father and we whispered our way through it and went off to bed.

Losing Cynthia was difficult for me. As the older female assistant, I felt a failure. I wondered if I could have done something different, been more motherly, or somehow provided her a greater sense of security. It took me a while to let go of these questions in spite of the reassurance of others. When, two or three weeks later, I was asked to fill in while one of the house leaders of a downtown home was on vacation, I declined because that house had recently welcomed a new young woman core member. I feared something could happen to her also. Phil agreed to take my place downtown, and I accepted to be acting leader at the Green House, where, by then, I had become comfortable filling in on his time away.

Cynthia had still been new to the community. Just as L'Arche has a trial period for assistants, it has a trial period for core members. New people will usually be making a strong effort to fit in, but, after a few months, they will not be able to sustain this effort and will become more themselves. At this point it will become clearer whether they can manage community life. As one consultant explained to us, some people cannot stand the informality or the intimacy and the expectations of the family-like lifestyle of a L'Arche home.

Gradually, I heard stories of other people besides Cynthia who, in the end, could not stay. In its early days, both in France and in Canada, L'Arche had wanted to welcome everyone who needed a home. At one point, Daybreak had welcomed a young woman who had been living on the streets. She may not have had much of an intellectual disability, if any, but she could not adjust to the expectations that she turn up for work and for dinner, and she would disappear for days. In the end, she returned to the streets. Sometimes, the community welcomed people who put others or themselves in danger, and in those days it was reluctant to say that it could not keep such people. One man had been angrily threatening and terrorized others in the house by wielding a knife. Another had a gentle nature, but his mood could change on a dime and he could pick up whatever was at hand – a ketchup bottle, a chair – and fling it at others across a room. The assistants tried to support him in many ways, drawing on professional help, but it was not until he moved to a more secure and structured setting with locked doors that he seemed able to relax and he got on much better.[2]

On the other hand, I heard of a young man named Mark, who, in fits of depression and anger, would storm around slamming doors and talking loudly to himself. He would throw out items that were precious to him – his radio, his favourite Beatles T-shirt. It turned out that he was developing schizophrenia. With good professional help and medication, he was able to stay in the community.

∾◦∾

During my early months in L'Arche, I often reflected on the mix of assistants, almost all of whom were ten to fifteen years younger than I. The people who had disabilities were the essential element. Without them, most of us would probably never have met. I liked all of the assistants and found some of them quite inspiring. Matthew, a tall, athletic fellow from Australia, had been invited to play representative rugby back home. He was full of energy (he could vault up the Big House stairs four at a time), but he was incredibly gentle with a man in his house who was ill. Veronica, a sixty-year-old nun who was loved by the members at the New House and who was usually in the group who went into town to the early Mass, could beat almost anyone at tennis; Gus and Debbie were Canadians who had met in L'Arche in France, married, and then lived in L'Arche in Côte d'Ivoire for three years. Phil's domesticity frequently surprised me. He had an English degree from the University of Toronto and had travelled extensively in Europe, but some late evenings I would discover him sitting in our small TV room darning the socks of the men in the house.

While seeming wise, caring, and responsible, the assistants could cut loose too. I heard a story from a few years earlier about Joe Egan having driven the getaway car as one of the other male assistants "streaked" across the local shopping plaza. And I had been in our van on an assistants' weekend when our house leader "mooned" the assistants in the L'Arche van travelling beside us. I was sure there were other ribald moments. But I wondered what kept these assistants in L'Arche after the first few months. They certainly had other options.

Assistants' days could be very long and tiring, and if something unusual came up, such as someone in their house being ill, they often needed to give up their free time. I knew from my CUSO training that people with purely altruistic motives usually do not last long in works of social justice. The people who work out well are getting something back from the experience – learning and growing and being changed in good ways. For assistants, I thought that deeper element was probably a sense of reciprocity or mutuality between the assistants and those they were there to help with the practicalities of life. It was mutuality that I had experienced in the blizzard with Mike. Almost all assistants who had stayed beyond a few months could name one or more relationships as a source of nourishment for their life in the community. Often, it was a member who in some circumstance had touched them deeply and "called" them to stay, as was the case with Joe and David.

As my three-month anniversary approached, I was enjoying our life together, and it seemed obvious I should stay through the summer. I began to ponder whether I should make the one-year commitment (from September) that Daybreak asked for in the spring. I ascertained with my department head at the university that I would still be able to return to my position there if I stayed on at L'Arche for the next year, but it would mean a financial sacrifice and the continued letting go of personal time and other lifestyle options that were not available to assistants, especially in those days. For example, there was only one telephone in our house. It was often in demand, and, in any case, the time I might have liked to call friends or family after they were home from work was also the time when we assistants were busy helping with tea time, the core members' own phone calls to their families and friends, their learning plans, dinner, evening activities, and nighttime routines.

Also, the question remained for me, was I a good fit at Daybreak? I found this difficult to judge. I was older and more reserved than most of the other assistants, and I was not good at teasing and creating the sense of fun that seemed so often to bring us all together. Sister Sue Mosteller, a Sister of Saint Joseph (Sue M., everyone called her), was a much loved and respected L'Arche leader. She lived in the Big House when she was not travelling as the international coordinator. I decided to ask her opinion. She responded, "From what I have observed, you are good here." Phil clearly did not want to put any pressure on me. He quoted an adage that he said he had heard from a wise Board member: "If it is good for you, it will be good for the community." That left the question Was it good for me? I was not used to thinking along these lines. I was rather duty-oriented and more likely to ask myself, "Is what I am doing useful, and am I competent in it?"

I had heard of others making a Jesuit-style (or Ignatian) retreat to discern important questions. Through Sue, I got in touch with

Father Bill Clarke, a Jesuit who was known as a wise resource for L'Arche people.[3] Bill had lived in L'Arche in France and now headed a small farm community similar to L'Arche in Guelph, Ontario. He arranged for me to spend a weekend at the Jesuit College and meet with one of his priest friends, Dan Phelan. Dan had lived in L'Arche too. He described to me a simple image sometimes used in Ignatian discernment. It is to envision water falling onto a rock, where it bounces off, and water falling onto a sponge, where it soaks in, and then to imagine making the decision in one direction. If the decision feels like water falling on a rock, it is probably wrong or not a good choice at this time, but if it feels like water falling on a sponge, it is probably right. The sponge-like feeling about staying was obvious to me, and I committed myself for the coming year. I came to understand that "good for me" had to do with whether I was feeling alive in my spirit and happy in the community. I could see that I was growing, becoming freer and more able to have fun and a little more outgoing than I had been.[4]

4. "Nice day, eh?": Community life and vacations

Community is a sign that love is possible in a materialistic world where people so often either ignore or fight each other. Jean Vanier

Numerous weekly meetings kept the community functioning smoothly and built a feeling of collegiality among the assistants and a sense of home among all who lived together in the houses. Most were planning meetings, but they nevertheless began with a check-in, during which each person spoke briefly about how they were (energized, stressed, or whatever), and ended with holding hands and repeating the Lord's Prayer. On Sunday evenings, all members met in their households to plan the week.

Mondays, there was a team meeting, followed by an all-assistants meeting, a team lunch, a house leaders' meeting, and a table meeting in each house over tea after dinner to share news from the earlier meetings. In the Green House, Peggy, who could read, would be called on to read aloud the Thought for the Week, usually a short passage from *Community and Growth*, and the other news. There was a triweekly meeting of Joe or Gus with the core members alone in each house – a time for them to voice concerns without the presence of assistants and for the leaders to take the temperature of the homes.

On Tuesday evenings, we all gathered in the Big House chapel for what L'Arche calls common worship. Responsibility for this time rotated among the houses. Members of the appointed house prepared a skit or mime illustrating the biblical reading for the day and planned the music. There was always a sustained period of silence, during which anyone could offer extemporaneous prayers. This concluded with the Lord's Prayer. Often local clergy from one of the three Christian denominations most represented at Daybreak (Anglican, Catholic, and United Church of Canada) came to help us, and often the Eucharist was celebrated. Catholic strictures around who could receive communion tended to irritate both Catholic and non-Catholic assistants, as they could lead to painful moments with core members who could not understand the theological differences. Some people simply took communion regardless of denomination.

∽◦∾

The most important meeting for assistants – the one that kept us well as a group and living in the communal spirit of L'Arche – was the Tuesday Morning Meeting. The Green House hosted, provided coffee and (except during Lent) coffee cake, and everyone crowded into the living room, half of us elbow to elbow on cushions on the floor. It was understood that no assistant would miss the TMM. Assistants' time away was scheduled beginning at noon on Tuesday. This meeting was a privileged time, and the invitation to attend was not extended to visitors or to very new assistants. Joe Egan, as community leader, would set the tone with a short inspirational talk. The rest of the morning was set aside for reflection on our life in community during the preceding week. There would be substantial periods of silence punctuated by assistants recounting moments, usually moments with core members, which had touched or challenged them or brought them insight. No one had to speak, and only a few people would speak each week. All respected that what had been shared was private – sacred, in a way. It was the intimacy and trust that existed in this meeting that sustained many of us and led us to decide to stay longer.

I think it often happened during a TMM that in the very act of telling a story, or listening to the story of another, we grasped anew the gift of our life together. Sometimes the stories were humorous. I recall one young man, Jim, who had the build of a football player and one year of university behind him, telling a hilarious story about his very frustrating experience accompanying Maurice – or Moe, as he liked to be called – while he made muffins. Maurice was not

48

much more than four feet tall, rotund, and approaching middle age. Except when dancing, when he could be light on his feet, Maurice was even slower than molasses. He also had a great sense of fun and loved to play the clown. He and Jim lived in the Big House, which was noted for its Monday Muffins Nights. All the house members would gather in the living room well ahead of time, awaiting the muffins and tea. After dinner and the dishes, Jim and Maurice would close the kitchen door and get to work.

Making muffins was an ILP – an individual learning plan – for Maurice – (such were government-legislated requirements), so Jim was not supposed to help him unless he got into serious difficulty. Maurice used a premix and had a recipe with a picture and a number for each step. After he had turned the oven on and assembled the bowl, wooden spoon, measuring cup, and tins, Maurice slowly measured the mix and the water, stirred the mixture, and sprayed the muffin tins. Then came the most exacting and slowest step: Maurice had to spoon the mixture into the tins. Jim described how it took every ounce of his self-discipline not to shove Maurice out of the way and do it himself. The pace was painful, especially for a man of Jim's age and energy. An hour or sometimes two hours after they started came the reward for Jim – seeing Maurice's smile and pride as he presented his muffins to the waiting household. All of us in the TMM knew Maurice, and we were in stitches listening to Jim's account, but what was most important and what shone through in his telling was his love for Maurice and the bond of friendship they shared.

I spoke with Jim not long ago about my memory of this story. He told me that their Monday evening muffin making had continued for three years, and that although Maurice's recipe was painfully methodical and Moe so slow, he eventually came to crave this quiet time together. He added, about the TMMs, "They were such a powerful, loving, intimate space for risking growth. They taught me about interiority, which for me as a twenty-year-old at the time was profound."

Maybe I knew a little about interiority when I came to L'Arche, but the TMMs taught me more, especially about the goodness of the trust in the group and about being open to speaking from my heart.

That day I was led to reflect on my first encounter with Maurice, who had an eye for women. I think he proposed marriage to every new female assistant who crossed his path. He had a very quiet voice, and he would slip up close to the newest arrival and get her to lean down and then whisper in her ear: "Marry me!" I needed to ask him to repeat his proposal three times before I got what he was saying. He knew that it would throw me, and he was amused by this. That morning, I thought about the loneliness of Moe and others like him in the community. I am sure he would have liked one of us to say "Yes!" And yet he had moved beyond this longing to simply enjoy teasing the assistants.

Joe's TMM talks were almost always based on Jean Vanier's *Community and Growth*, but he had an excellent grasp of what keeps a community healthy, and sometimes he chose a selection on life in community from another source. One time, when a problem of gossip had arisen, he quoted to us the strict rule of the Bruderhof. Basically, they insist that if a community member has something negative to say about another member, they need to say it privately to the person himself or herself, and never behind the person's back. [1]

At another TMM, Joe spoke about the Potter's House at the Church of the Saviour in Washington, DC, a community that reached out to the people in their neighbourhood who were struggling. The Potter's House members noted that each of the people they helped also had something important to contribute. L'Arche has a dictum that I think originated in this Washington community: "Every person is a leader at the point of their gift." It came to me that Lloyd, who was quiet and sometimes withdrawn, was a leader in his care for our house, faithfully taking out the garbage and compost each evening without being asked. And Peter, who did his best to avoid work and was a constant tease, was a leader in levity. Yet he also had an emotional fragility that called us to compassion. He could become anguished when something in the house was rearranged or even when anticipating some special event. (Peter had lived for a time in a large institution where, it was later discovered, there had been much abuse.)

Sometimes at a TMM or a regional gathering of L'Arche communities, an assistant would speak about an experience in another L'Arche, either in Canada or farther afield. Some had been asked to help out where there was a shortage of assistants; others had simply included a stint in another community as part of their travels. Clearly, opportunities for personal enrichment lay in L'Arche's being a network of communities.

∾⊶∾

Community life provided a good atmosphere for the kind of joking around that could include everyone. Once spring came, on some Saturday mornings Phil called together the men to help him wash the large old fourteen-seater brown van that was used for transporting people to work at ARC. The call was invariably interpreted as an invitation to a water fight. Luckily, there was no carpet on the hardwood of the Green House dining room floor. There were two doors leading outside. The door from the deck would open, and Lloyd or Francis would appear, carrying a bucket of water that he had filled at the outside tap below. They would dash across the room and out the front door onto the drive, where the van was parked, splashing half of the bucket's contents on the floor and eventually dousing someone with the other half. As our life together thawed some of my reserve, I found myself not just laughing but actually helping facilitate this activity.

Phil would come up with ideas for outings that the whole house could enjoy. One evening we all went to see a comedy at the Herongate dinner theatre. On Mother's Day, he ordered carnation boutonnieres for everyone and we all had brunch at a Golden Griddle restaurant. Mike, who was the only core member with a living mother close enough to visit, saw her later in the day. Occasionally, our entire household went black-light bowling together, even though some of the Green House folks also bowled on Saturdays in a Special Olympics league run by the Community Living Association.

Meanwhile some special events unfolded as spring progressed towards summer. One very celebratory day was Joan and Robin's wedding. [2] The entire house turned out in our best clothes, all the men looking spiffy in suits and white shirts and ties. I took a picture,

51

and afterwards, when I showed it to friends, I was pleased to find that they could not tell which people had a disability. "That is just it!" I exclaimed, a bit surprised at myself. "In the end we are not very different; we are all just human beings!"

The wedding, to which Joan and Robin seemed to have invited all of Daybreak as well as their families and other friends, was a delightful occasion to intermingle. Since I had a car, I was asked to take Peter's mother under my wing. She loved Joan – as did Peter – and she had made the all-day journey by bus down from the village where she lived in northeastern Ontario. Peter's mother was a strong woman, who, very early, was attracted to Jean Vanier's vision and had advocated persistently for her son to live in Daybreak even though Peter came from much farther away than the other Daybreak folks.

Another celebration was the wedding of Joanne and Allan in June. I did not know them, but I had a role as chauffeur of Thelus, who was the maid of honour. I learned that Thelus and Joanne had become friends while both women were living in the New House. Joanne and Allan had met at ARC. Allan had lived in the Big House for a time but later moved to a basement apartment in town, where he had support from a social services worker a couple of times a week. By then he had a job pumping gas at a local gas station. (After the pumps were automated, he worked at a supermarket bringing the shopping carts in from the parking lot.) Joanne was a volunteer at a nursing home.

Carmen, who was house leader at the Church Street house, to which Joanne had moved a few years earlier, was Joanne's closest confidante, and she organized the wedding. The flowers and dresses and the decorations were all beautifully coordinated according to Joanne's wishes.

Joanne and Allan had made the decision not to have children. Just looking after each other would be enough, and, as they both loved animals, they would bring a cat into their household. Nevertheless, the decision to support their wedding had not been easy for the Daybreak community. Some people thought they would not be able to manage. It was our consulting social services and mental health professionals who challenged the community's reservations. We assistants were perhaps judging their likelihood of happiness based on our own expectations. People who are struggling can still have satisfactory marriages, they pointed out.

In fact, Joanne and Allan had a long and happy marriage, even though they lived at or below the poverty line. They moved to a town north of Richmond Hill, closer to Allan's family and where they had good social service supports and a strong church connection. Joanne stayed in touch with Carmen and her husband, Steve, and some of the other early members of the community, and when the Daybreak Seniors Club came into being, a small group of the seniors used to drop in at their apartment periodically. In 2005, Carmen and Steve hosted a dinner for Joanne and Allan to celebrate their upcoming silver anniversary. I was again a chauffeur but was also present as a friend, and Thelus and Peggy and Bill V. were there. (Joanne passed away in 2013; Allan moved in with a family member and has since also died.) [3]

⌘

When I arrived, in early 1981, Carmen and Steve Ellis and their two young children were living in the Church Street house. Our Green House team was paired with the Church Street team for house accompaniment. Carmen and Steve were one of the early L'Arche couples who met in L'Arche in France. They were both Canadians, Carmen from Quebec and Steve from Ontario. When they returned to Canada, it had seemed good to them to come to Daybreak because Steve, a musician, would be studying in Toronto and Carmen could bring her previous L'Arche experience to a house leader role in the community.

Phil and Annette and I would have lunch with them and Marie (the young assistant on the team with Carmen), in a local restaurant after the Monday morning planning meeting. This was a social time and a time for relationship building, and if a question or a team tension had arisen, we could discuss it. Eating out was in itself a treat. I was happy to meet Carmen and Steve partly because they were close to me in age. We gradually became good friends.

"Accompaniment" was another practice imported from L'Arche in France. Besides the team accompaniers, everyone had a personal

53

accompanier – a person not in our house and also more experienced in community life with whom we could discuss confidentially how we were getting on. (Today, we use the word "coach" or "mentor.") A week or two after I had settled in at the Green House, Gus told me that Jo, the New House leader, would be my accompanier. This relationship worked out well.

That first summer I was given the task of leading a group on a two-week vacation trip to Winnipeg. The group consisted of one other assistant and four male core members. I knew none of the group except Gord, and I knew him only as one of the farm workers. The other assistant, a university student who was at Daybreak for the summer, also worked on the farm. We would travel by train and stay in one of the homes of the L'Arche Winnipeg community. (The Winnipeg community, in turn, was sending a vacation group to stay in one of our homes in Toronto.) I was a bit incredulous that this was my assignment, given that I was still very new, in my opinion at least, and given that I, a woman, was put with an all-male group, but I was beginning to learn that the decision making about who was capable of doing what in Daybreak was usually good. Assistants were called quickly to leadership. They grew into it and discovered new competencies. The one thing that made sense was that I knew Winnipeg, though the L'Arche Winnipeg community was far into the suburbs and I was not familiar with the neighbourhood or with getting around the city by public transit, as would be our lot.

During our first afternoon on the train, Mel and Gord let me know they were going forward to the lounge car to have a beer. A few minutes later Mel returned to say they needed me to come and vouch for Gord's age, as the waiter did not think he should be served. Mel, rather than Gord, had come, I recognized, because walking through the swaying train tended to make Gord feel ill. I was touched that Mel, who was legally blind and also didn't find it easy to negotiate the aisles as the train rocketed across the Canadian Shield, had taken the initiative to come back and get me. This sort of kindness was typical of Mel. He didn't want Gord to be excluded. Gord was actually twenty-eight, but like many people who have Down syndrome, he looked young.

In Winnipeg, we took a paddlewheel boat tour along the Red River, and we visited the legislative building, where, crowning its dome, we saw the famed Golden Boy carrying his sheaf of wheat, and inside, the two huge bronze bison that flank the grand staircase. We also spent a day at the new Manitoba Museum of Man and Nature and the planetarium. (Winnipeg had a planetarium before Toronto.) The museum had many impressive displays, including a full-size replica of the *Nonsuch,* the small ship that British explorer Henry Hudson sailed across the Atlantic and into Hudson Bay in 1668, as well as of a pioneer's sod house, and of an early-twentieth-century downtown street with a nickelodeon and a drugstore complete with soda bar.

At the end of our morning, my mother met us and took us to lunch. In the afternoon, we used our tickets to the planetarium. As soon as the planetarium sky started to rotate, Gord became dizzy, and he ended up sitting on a chair outside the theatre during the presentation. I think most of the others in our group fell asleep in the comfortable reclining chairs in the darkened room. On another day, my brother loaned us his big old Imperial for a trip to the zoo and Assiniboine Park. Long after, Mel remembered driving in my brother's very large car. Before we left, the people of L'Arche Winnipeg invited us to a barbecue. Gord was quite smitten with a young woman he met there. They spent most of the evening together on the two-person glider settee. When we got back to Daybreak, I asked Gord if he'd like me to help him write to her, but he thought Winnipeg was too far away.

In spite of my reservations, everyone had a very good time, and I came to see that the context of a vacation, a time when we lived a different and more relaxed rhythm with the emphasis on new experiences and enjoyment, was an equalizer and gave a fine opportunity to get to know one another simply as friends. The only difficult part of the trip was arriving back at Union Station in Toronto at 6:00 a.m. and quite tired. We could not afford sleeping berths on the train. While we spent only one night in the day coach on our westward trip, the rail timetable was such that we sat up for two nights on our return trip.

In October, Phil asked me to drive Peter and Peggy up to visit Peter's mother for the Thanksgiving weekend. (Peggy and Peter's mother had a long-standing friendship.) She had homemade cookies ready for our arrival and had planned Peter's favourite meals. She lived in a small house in a wooded area by a lake. I think it was a treat for all of us to be in Ontario's mid-north, nearly five hours away from Toronto. On Sunday morning we all attended the Anglican church together. But the highlight of the weekend was a lavish Thanksgiving banquet at the local Polish church, to which Peter's mother treated us.

A few years later I was asked to take another vacation group to Winnipeg. This time we drove one of the Daybreak station wagons. The group consisted of a young nun who was helping out at Daybreak for the summer, two middle-aged core members, George and Annie, and two younger members from downtown. The younger members sat in the very back on a seat that flipped so that they could ride looking out the back window. This time we were going to visit the Durners, a couple whom George and Annie remembered fondly from when they had lived at Daybreak. They had a romantic history in Daybreak lore as they had met and fallen in love there, George having come from North Carolina in the United States and speaking only English, and Danielle from Belgium and speaking French. George was now the community leader of L'Arche Winnipeg.

We stayed in a motel along the north shore of Lake Huron east of Sault Ste. Marie the first night. The next day, we set out early for our longest day of driving. We were enjoying the scenery north of Lake Superior and were making good time towards Thunder Bay, where we planned to spend a couple of nights at a retreat centre, when I heard Karen calling from the back that there was a police car following us. Sure enough! And I was definitely over the speed limit. I pulled over and the officer asked for my driver's licence.

Meanwhile, George, who was sitting beside me in the front, attempted to engage the officer in conversation: "Hello!" he said, in his gruff farmer's voice. The officer did not respond. "Hello," George tried again. Then, "Like your job?" he inquired. And when he still got no response, "Nice day, eh?" Meanwhile Annie kept up a quiet but audible running commentary from the seat behind me: "Oh, going too fast, Beth… Oh, getting a ticket, Beth… Tsk, tsk." I was hoping the officer might catch on to the nature of our group and maybe waive the ticket, but no, he was making no exception. In the end I was glad he did not become annoyed with George. For years after that trip, Annie and the backseat pair enjoyed reminding me of my speeding ticket. I think it was the most exciting part of the trip for them.

Of course, we wanted to see the Terry Fox monument. We stopped there at dusk on our way into Thunder Bay. In 1980, Daybreak members had lined Yonge Street in Richmond Hill to see this heroic young man, who had lost a leg to cancer and had set out to run across Canada to raise money for cancer research, pass by on his journey westward. We spent most of the next day at the replica of an Ojibwa village up on Mount McKay. It had guides in traditional clothing who gave interesting presentations. After a few minutes I missed George and found him talking with a man who sat in front of an easel working on a colourful Aboriginal painting. He had stopped work and was patiently responding to George's questions. Beside him was a modest sign with his name: Norval Morrisseau. Some of us had seen his paintings at the Art Gallery of Ontario, in Toronto. I counted it quite a privilege to meet him – a humble man with a gentle nature, it seemed to me.

Besides visiting with the Durners, the one other strong memory I have of that trip is of a Blue Bombers football game that got rained out. I have a mental picture of Annie, her British stoicism in evidence as she waited patiently, hoping the game might resume. The rain was streaming off the brim of her summer hat and down her raincoat.

I was on one Daybreak vacation with Michael. Our group stayed at a Board member's lovely country house near Wasaga Beach Provincial Park, with its long stretch of sand fronting onto the southern shoreline of Georgian Bay. We had just one minor crisis, when I was afraid Mike might have eaten a bit of nut topping at an ice cream stand and we needed to go to the emergency ward of the nearby hospital. He was fine, and I think he enjoyed the attention of the pretty nurse and young doctor who checked him out. Mike liked the house and he enjoyed the tours and spending afternoons at the beach, but he was bored in the evenings. The others had brought crafts and board games. Because he has very little small motor control, such activities are not possible for Mike unless done hand-over-hand. He likes best to be on the move, driving or flying. Michael has always been drawn to the colour red, and he loves speed and cars with special features. One year, Dan, who was teamed with Mike for Mike's vacation, suggested they rent a red Mustang convertible. The vacation was a great hit, and they rented another sporty red car the next year. They didn't need to go far – just toot about. Mike also flew with Dan to Newfoundland to visit Dan's family one Christmas.

On yet another vacation that I was on, a group of us were staying in a L'Arche house in downtown Toronto. One of the people in the group, a man whom I didn't know well, was learning to manage his money. The night before, an assistant was to give him his money for the next day's activities and he would place this in his wallet. We had planned a visit to public gardens for a picnic lunch and, in the afternoon, a new and much-anticipated movie. He had known he would need his money for the movie ticket, but when it came time to pay, his wallet was empty. It turned out that he had slipped out early that morning and spent his movie money on a couple of fancy donuts and a hot chocolate at a nearby Tim Hortons. Still standing next to him, I explained that he would have to miss the movie and that one of us assistants would stay back with him. He glared at me for a moment and suddenly punched me.

He did apologize, and later we discussed the incident with the consultant who was helping him with the money management program. For a while, he went back to the earlier arrangement of one of us assistants giving him his money just when he needed to pay for something. When he restarted the money management program, he was fairly successful with it, although I think his motivation to manage his money was not very great. I thought about my own role in the situation. I was standing too close, especially given that I knew this core member had sometimes punched people at ARC. I also wished I had reinforced more strongly the previous night the need for him to keep his money for the movie and the consequence of not doing so. A while later, Crisis Prevention training became available, and Daybreak assistants were sent to it. Although it is rare in L'Arche for people to hit out at others, I was not the only assistant who found the training helpful. There are usually signs when someone is beginning to become stressed and might lose control. We learned simple methods that will often de-escalate such situations.

5. *"Je m'abandonne à toi"*: Some months in Quebec

My vision is that belonging should be at the heart of a fundamental discovery: that we all belong to a common humanity, the human race. We may be rooted in a specific family and culture but we come to this earth to open up to others, to serve them and receive the gifts they bring to us, as well as to all of humanity. Jean Vanier

When I had some personal vacation time during my first summer at Daybreak, I drove down to Quebec to visit L'Arche Le Printemps,[1] the community in Saint-Malachie where my friend Marilyn had settled in as an assistant. The trip took eleven hours and would have been longer by train and bus. Leaving Quebec City, I crossed the Saint Lawrence river and headed south into a rural area. There, rolling hills mark the end of the Appalachian mountain range, which extends north into Canada.

Saint-Malachie is a charming little village that runs along the crest of a hill overlooking the Etchemin river. At that time it had a couple of stores, a post office, a very large old white clapboard church (unusual, in that old churches in Quebec were typically built of stone), and a sprinkling of traditional rural Quebec houses constructed of wood, some with gingerbread trim. Each had a front porch, and some had an outside staircase leading up to a second-storey porch and entry. The total population of the village would have been about a thousand.

L'Arche Le Printemps was financially much less well off than Daybreak, as it received only quite modest government assistance. It seemed to me that the people of Le Printemps lived a simpler life, closer to one another and to God and more in solidarity with the poor than we did at Daybreak, with the diversions of movie theatres, malls, and bowling alleys nearby. And yet, in almost all other ways, daily life and relationships within the two communities were much the same. It struck me how easily the pattern and values of L'Arche transferred to a different linguistic and cultural setting and a much more rural environment. The key elements of L'Arche were all there – the emphasis on welcome, on mealtimes, on doing things together, on mutuality in relationships, on being part of the wider community and knowing our neighbours, on meaningful work, the respect for each one's preferences, and the effort to balance these with life in community.

I began to think about moving there after completing my year's commitment at Daybreak. By the following spring, I had made up my mind, and I let both the Daybreak and the Le Printemps community leaders know that I would like to become an assistant in Le Printemps beginning in September. As it happened, the Saint-Malachie community was planning to open a third home, and I would be able to help establish it.

In the summer of 1982, I sold my car, knowing I would not have enough income to run a car in Quebec, and, with Carmen Ellis's help, I tried to bone up on my limited French. For a few weeks I stayed at the new Centre Street house in Richmond Hill, to which Peggy and Thelus had moved. It was a house for more independent core members, who now lived on their own with an assistant coming in to help them with some tasks. At the end of the summer, I met with Joe Egan for an exit interview. "Sometimes people discover that they already have put down roots and found a place of belonging and meaningful contribution only when they have left, or have decided to leave," he told me at the conclusion of our conversation, and he assured me that I would be welcome to return.

The Green House hosted a send-off party for me, which many Daybreak people attended. Some of the core members and assistants performed a funny skit about my trying to learn French. Then I was presented with an album of photos signed inside both covers with messages of thanks and good wishes from each one, and the gathering ended with a blessing and prayer that I would find life in my new community and bring goodness to them. A final surprise came just as everyone was leaving. John B., a man whom I had not come to know very well, pressed on me a small black-and-white photo of himself some years younger, as a Cub Scout. I did not want to take it as I was sure it was precious to him, but he insisted, so I added it to the album. John has difficulty finding his words, and it takes patience to wait while he is speaking. Reflecting later, I realized that on the occasions when we had been together in gatherings, I was one of the people who did remain present to him, waiting while he finished his thought. Perhaps that led to the bond he apparently felt with me.

I was very touched by the party, the gift of the album, and everyone's good wishes. I did not realize that in eighteen months I had come to be so appreciated and even loved by so many people.

∽∾∾

Le Printemps consisted of just two large and well-established homes near the south end of the main street of the village and a workshop that was down on the rural highway that ran along the river. Les Erables (the Maples), the newly acquired and renovated third *foyer* (literally "hearth"; *foyer* is the French word used for all L'Arche homes), where I was to live with four core members and two other assistants, was located towards the other end of the village, about a fifteen-minute walk along the rue Principale, from the other L'Arche homes. My housemates were Diane and Carmen and Dollard and Viateur and assistants François and Elizabeth.

In Saint-Malachie, there were none of the distractions of the city, and days were lived very simply. Most houses had a comfortable rocking chair or two on their porches, where the old people would sit. In front of one of the L'Arche homes, Léonard, who was by far the oldest member of the community, would occupy such a chair all day, smoking his pipe, offering a nod and toothless grin to passersby, and asking any woman who might seem less than middle-aged to marry him. As its oldest member, Léonard was revered in the community, and in a way, he came to represent for me the goodness that L'Arche brought to its members. He had lived almost all his life in an institution some distance to the south, until L'Arche was founded here and was able to welcome him.

Elizabeth, who was bilingual, had been in the community for some time and was our house leader for the first two months as the house got established. (After that, François and I shared that responsibility.) Carmen, Diane and Dollard were the other house members. Later, Viatur joined us. In all, the community at that time consisted of about two dozen people, including the community leader, Jean, and his wife, Cathy, who had a separate house with their children. Everyone walked everywhere in the village. There were visits of core members and assistants to local stores to pick up last-minute grocery items or to buy meat from the butcher, and there were frequent visits among the homes, and neighbours to drop in on. Monsieur le Curé clearly liked having the community in his parish and would invite us into the rectory for a few minutes' chat. Both Carmen and Diane enjoyed these visits.

Marilyn, who is very outgoing, had come to know several interesting people in the town apart from the usual L'Arche friends and parish folk. One day she took me to visit a professor who commuted to Laval University in Quebec City. He lived alone in a small, traditional-style but modern-seeming open-concept house with a kitchenette at one end. He invited us in, but I am not sure he was pleased to have our visit. To my amazement he made and drank cup after cup of espresso coffee as he and Marilyn discussed village news and I tried to follow. I would have loved a little cup of that coffee, but he made no offer!

Saint Malachie was an Irish saint, and I was curious to know how the village got its name.[2] On one of my trips to the post office to mail letters back to Daybreak and my family, the postmistress, who spoke English well, told me the early history of her family and the village. The founders had been Irish immigrants who came after the War of 1812, when Britain was wanting to increase the population of Lower Canada in areas between the Saint Lawrence and the American border. To this end it was giving out parcels of farmland. The descendants of these settlers continued to live in the village and intermarried with the French population of the region. Some still speak English at home, but they are fully bilingual and well integrated into the predominantly francophone Québécois culture.[3]

The Le Printemps community vehicle, a van, was used to transport people back and forth to work at the *atelier* (workshop) at the bottom of the hill. One night a week, a L'Arche group used the van to go to the swimming pool in the high school at Saint-Anselme, a town twenty minutes' drive to the north. There was a sauna with the pool – one sauna shared by men and women. Like the French in France, Quebeckers, I soon realized, tend to be more comfortable with the naked or near-naked body than the English. Diane and Carmen and I were sitting in the sauna fairly well wrapped in our towels when a man walked in totally nude. Not being aware of the norm, I challenged him in my faltering French, but he quickly set me straight, saying more or less, "What's your problem?" as he settled in on a bench across from us.

Life in the Le Printemps homes was simple and intimate and focused mainly on doing activities together at home. There were few places to go – no movie theatre or such. Besides the usual chores of cleaning and laundry and cooking, there were crafts and games and pastimes like colouring, and often a banner or sign to be made to welcome a visitor or mark a birthday or an anniversary. As in Daybreak, there were skits to be planned for community gatherings and prayer. The TV attracted only a little attention. Each home had a small prayer room with a candle, one or two icons, and cushions on the floor. Assistants and core members who wished would rise a bit earlier than the others and meet there to pray and read the morning office or the Gospel passage for the day. One assistant remained at home during the morning to cook the main meal, which was eaten at noon. Everyone else would go to the workshop after breakfast. At noon, the van from the *atelier* would return, dropping groups at each home for the *dîner* and a few minutes' rest before almost everyone, usually including the cook, would return to work for the afternoon.

The evening meal, the *souper,* often consisted of a hearty soup and bread and assorted cheeses. Local cheese was available as dairy farming was one of the mainstays of the area. Occasionally we would receive special cheese made by the Benedictine monks at the Saint-Benoît-du-Lac abbey, where one of the male assistants visited, or by the Trappist monks in the monastery at Oka. After the meal we would linger for a while chatting at the table. Dollard, who had few words but liked to entertain us, would often start a game by knocking with his knuckles on the underside of the table. Diane or Carmen would obligingly get up, open the door to the street, and return to let us know that no one was there. Everyone would laugh. Then a few minutes later the game would resume.

On Tuesdays after work everyone would gather for a community meeting in the living room of the largest Le Printemps home. New people were welcomed, plans for community events were sketched out, birthdays were marked, and Jean, as community leader, would make announcements of events or visitors for the coming week. In some ways this meeting served the same function as the all-assistants Monday morning planning meeting at Daybreak, but I liked it that here everyone in the community was present. One evening a week, there was a Mass celebrated by Père Gilles, a gentle and wise Jesuit priest who travelled down from Quebec City. He would spend the day in the community and meet with core members and assistants who wanted to see him. Although many of the francophone assistants were not religious and some held the Catholic Church in disdain for its history of aligning itself with the wealthy, usually anglophone, business class, everyone seemed to respect Gilles, who lived very simply and was attentive to each person. On Sundays, almost all the core members and enough assistants to support them would attend Mass at the parish church.

Each week there was a *soirée de famille* in our *foyer,* a special candlelight evening meal without guests and sometimes eaten in silence or to quiet music. It was followed by some entertainment created by those in the house. This might include French folk or popular songs, especially if someone present could play the guitar. There was a time for each person to speak about how they were doing, as in the house meetings in the Green House, and a time of communal prayer that ended with singing the L'Arche prayer, which addressed Mary: "O Mary, we ask you to bless our house... May L'Arche be a true home... a refuge of peace and welcome for the poor and for little people ...Help us to welcome with tenderness and compassion those you send us ...".[4]

Almost everyone in the community worked at the *atelier*. Most of the men worked on the paper recycling project, and the women joined a talented Swiss assistant who worked with them to create beautiful cards using pressed local wildflowers. I was usually asked to help Christiane or Madeleine with the cards. A couple of core members had their own projects. Carmen made curtains, by stringing together cut-up coloured straws. They were like those often found in open doorways. Benoît specialized in creating wood burnings of the San Damiano cross of Saint Francis. One of the *atelier* assistants would prepare and sand the cross-shaped pine boards for him. Each cross was unique, revealing Benoît's own profound religious sensibility.

Benoît was a mystery. He could be easily frightened, and he shied away from crowds and from being touched. He seemed very gentle and delicate. He moved slowly and talked rarely and only in a murmur. I had the impression that he had suffered a lot and wondered what trauma he might have experienced. Everyone loved and respected him. Elizabeth was close to Benoît, and, through her, I came to know him even though we were in different houses. I think we shared a bond because he understood that I also, with my limited French, could not communicate in the same way as the others and sometimes felt lonely, and because I appreciated his work. He was a compassionate man – maybe a kind of Christ figure in the community.

In those days Saint-Malachie had only one little restaurant, a diner down on the main road not far from the *atelier*. On Friday afternoons each worker would be paid two dollars for the week's work, and the entire van load of L'Arche people would crowd into the restaurant and spend all their pay, almost always on a plate of *patates frites* and a Coke or other pop. This was in a time before the popularity of poutine, although in the village grocery store I discovered cheese curds – a tasty and popular local snack then, and later an essential ingredient of poutine.

The house food budget was quite modest. One morning a week, whether or not we needed a major grocery shopping trip, an assistant would take the van up to Lévis, the smaller and more industrial city that faces Quebec City across the Saint Lawrence

River, where the produce manager of the supermarket had a soft spot for L'Arche and would save their reduced produce for us. It would be distributed among the three L'Arche homes and was our primary source of vegetables for salads, soups, and main meals. The community also had a membership in a co-op, where it obtained large supplies of various kinds of dried beans, lentils, seeds, rice, and flour. Occasionally, a batch of one or another would be infested with weevils, so we had to check our cupboard regularly. One luxury we had was a gallon of maple syrup given each house by a local producer. Besides using it on pancakes, for a Sunday breakfast treat we would fry eggs in maple syrup. I was devastated when, after a few months, it fermented. We had barely used half of it. I had not realized that it needed to be kept in the fridge!

One day when I had returned from the Lévis trip and was home making the noon meal, I received a surprise call from Joe Egan. He wanted to tell me that Bill Rous had died. Like others, I had visited Bill from time to time in the New House, sitting by his bed for a few minutes. I knew that Bill was important to the members of the Daybreak community who had known him when he was well and able to interact with them. I gathered from stories I'd heard that Bill had been quite a character. But I had hardly known him. I was a bit mystified as to why Joe had called me with this news. However, I did mention Daybreak's loss of a long-time core member at the Tuesday afternoon community meeting when there was an opportunity to share news. Others seemed to take this news in a more heartfelt manner than I did, and one of the homes was assigned to make a sympathy card for the Daybreak community. I had not yet fully grasped the bond that exists among L'Arche communities.

As I grew in my sense of belonging in L'Arche, I appreciated this bond. We really were all part of one body, in some sense. And someone's death was a time to step back and appreciate that person anew. Visitations and funerals in L'Arche are usually big celebrations of the individual's life. Many stories are shared and photos albums displayed. Most people in L'Arche become comfortable with death and saying goodbye to friends because L'Arche welcomes people of varying ages – some people live at home until their parents are very old and they are already older themselves.

None of the assistants in Le Printemps had cars, and, unless they had friends or family nearby, they would usually spend their day away in the little assistants' apartment that was attached to the house of a friend of the community. For our monthly weekend we might travel up to Quebec City if there was space to stay in the L'Arche community there, or we female assistants could go to the Trappistine monastery in Saint-Romuald, where the elderly sisters graciously welcomed us for a small donation. Father Benedict Vanier, Jean's older brother who was a Trappist monk, served as chaplain there for many years and met with assistants for spiritual direction if they asked. When I would arrive tired from trying to speak French, he would kindly urge me to take a break and speak English with him and to read English books from his library. I remember borrowing books by Thomas Merton while there.

One core member at the *atelier* was a particular challenge for me. He was saucy and uncooperative and made it clear that he didn't like me. I recognized that my poor French contributed to the problem. I wasn't able to joke with him, as were the other assistants. This man's family, like many Quebeckers, were strongly separatist, and I wondered also if he disliked me because he knew I came from English Canada. Only two years earlier, in 1980, Quebec had held a referendum to decide if it wanted to secede from Canada. (Some assistants were separatists, but I never picked up any negativity from them. I think they were pleased that I had chosen to join them, and that I was trying to learn French.)

∾∽

In mid-October, at the six-week point, I hit the wall. I knew the signs of culture shock from my CUSO experience, and I knew it would pass. However, one day I was particularly exhausted by the busy pace of life and my efforts to speak French, and I was feeling the isolation of not having enough of the language to join in the interesting, sometimes philosophical conversations among the other assistants. In addition, I had become aware that I had no love at all in my heart for the challenging core member. In fact, I strongly disliked him. I was feeling a complete failure as an assistant. I went into the tiny attic chapel attached to the assistants' apartment and wept a long time, admitting to myself and God my total inner poverty.

It was a cathartic moment that opened the way to some significant spiritual growth. My two favourite Rublev icons were in that chapel – the one of the Trinity, which L'Arche people often display because it depicts both the community shared by the Trinity and the hospitality of Abraham to the angels, themes central to L'Arche, and the one known as Christ the Redeemer. That day, I was drawn to the latter. The iconographer is meant to paint the subject's eyes as looking straight back at the gazer, and it seemed to me that this was the case at that moment. It seemed a gaze of knowing acceptance. Beside the candle, someone had left a small card inscribed with the Prayer of Abandonment of Charles de Foucauld. *Mon Père, je m'abandonne à toi,* it begins. *Fais de moi ce qu'il te plaira....* (Father, I abandon myself to you. Do with me what pleases you.) I still prefer the prayer in French, where the second-person singular pronoun conveys an intimacy with God that the English misses.

As I read this prayer I knew that it was okay and even good to be so utterly empty and so *incapable.* (The French pronunciation seemed to better capture the experience.) Feeling *incapable* was a new experience for me. Maybe I was often that way but didn't see it and certainly did not think of "abandoning" myself to God or anyone else. But in this place of emptiness, everything was all right. Accepting that I was "incapable," I discovered the grace to continue, and as I lived the ensuing days with greater inner freedom, almost immediately I found myself more able to cope with daily life.

This experience of poverty of spirit as a source of blessing (it *is* one of the Beatitudes) has nourished and formed me in a fundamental way over the years. My understanding and the imagery I tend to use to describe God has changed, but the fundamental truth of our contingency, and, I believe, of the enormous creative power of Life and Love that sustains us and our universe and all the universes beyond, remains. Rabbi Michael Lerner's description of God as "the spiritual energy of the universe that makes for transformation and self-transcendence" speaks to me.[5]

I lamented the core member's rejection of me to François, and he pointed out my problem with verbs, particularly with *falloir*, and suggested the more delicate and gentle verb form. I was using "Il *faut* que tu ..." rather than *faudrait* (in effect, "You must" ... rather than the more delicate, "It would be better ..."). I surely had come across as bossy when I told the man that he "must" put his work here, or "must" hurry up because the van was leaving. I learned to say instead, "It would be good" to do whatever ... I seemed to turn a corner with the young man, even as my French seemed finally to be improving.

Our life together at Les Erables and the *atelier* continued, and then, in late November, a letter arrived from Phil. In short, he told me he had decided to leave the Green House and L'Arche in the new year, to explore his future life direction – whether marriage or a vocation to religious life. Instantly, I thought of Michael and Lloyd and Francis and Peter, whom I loved, and of how difficult this news would be for them. I felt I should return. I had made a commitment to Saint-Malachie for the usual three-month *stage*, with a view to continuing if all went well, as seemed the case at that point. On the other hand, I recognized that I had a heart commitment to the well-being of the people in the Green House that went quite deep. In a way, without my realizing it, they had become "my people." Because I had often covered as house leader for Phil during times when he was away, I knew I was an obvious person to take his place. I had no doubt about the decision I should make.

For some reason, it seemed urgent that I let Daybreak know, and I placed a call to Joe Egan that afternoon to tell him I would come back. As it happened, I called in the midst of a Daybreak Council meeting and exactly at the point when they were discussing Phil's replacement. And so it was decided. At the same time, I explained to Joe that I wanted to stay on in Le Printemps until I could be replaced. In conversation with Jean, the community leader, it was agreed that I would leave in mid-January, as there was the promise of another assistant arriving around that time.

I went to L'Arche Le Printemps in good faith, intending to spend a year and perhaps much longer, but, in fact, in the grand scheme of things it seemed I went so I could discover and accept first, that

I was not always capable and that this was okay, and second, that I *belonged* at Daybreak and to certain people there who were calling me back. A third discovery was that, because of my time at Le Printemps, our two communities could share a friendship across language and cultural differences.

∽◦∾

I have never lost track of the album that the people of Daybreak gave me when I left for Saint-Malachie in early September 1982, or of the few pictures that I took there and added to that album. Today, when I look at the messages written by Daybreak assistants and core members inside its covers, I see how it was so right for me to go to Le Printemps and also that it was so right to return to Daybreak. My Daybreak friends sent me with love, proud to be sending one of their own to a sister community. They were more aware than I of the bond they had come to share with me, and they expressed it in their comments. A few seemed to know that Daybreak would draw me back one day. I am touched again as I reread the notes: "Hope to see you again," "I'll always remember the friendship you showed me," "Thank you for your thoughtful presence to our family," "Please keep in touch," "Bonne chance au Québec. I am sure you will make many friends there," and "Remember us with these pictures until you return." I had been at Daybreak only a year and a half, and, in my usual cautious and reserved manner, I had kept my heart's commitment somewhat in abeyance, but somehow, I had already come to belong there. At the same time, I have never stopped carrying the people of L'Arche Le Printemps in my heart. For me, those four months in Saint-Malachie, where I experienced the intimate ethos of the village and community life, and where I came better to know and accept myself, were profoundly enriching and life-changing, and, long after, they continued to nourish my spiritual journey. I had grown to love the people of Le Printemps – especially the core people and assistants with whom I had lived or worked closely. Some of them had loved me, and all attested that the feeling of connection was mutual. What was more, I sensed that I was not just one anglophone person who had come to live their life for a little while. I also represented a bridge between our two communities – this small, rural Quebec francophone community and the large, semi-urban anglophone community of Daybreak, the oldest and biggest L'Arche community in North America. Daybreak had sent me to them, and now they sent me back to Daybreak. It seemed obvious we should find a way to maintain the connection.

∽o∾

In French Catholic tradition, Christmas is celebrated as a religious feast only. Gifts are exchanged not at Christmas but at Epiphany, la fête des Rois, the twelfth and final day of the Christmas season and the day when the Magi, the Three Kings from the Orient, arrived bringing gifts for the baby Jesus. In 1984, at the beginning of my first January back at Daybreak, I organized a little group of Daybreak folk – a van load – to travel down to Saint-Malachie for the celebration of Epiphany. The visit was a great success for all of us in both L'Arche communities, and for me it was a wonderful opportunity to renew friendships there.

The Epiphany visit became an annual tradition. Each time, we were welcomed with the same wonderful Le Printemps hospitality. On one of these trips, both Lloyd and Michael came along. At the large gathering of community members and friends, there were special sandwiches and other refreshments and, for dessert, as usual, two cakes, one to be served to the women and one to be served to the men. Each cake had a single bean hidden in it. One of the Epiphany traditions is to crown a king and queen. They then distribute the gifts. The roles of king and queen are assigned to the two people who find a bean in their cake. I am sure that the planners had organized behind the scenes that a male member of the Daybreak group would get the piece with the bean from the men's cake. As it turned out, Lloyd found the bean in his cake and became the king, and Madeleine from Le Printemps became the queen. To this day I have a mental picture of them sitting on their "thrones," wearing their foil-covered cardboard crowns and grinning from ear to ear. That year, our Le Printemps hosts presented us with the very special gift of wood-burned crosses made by Benoît – one for each of our (by then) eight Daybreak homes.

The winter snowfall can be enormous in Quebec, often mounting well up to the second floors of houses. We finally discontinued these January trips after nearly ending up topsy-turvy in a ditch one dark evening while negotiating a tight curve in a Quebec snowstorm. Frère Rolland, a Capuchin brother who was an assistant at Le Printemps from its founding, drove a van of folks from Le Printemps to Daybreak for Easter weekend a couple of times, and he did the same for Halloween another year, but I felt that our welcome of them never quite compared with our mid-winter experience of celebrating Epiphany in Saint-Malachie.

❧

In the later 1980s and the 1990s, I became busy in various roles in the Daybreak community, and I studied for a few years. It was not until I was working on educational resources for L'Arche Canada that I had occasion to travel to Quebec again. I was gathering stories from L'Arche communities across the country for a best-practices book, for which we had received a federal government grant. Twenty years had passed when I called the L'Arche community in Saint-Malachie to ask if I could come for an afternoon visit to their *atelier* and perhaps have dinner in my old *foyer*. I knew that some of the core members had died, and all of the assistants whom I had known had left and new people had come. Nevertheless, there was still the same spirit of welcome, and I was delighted when I walked into the *atelier* and first Madeleine, and then Diane, Carmen, and Christiane all recognized me.

Diane rushed over and gave me one of her special hugs, and I was immediately reminded of the kindness and sensitivity this silent little woman had shown me back in 1982. On days when I was struggling, she would seem to sense this and would wrap her arms around my waist in the same warm hug. Among those who greeted me warmly was the man whom I had found so difficult to like. Things did improve greatly between us before I left, and I think we had both overcome any ill feelings. Everyone stopped work for tea, and we had a great reunion. They then showed me the work they were doing now. They were making modular pinewood shelves, a product that sold well and that was a collaboration with the woodworking shop in L'Arche Vancouver.[6]

Benoît, I learned, had retired and was no longer making his wood-burned crosses. I would need to see him at his *foyer,* a home that had opened in the intervening years. When I introduced myself at the door, the assistant called Benoît. He approached me slowly, looking bewildered. Then, I could see that he was pulling back the memory of me gradually as I spoke to him. His face broadened into a beautiful smile accompanied by a lively murmur and the sign of happiness he used to make with his hands. That visit and the dinner in Les Erables, where Diane and Carmen still lived, were special blessings for me, and I think this was true for my old friends as well, but they also awakened the poignancy of years passing. I wished I had made more of an effort to stay in touch.

6. *"P'zatt!"*: A deepening belonging

Gradually we discover what a richness it is to live with such a diversity of people, and such a diversity of gifts. Jean Vanier

In mid-January 1983, Phil and Jane picked me up at Union Station in Toronto. Jane was a core member who had arrived in the Green House while I was away. She had come from an institution where she lived after her mother died. Returning, I felt much more settled interiorly, ready to follow an emerging sense of long-term vocation in L'Arche. I was eager to see my friends Peter, Francis, Michael, and Lloyd again, and to get to know Jane. Peggy was doing well at the new Centre Street house in the company of others who were more independent. I would miss Annette, who had returned to university, but I was happy to learn that Sharon, who had come in the spring before I left, was still there. She and I and a male assistant who was yet to come would be the team when Phil left. Apart from Jane's arrival, there had been few changes in the four months I was away. There was a smooth transition when Phil moved to an apartment downtown at the end of the month.

My life became busier as the number of meetings I was expected to attend increased, but at the same time there was a good feeling of collegiality throughout the community. Soon after I returned from Quebec, there was an all-community discernment for new Daybreak Council members, and I was elected. The Council, which met every two weeks, was an advisory group for the community leader. It contributed to major decisions and envisioned future growth. This ongoing involvement in helping to shape the community increased my sense of belonging.

Jane proved a hardy person, temperamentally a survivor. She knew what she liked and wanted. She was both an endearing and a challenging member of the Green House. She loved to have fun and play little jokes. On small pieces of paper she would draw pictures of what looked like ghosts – she called them nightmares – and put one of the drawings at someone's place at the table or into the pocket of someone who was in her favour. I think she gave them only to assistants. These were gifts and meant to surprise and please us, and she would smile and laugh with delight when we discovered them. Jane showed a lot of initiative when something interested her, for instance, doing her rug hooking (at which she was skilled), and a lot of resistance when something did not, such as going for a walk or coming swimming with others in the house. If pushed into exercising, she would complain loudly.

Jane could learn simple procedures very well when they were demonstrated for her. While I lived with Jane, she had some teeth out and got new partial dentures. I was with her as the dental hygienist showed her how to brush her teeth and care for the dentures. Jane grasped the procedure, which involved a number of steps, and followed it unfailingly for years. In a way, Jane had taken Cynthia's place at the Green House, but she was very different from Cynthia, sturdy and confident in herself, whereas Cynthia had been fragile. Obviously, no one can ever replace another person. Certainly, Cynthia remained in the hearts of all of us, her former housemates.

Michael was the most physically limited person at Daybreak, but I think he was also the most passionate when interested in something. The remarkable capabilities of Superman inspired him then and still do today. One of the ways he expresses this interest is through gathering up his breath and doing unusual things with his throat and mouth to produce certain sound effects. One winter morning when it was time for Mike and the others to leave for work, the front door of the Green House seemed to be frozen or locked shut, and neither Cathy, who was helping out at that time, nor I could open it. For Mike to exit through the mud room door was risky because descending stairs could trigger a seizure. We needed the front door to open. When I explained the problem to Mike, he told us authoritatively, "Stand back!" He held his arm straight out and approached the door, uttering a loud *p'zatt!* sound, as in the comics. He then turned the knob, and the door opened easily. Cathy and I stood mouths agape as he matter-of-factly walked through the door and to the waiting van.

As a few months had passed since Peggy moved out, we were asked to welcome Margaret, not yet age twenty-one, who had been living with younger children in a foster family but was now too old to continue living there. Margaret had lost both her parents, but she had an elderly, caring aunt who was a good advocate and a loving presence for her during the transition. Her aunt passed away a year or so later.

It was clearly a tremendous adjustment for Margaret to move into an all-adult household with four men, two of whom were more than twice her age, and Jane, who was also somewhat older and very different in temperament. Jane could be quite boisterous. Margaret was quiet. She must have felt a little lost. She seemed to be sad and not to have a lot of self-confidence. She related sometimes to Francis and Lloyd, but not much to Michael and Peter, the more disabled house members. She spent her free time either alone in her room or sitting in the living room rocking chair. Sometimes she spoke aloud to herself about the people in the house and their actions, apparently trying to figure them out.

Sharon and I tried to spend one-on-one time with Margaret when possible. Thinking she was homesick, one day I drove her back to have a little visit with her foster family, but seeing them again did not seem to be especially meaningful to her. For Margaret's twenty-first birthday, the Green House hosted a barbecue in our backyard. Most of the people in the other two homes on the farm property came. Her twin brothers came, and her aunt came early with the gift of a new, very chic polka-dot outfit. She looked smashing, and everyone complimented her. She seemed happy that day. However, it was clear that the Green House was not a good fit for her. When an opportunity came to live in town with more independent people, Margaret moved, and then she moved again to one of Daybreak's downtown houses.

Phil's musician friend Steve Mosher sometimes visited the Green House when not on tour with the National Ballet Orchestra. After Phil left Daybreak, Steve continued his visits. Sometimes, he would take Peter and Lloyd for a beer at the local pub, an experience that they all seemed to relish. When we were short of assistants or during Daybreak vacations, if he was free Steve would become a temporary unpaid assistant. In the summer of 1984, he benefitted from covering for my personal vacation in a way that I am sure he did not anticipate. Alida, a young teacher, had also come to volunteer at the Green House, and Steve and Alida got to know each other that week. (It was later that Steve formed a close friendship with George, at the Church Street house, and, in time, with Mel, who had moved in the 1970s to one of the downtown houses.) Steve had seemed to be a sworn bachelor, but several years later he and Alida married.

I enjoyed being back on the Daybreak farm. During lambing season, if there was a runt rejected by its mother, Jean Lomas, the wife of our farm manager, Len, would take it into their house and feed it with a milk bottle. When I was free, I would drop in to assist with this and to hold the little creature for a few minutes. In the summer, if I had some time, I would stroll along the farm lane, which stretched almost to the Canadian National Railway main line, a twenty-minute walk. Lilac and honeysuckle bordered the lane here and there, and at the end of the lane, just before the last large field of grain, there was a big old oak tree, under which I would sit. I loved seeing John S. or Len on the tractor working the fields, and the cows and sheep grazing.

I signed up to help with the farm chores one weekend. There were two sign-up slots, one to feed the chickens and gather the eggs, and one to feed the cows. I chose the latter. Filling the water troughs was easy, and I managed to drag the two heavy bales of hay to the door of the loft and push them down into the midst of the waiting cows in the feedlot. The cows were also to have a pail of grain, and some of them waited at the empty trough inside, knowing this was coming. The location of the grain was not, however, evident, and John, who was to look after the chickens that morning, had not yet shown up, but I needed to get back to the Green House to help with morning routines. I looked around and finally found a bin that appeared to be grain and dumped a pail of it into the cows' feed trough.

When I mentioned to Len a few days later that I had been uncertain as to where the grain for the cows was located, he asked what bin I had fed them from and then said, "Ah, that's why the cows have been constipated!" I had fed them the chickens' grain. Len didn't seem too concerned, but I felt terrible and my stomach ached for the poor cows! The chicken chores took more courage, but I did do them a couple of times, holding my nose and constantly fearing that the roosting hens would give me a big peck as I reached under them for their precious eggs, or that I would step on the feet of the avian masses that crowded around as I put the food into their feeder. The experience increased my admiration for George and Gord and John S., each of whom was responsible for the chickens at various times.

∽◦∾

John was in the habit of dropping in to the Green House some evenings after the New House finished dinner. He usually arrived just in time for dessert. He had the gift of an entertainer and would take over the room for a few minutes. If there were guests, he would ask their names and where they were from, and then, while everyone was still at the table, he would launch into a short speech that was difficult to follow but during which he would announce clearly the name of each person present and elicit applause for that person. If he remembered the person's hometown, he might identify them in this way – Mr. Halifax! Miss Ottawa! His "speech" would end in a crescendo as he called the name of one more person and awarded that person the quarter or the chocolate bar that he had been holding up, thereby riveting our attention throughout his oration. He was truly a community builder. I think his sensitivity guided him, as often the prize went to the guest, if there was one, or to someone who needed lifting up at that moment. Later, when Clara or Chris gave student retreats, John would often drop in to greet the retreatants and animate the gathering for a few minutes, calling the young people out of their shyness to tell him their names.

John had grown up on farms – on the family farm until his parents died, and then on his uncle's farm – and he brought his farming skills and aptitude to Daybreak. He had learned to drive a tractor skillfully. When Len came as the farm manager, in the mid-seventies, he adopted John as his right-hand man. More than that, John was like a son to Len and Jean, and a brother to their five daughters.

John differed from others I knew who had Down syndrome in that he had a lean build, but he did have the usual outgoing, kind nature and sensitivity. He had a few standard questions and phrases. He would greet people with a cheery wave, calling out, "How are ya?" or "How's your mom?" even though some people had told him repeatedly that their mothers had passed on. "Oh, that's right," he would say unapologetically. Every Saturday and some weekday summer evenings, John walked the three kilometres into the heart of Richmond Hill, dropping in to visit in each business along the way. He had friends among the employees in all the car dealerships, coffee shops, hardware and appliance stores, and even the local bank, and he had quite a collection of business cards, hats, badges, and other memorabilia from these establishments.

Besides being a farmer, John was a musician. As a boy he had often attended country square dances with his family. Later he would accompany his uncle and guardian, who called the dances or played the drum with house bands that performed in the neighbouring area. John would take a pair of kitchen spoons and play along with these groups. He had a fine sense of rhythm and timing and a touch of showmanship. Daybreak assistants would regularly take John to play at local pubs where a country band or an Irish group was performing. The bands recognized John's skill and welcomed him. After a couple of numbers, he would stand, bow to the loud applause, and then urge applause for the lead player and other band members, pointing out each one. After Henri Nouwen came to Daybreak, he brought back a fine pair of joined, highly polished wooden spoons from one of his speaking trips – a gift for John. John was delighted. He played those spoons for many years and would always mention Henri as having given him his spoons. Much later, some assistants contributed to buy him a new pair.

Not surprisingly, with his experience on farms, John had a way with animals. Late one evening, after Clara, one of John's assistant friends, and John had gone downtown so he could play his spoons with a group at a popular pub, they discovered their car had been towed because they had accidentally parked illegally. After managing to flag a cab, they arrived in a desolate area down near the harbour, where the barbed-wire enclosure that was the car pound was located. A large, chained German shepherd was guarding the entrance and barked furiously at them. In spite of Clara's cautions, John stooped down to the level of the dog and, in his quiet voice, began coaxing it: "Here, puppy, puppy, puppy…" Gradually, the dog stopped barking and came closer. John allowed it to sniff him, and then he was able to pet the dog. Inside the small trailer that served as the car pound office, John chatted up the two burly guards while Clara paid the fine.

Beginning in the 1990s and until today, once a year everything in the upper level of the Daybreak barn is pushed back to the walls, the floor is swept, lights and decorations are hung, and the community holds a barn dance to raise funds for our sister L'Arche communities in Honduras. For John's fiftieth birthday, his assistant friends decided to hold a barn dance party for him. They invited friends of John who were professional musicians. One played the fiddle, another the Irish bodhran drum and keyboard. John's uncle called some of the dances, teaching the essentials so everyone could join in. John played with the band through the evening, giving out his well-honed western hoot every so often. It was a regular country hoedown with people dosey-doe-ing and weaving in a very large circle. As usual at Daybreak dances, it included members whose partners twirled them in their wheelchairs.

One of John's New House assistant friends, Deiren, was studying filmmaking. He created an award-winning, ten-minute video about John's life titled *Where's Your Home?* The title is a question that John invariably asked when meeting new people. The film has often been shown to introduce L'Arche to visitors and to help teach high school students and others about the gifts and abilities of people who may seem very different from them. It is easy to sense Deiren's love and respect for John in that film. Deiren began to make a feature film with John, to be titled "The Spoonman," focusing on John as a performer. On one occasion, Deiren and Chris drove John down to the States, where John played with the famous Irish band The Chieftains. For another, Deiren contacted Natalie MacMaster who invited John to perform with her and Donnel Leahy's Celtic country-style band. John got a standing ovation. Deiren described John's response: "Moving to centre stage, arms raised in a glorious V, he took his bow, and then, as any gracious star would do, turned to Natalie and the Leahys to share the ovation with them." (Subsequently, John developed some serious health problems, and the filming needed to be put on hold.)

John was also known for miming. I would see him standing alone on the far side of the Daybreak pond making elaborate gestures to an audience of evergreen trees and then bowing. On one very cold winter day when some visitors to the Green House were ready to leave, their car would not start. The visitors had clearly been uncomfortable meeting people like Peter and Michael and Francis. They were eager to leave and not keen to reenter the household of "strange" people to seek help. Just then, John came along. He stood in front of the car, opened the imaginary hood, fiddled around in the imaginary motor for a minute, closed the hood, and pointed to the driver to turn the ignition key again. The car started. John was nonplussed, but his apparently magical abilities must have left the visitors with something to think about as they drove home.

In many ways John was a goodwill ambassador for Daybreak. I didn't live or work with him, but I was John's driver one evening when he returned from playing his spoons with a popular country group at a teachers' conference. The performance had gone very well, and the large audience responded with great enthusiasm. As we drove home, I praised his playing and, eager to help him savour his success, tried to engage him in conversation about the evening. He seemed shy and reluctant to respond. We drove on in silence for a while. Then I heard him ask, "Monica there?" Monica was a much-loved assistant at the New House. I glanced over to see he was holding his hand to his ear and the side of his face, shaping his thumb and little finger to imitate a telephone. When Monica apparently "answered," it seemed she posed several questions about the evening, each of which elicited a little more information from John about the experience and the pleasure he was taking in his success. The imaginary conversation concluded with John telling Monica that he would like a slice of his favourite pie when he arrived home – a message I made sure to convey a few minutes later, when the real Monica greeted us at the door.

∽o∾

Early one bitterly cold February Sunday morning when I was making the coffee in the Green House kitchen and Gene, a Jesuit novice who was the team member with me that day, was taking some quiet time before the core members awoke, I heard the mud room door fly open and someone enter. A husky voice shouted, "Hey! Anybody here?" Looking down the stairs, I saw George, whom I knew from farm team lunches. George had a reputation for being totally reliable, and he would not have failed to come that morning to do the farm chores even though the temperature was at least 30 below. He knew Len counted on him. George was very big and strong – six foot two and 265 pounds, he had told us over soup at the Green House one day. Before he came to Daybreak he had worked in a mill in the town where he grew up, heaving hundred-pound sacks of flour into trucks. He liked to let people know that he was tough – tough not in the sense of nasty but in the sense of being strong and able to endure and put up a good fight. He was no "sissy."

George tramped up the stairs into the dining room and silently held out his huge hands, which were bluish grey, as Gene and I converged on him. Looking at them with concern, he said, "Can't bend my fingers." George, who had previously lived at the New House, had moved into town, to Daybreak's Church Street house, the previous autumn. As was his daily custom, at eight that morning he had left the house and walked up to the Daybreak farm. Proper work boots were a requirement for all the farm team, and fortunately he did have his winter work boots on that morning, along with his heavy winter jacket and his much loved and well-worn Montreal Canadiens toque, but he had forgotten his gloves. The condition of his hands was exacerbated by the fact that it was Sunday and shops along the way were closed. His custom on other days was to stop along the way to say hello and warm up.

Having grown up on the prairies, I knew that trying to warm frostbitten parts of the body too quickly could do serious damage, because the blood vessels would break. I brought George a large basin of very cold water to put his hands into. He clearly was in great pain. I came to know George very well in the years that followed, when he had to have one of his hips replaced twice and, in the process of recovery, suffered a fractured femur, but I never saw him in more pain than on that day. When Gene suggested he take George to the emergency ward at our local hospital, I agreed. I could help the other six house members get ready for the day and have breakfast. I called Len to let him know George could not do the farm chores and Church Street to tell them what was happening. Then I knocked on each person's bedroom door. I think all the Green House members grasped the potential seriousness of George's frozen hands when I explained the situation over breakfast. Everyone was extra helpful and ready for church on time.

I visited George a few days later. The doctor who'd looked at his hands at the hospital said that he might lose some fingers. It would be touch and go. George's hands were thoroughly bandaged, and he had to keep them close to his chest. A nurse was coming daily to dress them. He was home from work for some time. Years later, when George asked friends and former assistants to write memories of him for his life story book, Nick, who had been an assistant at Church Street, wrote of George's frostbitten hands, the loss of all his fingernails, and the fortitude and patience George had shown, allowing Nick and others at Church Street to care for and feed him.

When George finally returned to his job on the farm, a couple of his fingers were still bandaged. Fortunately, his hands did heal and he had the full use of them for many more years.

During the eighteen months between when I returned from Quebec and when four of us in the Green House moved into homes in the Town of Richmond Hill, our team included a series of male assistants, some more given to the role than others. We were fortunate with Gene. Early in my experience as a house leader, we welcomed a male assistant who was strikingly clean-cut and neat.

He had not held any previous job for long for various good reasons that he explained, and we hoped L'Arche would be the right place for him. After he moved in, he would continually reposition certain items. One was the wastebasket near the small desk, phone, and bulletin board. We explained that we had discovered this to be the handiest place for it, but he continued to move it.

One evening in the early fall, all of us in the house, except Lloyd and this new assistant, were heading off to the swimming pool. The farm had an abundance of apple trees, and he announced that he and Lloyd were going to make apple pies while we were gone. I offered to find him the various items he would need – a hand pastry blender, the rolling pin, and so forth. But he declined, assuring me he knew what he was doing. We returned a couple of hours later to find him, with Lloyd's help, scraping goo off practically every surface in the kitchen, including the ceiling. He had tried to blend the pastry in an electric blender without the lid... I learned that he actually had never made a pie before. There were other difficult moments and disagreements. Soon, in consultation with the community leader, it was decided that we needed to ask him to leave. He did not protest. I think he actually held us in some disdain.

Then, for over a year, the Green House had a young assistant who was very enthusiastic but tended to be scattered. One afternoon on a weekend when Sharon was away, I returned from some errands to learn that the house had just had a number of "fire drills" in rapid succession. Each time, everyone had left the house and assembled outside, and the assistant had turned off the alarm and checked for any signs of fire, then reset the alarm. And each time, very shortly after, it had begun ringing again, and everyone had again left the house. Only after their third or fourth exodus did the assistant open the upstairs bathroom door. The tub was overflowing and the water draining into the heating vent, activating the alarm and pouring over Sharon's best clothes hanging in the closet of the bedroom below. The assistant had started to run Michael's bath and forgotten about it.

In the spring of 1984, Len and the farm team planted the usual large garden. The homes were free to harvest from it, and surplus produce was sold in town on the weekly egg route delivery.

One warm June afternoon I took Peter with me to pick some strawberries. In the strawberry patch we met a young woman who had just arrived from Manchester, England, and was living in the Church Street house. In her strong Mancunian accent, she introduced herself as Julie Gittins. We chatted a bit as we picked, and Peter seated himself among the strawberries and ate all that he could reach, teasing me by helping himself from my basket every once in a while. "Ah...ah...ah... Beth!" he would say as his hand got closer, and, if I did not move the basket away, he would take a berry and then slap his offending hand lightly – evidently the response he expected from me.

I learned that Julie had trained as a teacher and had tried teaching for a short time but decided that it was not for her. Like many young assistants, she thought a year abroad in a L'Arche community would give her the opportunity to rethink her direction. She dressed in the punk style, which was just coming into fashion in Canada – hot pink and bright orange, I recall – colours I would not have dreamed of putting together. She seemed a cheery, straightforward person, and I immediately liked her.

That summer of 1984 there was a strong sense of solidarity and energy in the community as we looked toward celebrating L'Arche's twentieth anniversary and Daybreak's fifteenth anniversary in October. The community had begun to grow and was on the cusp of further growth. We all embraced the mission of providing more day or work settings and homes, and welcoming more people, thereby helping to empty the institutions. At the end of the summer, Daybreak opened a new rented house on Mill Street in the Town of Richmond Hill, about a fifteen-minute walk from Church Street. Lloyd and Francis and Sharon moved there with two other core members and an assistant, thus relieving the Big House, which had become overcrowded, and creating spaces in the New and Green Houses. Sharon became the Mill Street house leader. I was asked to go to the Church Street house, where a house leader would be needed.

I was finding the busyness of a household of nine tiring, and, although I knew I would miss the Green House members, I was relieved to be moving to a house of just six people, with its four core members being more independent. It also seemed easier that Lloyd and I would not live together, since I sensed that he still had some attachment to me. Lloyd was friends with George and Gord, who lived at Church Street, and we would no doubt still encounter each other, but in a less intimate setting. The Green House members who needed more support with their daily routines stayed back that year, but within a few years all the former core members except Peter had moved to homes in town. Peter was adamant that he did not want to leave the Green House.

∽∾∿

Michael, Jane, and Margaret handled the news of our upcoming moves without seeming overly upset, but when I explained to Peter that I would be moving, he showed his sadness by repeating this reality over and over: "You going, Beth?" It was hard to hear him, and I think he knew that. Only a few months earlier, when he had expressed delight on my arrival home after a weekend away, I had sung him the refrain from the Debby Boone song "You Light Up My Life," and he had responded with a huge smile. Now, I would see him much less often. Although it felt right to move, I struggled with the feeling that I was abandoning Peter. Indeed, I saw little of him or the others for the next few years. But Peter made new friends – including some lasting male friends. Carl was one. He was house leader of the Green House in the early 1990s and continued to live in the house until 2010, while carrying other responsibilities. Even after Carl moved out and right up until Peter died, they were cooking partners for the Green House Sunday dinner.

Peter also made a longtime friend in Rob Ens. Rob was a Mennonite who was drawn to Henri Nouwen's writings. After Henri had moved to Daybreak, Rob spotted him in a Toronto eatery one day, and Henri invited Rob to dinner at the Green House. Rob was fascinated by Peter, who continued to be a tease and also sometimes became very anxious. Like a number of other core members, Peter did not give information in a direct manner, and his anxiety complicated interactions. To read his signals, it was important to come to know him well. Rob could see that Steffen,

89

an assistant from Germany, and Peter shared a special relationship. Steffen modeled for Rob how to relate to Peter, and the three became very good friends.

Rob would devote his Friday evenings to Peter. He would come to dinner straight from his work in the far west end of Toronto, they would attend common prayer or community worship, which by then was on Friday evenings, and then they would go out with a few others to the local pub. Peter would drink his own beer and then tease Rob by taking sips from Rob's beer when he was not looking. At the end of the evening, Rob would take Peter home and help him with his nighttime routine. "See you in the morning, Rob?" Peter would query several times as he got into his pyjamas, laid out the next day's clothes, and brushed his teeth. The next morning, Rob and Peter would join the men's group for breakfast at a local diner. Rob's other longtime commitment to Peter was to take him each year to the annual Santa Claus Parade. Peter was fascinated by Santa and always very anxious that he might miss seeing him. Come November, he would talk of little else.

Steffen returned to Germany but later came back to spend three more years at Daybreak. Along with his housemates, Peter travelled twice to Germany to visit Steffen and also Ralf, a much loved German priest who had spent a sabbatical at Daybreak. Rob helped lead one of those trips. Away from the group, he and Peter spent a peaceful afternoon driving down the winding road beside the Mosel River. Rob recalls that Peter very much liked the honor-system bar fridge at the Marienburg castle. When Rob married Namju (a Daybreak Craft Studio assistant) in 2011, Peter and Steffen celebrated with them.

Peter passed away suddenly of a heart attack on New Year's Eve 2015. The community had gathered for Taizé prayer at the chapel and then brought in the New Year early with fireworks and a champagne toast. Peter had had a good evening and had seen many friends. John S., who had been in hospital, came in a wheelchair and sat near the front, where he could play his spoons with Clara, Chris, and the other musicians. Peter had gone across the room and extended his hand in welcome to John. The heart attack struck as Peter and others were walking home to the Green House.

Not long before he died, I had a few minutes alone with Peter when Rob was away and it fell to me to drive him home from the pub one Friday evening. It was rare for just the two of us to be together. Reminding him of the fun we had had in the Green House long ago, I sang the opening lines of the popular Gene Raskin song "Those Were the Days." I looked over at Peter in the passenger seat and saw that he was smiling.

7. A Decade of Growth and Change on Daybreak Farm

The communities wish to secure for their members education, work and
therapeutic activities, which will be a source of dignity, growth and fulfillment
for them. Charter of L'Arche (v. 1993)

One of Jean Vanier's convictions in founding L'Arche was that every person, whatever their abilities, should be able to have a meaningful day – in contrast to the men he had seen pacing endlessly in the institution he first visited. Today, Daybreak has good options for dignified and creative work or daytime activities. However, when I arrived, those who did not want to work on the farm or were not up to such work had to work at ARC. Peggy worked in the ARC kitchen and later, when her ankle was giving out, in the ARC office answering the phones. She missed her work in the Daybreak bakery, which was not financially viable and had had to close, but she found both the ARC jobs relatively agreeable. She was well spoken, and this and the fact that she could read made her an ideal person for the front desk. Francis was happy at ARC for two reasons: he could see Linda at lunchtimes, and his job disassembling hydrometers engaged his love of using tools and his skill working with his hands. The ARC staff set him up in a separate closet-like room where he could work undistracted. I think this made him feel special.

At ARC, most people worked on packaging contracts at tables with six or eight others. They placed wrapped chocolates or Christmas lights or other small products into boxes. Lloyd sat at one of these tables. Some people enjoyed the work and the chance to socialize, but Lloyd detested both the work, which was too easy for him, and being with people who sometimes behaved strangely.

However, he did not want to work on the Daybreak farm. Perhaps if Daybreak had had a Holstein farm he would have been interested!

Michael's grumpiness on weekday mornings was totally predictable. Besides whatever negative effects his medication had on his mood, he did not like ARC, where he was in the recreation program with Peter. Intellectually, Mike would have been capable of doing the packaging work, but he lacked the required fine motor coordination. Not only was he bored but Peter, who enjoyed the recreation program, persisted in teasing Mike there, just as he did at home.

One concern of the Daybreak Council was to find better work opportunities for Daybreak people. Over several years the community had paid for special nursing for Bill Rous, who had passed away while I was in Quebec. These funds, no longer needed to pay for nursing, and some additional money provided by the Daybreak Board of Directors, made the creation of a new work setting possible. The farm workshop opposite the barn had previously housed the community's small bakery project. The building now served as farm office and the egg-grading and storage room. The plan was to convert it into a woodworking shop. It would be led by Joe Vorstermans, an experienced assistant who had recently completed an intensive cabinetmaking course. An extension was built onto the west end of the barn near the silo to serve as an egg room and office.

Michael would have to wait a few more years before Daybreak had a suitable daytime place for him, but the woodworking shop would address Lloyd's desire to leave ARC, and David's need for a job that would interest him. David otherwise tended to lose focus and wander off, whether working at ARC or on the farm. Some on the Community Council were concerned that a woodworking shop would not be safe work for David, but Joe Egan, who shares an enduring bond with David, advocated for him, knowing how much the job would mean to David. He already had his own small shed, where he enjoyed nailing boards together. Lloyd was thrilled with the idea of this new opportunity as he had a brother-in-law and a nephew who did woodworking.

A competition was held to choose a name for the woodworking shop. Stephanie (who was married to Joe V. – they had both been early Green House assistants) won the contest for her suggestion: the Woodery. It was a play on the Bakery, and a reminder that the bakery had previously occupied the building. Most of the community and several Board members gathered at the Woodery to mark its opening, and a bottle of champagne was produced. When David, as the Woodery representative, popped the cork, it flew up with such force that it shattered the fluorescent light fixture! No one was hurt, and this incident added to the sense of celebration, though there was not quite as much champagne to pass around.

Joe V. had researched products that the men could make fairly independently and had decided on a collapsible deck or patio chair made in two parts, each consisting of several well-sanded and polished sturdy cedar slats held together with screws. He created jigs so that the workers would be able to position the screws and keep them in place as they put them in.

The Woodery was a great success as far as work for Lloyd and David was concerned. Both men were much happier. One day, a couple of weeks after the Woodery began, all of us in the Green House stood around a beaming Lloyd as he displayed the first chair they had made. Everyone had a chance to try it out.

Joe V. came up with ideas that gave the men a greater sense of the dignity of their work. One of these was a uniform that they all wore each day. Another was a weekly Woodery team meeting, which everyone attended. There, they learned about any new contracts and the schedule of work to be done during the week, and they received instruction on new procedures or tools. There was also a daily check-in, and workers who arrived on time and wearing their work boots and a clean uniform (khaki pants and matching shirt) received a bonus with their pay. The pay at the Woodery was good for a sheltered facility.

When the collapsible deck chairs proved difficult to sell, the Woodery shifted to making sets of children's blocks from poplar wood. These sold better. When they had time, they also made some very nice pine bookcases that were bought by assistants and friends of the community. However, the bookcases required fine finishing that only Joe V. could do. They were always a sideline. For the skills of the workers, an ideal product proved to be wooden pallets that they made for an appliance company in a neighbouring township. Around this time, Nick, an experienced assistant from England, came to the Woodery, and it welcomed three more workers. George had long worked on the farm and, for a couple of years, on Daybreak's recycling truck. When the recycling job ended, he had been looking after the eggs, but he was asking for different work. Gord took on the eggs. George's steadiness and his strength were appreciated in his new job. The Woodery was able to take over part of the loft level of the barn. They had only a couple of gas heaters and it was cold, but they constructed and stored the pallets there. The pallets became the Woodery's biggest and most financially successful product for several years.

Meanwhile, in the winter and spring of 1984, Daybreak tore down the dilapidated old chicken coop opposite the community garden and built a beautiful, accessible, and airy meeting hall. It accommodated the entire community, so that we no longer needed to rent church halls for meetings, and it provided space for daytime programming for people who had much higher needs. These people would include Michael's younger brother, Adam, for whose coming Michael had long prayed. The building was full of light. It had a high ceiling and a mezzanine, a large kitchen, and double doors opening to a long, south-facing porch that looked onto pasture and woodland. To lead the Day Program, the community recruited Mary Bastedo, who had an occupational therapy degree as well as experience in L'Arche Edmonton. A nurse was also part of the team. They began in the late spring of 1984 with the visits of a tiny, bent young woman named Rose. Abandoned from infancy, she had lived much of her life in a covered crib in an institution and had never learned to walk.

Three Daybreak people who were not doing well at ARC were able to join the Day Program. The program had a carding drum, and initially some of the core members would card the wool of the Daybreak sheep, and, with an assistant or a volunteer, they put their skills together to prepare the soup or salad for the farm team lunches. A while after Rose came, Adam moved into a renovated and fully accessible wing of the New House, which he shared with Rose and Michael B., a man who has cerebral palsy and uses a wheelchair and also had come as a Day Program member. Mary brought in an expert in neuro developmental therapy, who helped Rose and Adam make progress in walking. In time, a Snoezelen room[1] was created, where individuals could relax if need be. A fine cadre of volunteers meant there could be lots of one-on-one time. Making good use of a donated wheelchair van, everyone in the Day Program engaged in a variety of therapeutic, social, and recreational activities, including horseback riding, exercise at the swimming pool, crafts, artwork, and visits to parks and the local mall – the principle being that people like Rose and Adam and Michael, who looked different, should be out in public like any other citizen.

Often house assistants and people in the Daybreak office would bring a sandwich and join the lunch group of Woodery and farm workers and Day Program members, so that a vibrant noon-hour gathering was created. There was a stereo and a piano, and music added to the convivial atmosphere. George was particularly taken with Rose. After he had eaten he liked to help wheel her along the farm lane in her stroller. He was thrilled when she began to walk and would take hold of one of his large fingers to steady herself. I loved seeing them together – big George and tiny Rose.

The opening of the Meeting Hall and then, in October 1984, Daybreak's fifteenth anniversary celebration and the twentieth anniversary of the founding of the original L'Arche community in France were big events. At the end of the speeches that marked the Meeting Hall opening, we all headed outside to release a host of helium-filled balloons into the early evening sky.

For the anniversary dinner, Julie, my strawberry patch acquaintance and, by then, my teammate at Church Street, was the key person in creating the decorations. Before the celebration, Julie fixed a huge brown-paper "ark" to an end wall of the Meeting Hall, and everyone in the community drew handprints, coloured them brightly, and pasted them onto the ark so that the "hands" covered the entire hull. A large painted rainbow arched over the cut-out torsos and heads of three figures in the boat. (The boat had many manifestations in earlier days. It is now standardized and is a registered logo used by all L'Arche communities.) Julie also painted a long banner that was mounted over the makeshift podium, declaring "Fifteen Years of Faithfulness!" Looking back from a standpoint of *fifty* years of Daybreak faithfulness today, fifteen or even twenty seems a small number. I marvel at the trust that parents and Board members placed in the new little community in those early years.

For the same occasion, Joe V. made a cut-out plywood tree with many branches, on which were mounted small candles representing all the communities of L'Arche around the world. Several large round tables were set up, and a formal, catered roast chicken dinner was served. All looked splendid! Everyone in the community was present, including Board members, and some special guests. There were speeches and toasts and a celebration of some recent achievements. Len and team gave an update on the farm; David and Lloyd and Joe V. described the new Woodery and showed the chairs they were making; Mary outlined the activities of the new Day Program, and Michael and I even had a spot standing at the mic in our winter parkas to relate our "Arctic Adventure." Providence seemed in evidence in every account.

෴

Joe Egan had said that Bill Rous in his last years, because of his need for total care, was at the centre of the community and kept us faithful to the essence of the mission of L'Arche – to welcome those who are most in need, most "poor" in their bodies and minds. When Bill died, something was lost of this spirit. Everyone who remained was ambulatory, could speak, and was at least partially independent with some tasks such as personal care. Now it was obvious to all of us that it was good to have people among us again who called us to slow right down and be more attentive.

Rose had problems eating and needed surgery on her esophagus. With difficulty, a doctor was found who was willing to perform this operation, and Rose began to gain strength and grow and mature as a woman. Rose and Adam both had their own followers – people whose lives were changed by coming to know them. Debbie, who especially had a heart for people with multiple disabilities, had pushed for the welcome of Rose in spite of her medical problems, and she lent good support to those around Rose. The New House had a strong team of female assistants who cared for this tiny woman – Ann P., who was a nurse and had cared for Bill Rous; Zenia; Regina, who was a physiotherapist from Brazil; Heather; Clara; Liska; and over the years many others. Each one was profoundly touched by Rose.

Among Rose's numerous friends, Zenia stood out. She was a concert pianist who came to Daybreak and found her second vocation in L'Arche. Coming to know Rose completely changed Zenia's life, and Zenia and others changed Rose, who for quite some time would not even make eye contact and seemed closed in her own world. She would sit for long periods on the floor rocking and spinning a pasta measuring stick or anything else she could twirl, seemingly mesmerized by it. She made small sounds, but if someone she didn't know touched her, she would scream and slide away. Gradually, Zenia and Rose's other friends were able to call her into relationship. The New House assistants would bring Rose to community worship, where she would be in constant motion, inquisitively walking from person to person, holding on to each one or the arm of their chair. There were a couple of couches in the chapel. Rose did not know me well, but one evening when I was sitting on one of the couches, she paused to balance herself by holding on to my knee and then climbed up on me. I remember feeling honoured by her trust and trying to stay very still so she would not flit away.

Rose never talked, nor did Adam, but they transformed people who came to know them. Like Rose, Adam needed total care, but while Rose was an active little person who laughed and skittled about on the floor, leaning back and using her hands and feet, Adam was generally still and silent. He was a deeply peaceful man, and he seemed to have the gift of bringing peace to all those who came to know him over the eleven years he lived at Daybreak. One of the people touched by spending hours simply sitting with Adam was an abbot of a Camaldolese monastery who passed part of his sabbatical at Daybreak. Another whose life Adam deeply affected was the priest-writer and pastoral theologian Henri Nouwen, who became Daybreak's pastor in 1986.

Henri Nouwen was known to some of us through his books on spirituality. When Father Henri arrived at Daybreak, he was asked to live with Adam and others at the New House and to help with Adam's care. Later, when Henri moved from the New House, he remained on a roster to help Adam with his morning routine of bathing, dressing, and having breakfast. If assistants rushed Adam, he would have a seizure, and then the morning routine would take twice as long. Henri was accustomed to dashing from one task or meeting to the next. He came to regard Adam as his teacher, calling him to slow down, to be present, and, more than that, to understand the incarnation more deeply by recognizing God's presence in Adam's frail body. [2]

Henri lived in the New House for his first year at Daybreak, but, given the frenetic pace he kept, his many visitors and his frequent trips to give lectures, the situation was hardly ideal for him or for the household. Meanwhile, Richmond Hill was growing northward. The writing had been on the wall for some time, and, in 1985, the community had learned that the leased land it had been farming had been sold to a developer. The farm was gradually closed down in the ensuing eighteen months, the animals sold, and then finally the laying hens. In 1987, Len and Jean and their family moved a twenty-minute drive north to the Humane Society farm in Newmarket, where Len had taken the job of farm manager, and the bungalow became empty. At an all-community meeting, it was decided that this house could become a small spiritual centre for the community. By community consensus, Dayspring was chosen as its name.

The original chapel in the Big House had caught fire one late evening during Advent of 1985. All the Big House members exited safely from the second and third floors, but the main floor had to be gutted. New office space was constructed there, and a very small chapel was created in the Big House basement to provide space for private prayer. Since that time the community had used the Meeting Hall for worship gatherings. The plan for the bungalow included a chapel that would occupy most of the lower level of the house. Thick wall-to-wall carpeting was laid there, as most of us would sit on the floor. Benches around the side would provide a place for those who could not get up and down so easily. The upper level had the existing kitchen and large open dining and living room, and bedrooms for Henri and for three visitors or retreatants or community members who wanted to spend a quiet day.

Everyone in Daybreak was on a work crew to help with the renovations, with a view to each person feeling a sense of ownership of our new spiritual centre. Gord and I and Paula (a Marquette grad studying social work at the University of Chicago) and a couple of others spent an afternoon together scraping wallpaper as part of this project. When the house was ready, Henri brought his extensive library and some of the furniture that he had had at Harvard and that came originally from his home in Holland. The living room, lined with bookshelves and with its inviting fireplace, became a favourite room for small gatherings.

By 1987, bulldozers were ripping the topsoil off the land around the community, and the infrastructure for a new housing development was being installed. The digging muddied the water in our well, bringing an end to its use. The changes to the land were very difficult to watch. One of the Green House assistants, furious to see the farmland being torn up, nailed a large bedsheet to the roof facing in the direction of the bulldozer operators with the words "Land Rapists" written in red paint. Joe Egan intervened and asked the assistant to take it down. The workers were just doing their job, he pointed out. But we all mourned the loss of the land and the animals.

Daybreak held on to the property it owned. This land included the pond and all the buildings – besides the bungalow, the Big and New and Green Houses, the barn and Woodery building, the Meeting Hall, and a small white clapboard house donated by Pickseed company in the 1970s. It had been towed a kilometer up Yonge Street and installed just north of the Big House and was where Gus and Debbie and their family lived for some years. By the end of 1989, the community had two more homes in town, and the people who had lived in the Big House moved to homier settings. The upper floors of the Big House were renovated to provide an apartment for married assistants, more office space, and some guest bedrooms.

After three or four years, the brighter side of the land development became evident as we saw that some of the large new houses being built around us might suit us well as Daybreak homes. Becoming part of a neighbourhood might have some advantages also for those who lived in the New House and the Green House. Further development was inevitable. Following the town's official plan, a few years later a north-south road was built through the Daybreak property, separating the Green House and bungalow (now called the Cedars retreat house) from the rest of Daybreak. The town agreed to curve the road around the New House and Meeting Hall, which otherwise would have been demolished.

∾o∾

After the collapse of the Soviet Union and Ukraine's declaration of independence, in 1991, Zenia went to Ukraine, a natural draw for her since she was of Ukrainian heritage and spoke the language. In this she had encouragement from a little support group at Daybreak that consisted of Sue M., Henri, and one or two experienced assistants. Of course, there was no L'Arche in Ukraine, and Zenia found that services for people who had intellectual disabilities were almost nonexistent. These people and their families were isolated in dreary Communist-era apartment buildings. Zenia became acquainted with some of these families. At the same time, she developed relationships with parishes and made contact with students and local professionals. She brought these diverse people together, and soon several Faith and Light communities were flourishing.[3] They consisted of the families of people with disabilities and young people, often students, who became their friends and wanted to lend their support.

On return trips to Canada, Zenia solicited funding that allowed her to help create a large children's rehabilitation centre, to help establish an outreach centre for persons with special needs at the Catholic university, to establish several Faith and Light communities, and to sow the seeds for L'Arche to begin in Ukraine. For several years Joe V. travelled to Ukraine to give retreats to youth volunteers and families. Rose died in 2005, but not before she had flown with two of her assistant friends to Ukraine to visit her friend Zenia and the Faith and Light communities there. I am sure that no one who knew Rose before she moved to Daybreak could have imagined how her life would evolve and how many people she would touch.

∞∞∞

In the early 1990s, Joe Child assumed management of the Woodery. With the closing of the farm, the Woodery had taken over the entire barn and employed a growing number of people. Joe Child, a professional cabinetmaker who had had his own large shop in Massachusetts, had come to Daybreak mainly for the sake of his wife, Kathy Kelly. She had spent time in L'Arche Paris, and she wanted to revisit that experience. They even wondered about starting a L'Arche in their home area of Northampton. Joe and Kathy planned to stay at Daybreak only two years, but they soon found themselves at home and stayed on, becoming great assets to the community.

Joe had never worked with people with intellectual disabilities before, but he had a kind and welcoming heart, and he was soon much loved by all the workers. He recounts needing to learn how to choose suitable contracts and break down the tasks at the Woodery so that everyone had something to do. Often, people with intellectual disabilities cannot readily express discontent. If workers felt left out or bored, they sometimes resorted to other means of communication, such as hiding important tools.

Previously, the Woodery had had to use a bathroom across the lane in the old Woodery building. Plans were afoot to convert this building into a craft studio that would provide another place of employment for Daybreak members. So a bathroom was installed in the barn, and when the Woodery team had time between contracts, they worked on insulating the downstairs of the barn and, with the help of a high school shops class, laid a new plywood floor on the upper level. New doors were installed also, so that the pigeons and raccoons could not take up residence inside.

The Woodery began a new contract, making thousands of surveyors' stakes each month. It proved to be good work for everybody. In spite of the fears of some that David would wander off or not be safe in the Woodery, he worked there for many years, until he retired. David's kindness and gentle affability helped create the sense of community in the Woodery. He had a tremor that kept him from working with the saws. However, the top end of each cut and sharpened stake had to be dipped in red paint. This was one of David's tasks. His green coveralls often resembled an abstract Christmas painting. David also operated the bander. He would gather the stakes into a square stack and press a button, whereupon a metal arm reached down and around the stakes to bundle them together.

During Joe C.'s time, the Woodery grew to employ another cabinetmaker and more workers and assistants. Ellen was one of the women who found good work there. She was often given the role of pressing the button to operate the saw. When Ellen was unhappy, which could happen when one of the other women had more of Joe's attention, a warm hug from David and a reassuring "Don't worry, hon," would bring her around.

Joe tells a story about David that, in a way, captures the essence of L'Arche. For years, the entire Woodery has gone out to a favourite hamburger and falafel place for lunch on Fridays. One particular week, Joe had had a difficult couple of days. He was tired and didn't feel like going, but he knew the others would be disappointed if he backed out. He climbed wearily into his car, and a number of core members joined him. As they waited for the other car to fill up, David, who was sitting behind Joe, reached forward and began to massage Joe's shoulders. After a minute or two, Joe responded, "Keep that up, David, and I'll give you a raise!" David replied, "I don't want a raise, Joe. I just want to be with you."[4]

I think every person who has ever worked in the Woodery has loved their job. There is a sense of collegiality, and they know themselves to be productive workers making products that are needed. All of the early workers have retired now. However, the Woodery today is a thriving operation. Each week, large trucks arrive to unload lumber or to load up their products – still mainly stakes. These days, one or two of the workers on any given day are high school students who have a disability and are on placements, and a few of the full-time workers are day participants who live with their parents. An addition has recently been built at the west end of the barn so that the Woodery can give employment to more people.

∽∾∾

When the Daybreak farm finally closed, John S. worked for a while with Len on the Humane Society farm. Later, he worked mornings north and east of Richmond Hill, first at a stable where he fed and groomed the horses and then at a petting farm that welcomed schoolchildren. John's competent gentleness with the chicks and lambs and other animals was appreciated by the people who owned the farm. House assistants would drive him to work and pick him up. Riding the John Deere mower, he also cut the several acres of grass on the Daybreak property. In winter, he plowed the lane and parking areas with the Kubota snowplow.

In his late fifties, John developed some serious health problems and was hospitalized on and off. Finally, when the house assistants could no longer manage his care, he was admitted to a long-term-care facility. A few months later, in March 2017, he passed away. He was sixty-six, old for someone with Down syndrome. John was one of the founding members of Daybreak, and the celebration of his life at his visitation and funeral brought back a great number of old friends and former assistants who had been welcomed and loved and inspired by him. Len and Jean had died, but all of their daughters came. Lou Moore, the leader of the country band with whom John had often played the spoons in recent years, brought his acoustic guitar, and, at the beginning of the service, he led us all in "Will the Circle Be Unbroken?" Deiren still hopes to finish the Spoonman film.

8. "Tell me, which one is which?": Our life together on Church Street

Forgiveness and celebration are at the heart of community. These are the two faces of love. Jean Vanier

Daybreak's Church Street house is located on a well-treed residential street in the old part of Richmond Hill, where many houses have been designated historic. A solid three-storey red-brick edifice built in the early 1900s, the house had been nicely renovated, preserving most of its traditional features. It has a fairly deep lot that allowed for a deck to be constructed in recent years without losing either back lawn or garden. A driveway runs along the north side of the house, bordered by a white cedar hedge. The house is just one block off Yonge Street and an easy walk to banks, restaurants, a pharmacy, and other services, and thus is ideal for core members who are more independent. From its beginning, house members had cultivated good relationships with shopkeepers and neighbours.

On Labour Day weekend in 1984, I was welcomed into the Church Street house with a backyard barbecue organized by Carmen. (She and Steve and their children were no longer living in the house, but Carmen was the house accompanier.) At the same gathering, Colleen, the outgoing house leader, and John O., who had been an assistant in the Big House for a year, were being sent off – Colleen to begin university and John to graduate school, where he was to study with Henri Nouwen. Gus and Debbie came with their children and people from the Big House. Gus gave a short speech thanking Colleen and John. Everyone in Church Street was there: Julie from Manchester, and George, whose frozen hands we had ministered to at the Green House, and Gord, with whom I had been on vacation to Winnipeg three years earlier, and Anne

Marie and Helen, both of whom I knew only slightly when I moved in. Nick, the Church Street work assistant, had started to live out of the house but would be continuing to help out regularly. As the barbecue ended, George, his large fifty-seven-year-old bulk hovering over me and a potted yellow mum held firmly under one of his arms, planted a kiss on my forehead and then handed me the mum, my welcome gift from the house. And so began a new phase of my life in L'Arche.

Helen was a very early member of Church Street. Anne Marie and Gord and George had all moved there from homes on the Daybreak farm when spaces had opened up in 1981 and 1982. Anne Marie and Gord were about thirty. But George and Helen were nearly a generation older. Helen, like Gord, had Down syndrome. In this regard, Church Street was rich. It is often commented that every L'Arche house should have at least one person with Down syndrome, as people who have the extra chromosome are usually gifted at creating a sense of community and celebration, and they can be good animators. Both were wonderful people to live with and also challenging at times.

I had first met Helen on a cottage vacation in the summer of 1983. Her reputation for mischief had preceded her, and, hearing also that she was usually drawn to younger female assistants, I had suggested that Theresa, a fun-loving young American assistant, be Helen's primary reference on the vacation as I was concerned that I might lock horns with Helen. Colleen had warned me never to get into a power struggle with Helen. Whoever did was bound to lose.

Linking Helen with Theresa had turned out well. Helen, who had worked in the Daybreak bakery, loved to bake and was quite good at it, providing she had a partner. Helen was a diminutive person, but she could knead bread dough and roll out pastry like a professional. Helen and Theresa made bread and pies, which the rest of the vacation group happily consumed. The cottage had a small beach and a paddleboat that we could use, and we enjoyed touring towns in the area, taking a boat tour of the Thousand Islands at the eastern end of Lake Ontario, and visiting a country fair where Theresa and Moe mounted the stage and joined in the dancing. Helen sat in a folding chair wearing a coat that was too warm for the day, a beige babushka, and her enormous sunglasses. Smoking and surrounded by numerous bulky tote bags, she looked for all the world like the bag lady queen. It was obvious Helen enjoyed being different. (On the other hand, when we were out in public and someone stared at her, she could be sensitive and annoyed. She might tell them, "Get a camera!")

Julie was an upbeat person, and she had already been at Church Street for three months and had established good relationships with the other house members – especially Helen. Through Julie, who was much younger than I, I came to know about U2 and Bono and Bruce Springsteen. (Julie was considerate about the volume of our stereo when others were home.)

I was not sure what to expect from the core members when the six of us began living together. Other assistants sometimes referred to the house, and likewise each of the individuals in the house, as a "challenge." I settled in, and the transition seemed smooth, although I am sure the others missed Colleen, and for a few weeks I pined for the intimacy of the Green House, with its simpler relationships and few interpersonal conflicts, and where the core members needed more practical help from the assistants. No one at Church Street needed help brushing their teeth or shaving or doing their laundry. We did cook in pairs, but most of the core members were fairly capable in the kitchen. I knew more about the shadow sides of the Church Street members' reputations – that not everyone was always straightforward and honest, and that individuals would need emotional and psychological support – than about their gifts. I wondered what they had heard about me as a house leader.

Helen had her own rhythm. She liked doing handiwork and she liked being out and about by herself or babysitting the small children of some of the married assistants with Julie or me. She enjoyed being part of interactions when assistants from other houses would drop in. She seemed to have a comment about almost anything that was going on. She could be quite funny or facetious.

After Gord had been refused service in the lounge car on the train to Winnipeg in 1981, he had grown a beard to make himself look older. It was a light reddish brown and suited him, complementing his reddish brown hair. At thirty, Gord was one of the best-looking younger men in the community, and even before I moved to Church Street I was aware that, among the core members, more than one young woman thought him attractive.

I knew George from farm team lunches. He had a reputation for being honest and responsible and for never swearing. He sometimes seemed a bit dreamy, as when he talked about professional wrestlers he'd met, and I wondered if he was all there at such moments; however, I knew he was a valued worker and I had seen his presence and gentleness with people who were physically much less able, such as Rose at the Day Program. A man of few words, he rarely raised his voice, though he could be cranky at times, usually because someone had moved or hidden something belonging to him. Apart from his work, sports seemed to be the most important aspect of George's life. He had his favourite teams – the Los Angeles Dodgers for baseball, the Hamilton Tiger-Cats for football, and the Montreal Canadiens – or Habs (for "Habitants"), as they were popularly known and as George liked to call them, for hockey. After signing his name he often wrote "Habs" or drew the Canadiens' logo.

Anne Marie seemed a fairly self-confident young woman. She was of medium build and height, with dark brown hair that had been cut in a becoming bob at Carmen's suggestion. I knew her from the New House as someone who was curious about others, especially visitors. Still today, she has a prodigious memory and can recall the names of people she met years ago and of their children and siblings. This can delight and touch visitors. She likes to engage them in conversation, but in her questioning, she is not always sensitive to others' desires for privacy. She is known for her personal questions about people's families and about babies, especially if she meets someone who happens to be pregnant. I am quite sure she has often thought about what it would be like to have a baby herself. Sometimes she is silent for a minute in such conversations and then will say, more to herself than to others, "But then you have to take care of the baby!"

Anne Marie has mild cerebral palsy, and it is not unusual for her to explain this to people she meets. The CP affects her gait, but she could still walk well when I lived with her. It also sometimes causes a hesitation in her speech, but she can enunciate clearly and can speak with conviction. Anne Marie can assimilate knowledge and use it when she wants. During the time I lived with her she saw the film *My Left Foot,* about a man who also had CP, and she often spoke of it. I think it helped her relate to her own situation.

The previous year she had broken her ankle, and when I arrived at Church Street this was one of her favourite topics of conversation. She seemed to enjoy describing the throbbing pain it had caused her. She liked the word "throbbing" and would work it into two or three sentences in succession. The word certainly does not evoke comfort, and I would find myself trying to steer the conversation away from her ankle.

Anne Marie was and is still known for not liking silence. I think it awakens her anxiety. She will speak out loudly, sometimes sounding angry, during the minute or two of silence that can occur during prayer around the table after dinner, and still today she chooses not to attend community worship. When I tried to discuss the issue with her, she would smile and respond a bit shyly, "I like to talk." She went on a retreat just one time. Jean Vanier was the speaker. She said he spoke too personally – too close to her heart, I understood her to mean – and that she did not like the times of silence there either.

Our first autumn as a new team was quite busy, not only with the usual medical and dental appointments but also with the preparations for Daybreak's fifteenth anniversary events. Julie and Gord were on the community's celebration committee, which held several meetings. Julie and I worked well together. I have always found it difficult to be with people whom I felt I needed to second-guess. Julie was comfortable speaking her mind with me, and I liked this. One small incident that occurred several months into our three years together illustrates the gift this can be. After a tiring day at the Daybreak office, I came home just in time to cook one evening. I had called earlier in the day and left a message asking Julie to take a package of meat out of the freezer for me. I found she had not done this, and I barked at her. She barked right back that she had not received the message. We both dropped the issue and I went on to prepare dinner. The meal, after-dinner prayer, and clean-up proceeded with no further reference to the matter and, I believe, no further thought of it on our parts.

At that time, a new young male assistant was with us for a trial period. The next day he told me that he had tensed right up, expecting the sky to fall in the moment he heard our sharp exchange. He said he had never experienced angry words between people that had not resulted in one or other of them storming out of the house and not returning for several hours. That had been the nature of his family life.

Our most enjoyable times together as a household usually involved food. Even if there was an ongoing spat between core members, almost always everyone would show up for the evening meal and for our Sunday evening house meetings. We did not often have dessert on weeknights as everyone was supposedly watching their weight, but at the house meeting we would have a special dessert and tea in the living room, often with a crackling fire if it was wintertime. There was something about that room, with its dark wood mantelpiece, its fireplace, its large oriel window, and its comfortable furniture, that called us together. But food was indeed a unifier. Sometimes we would go out to dinner as a household to celebrate a birthday or other special occasion. We liked a restaurant at the nearby mall that had nice decor, including candles on the tables, and a varied menu which suited everyone. (A hamburger platter or chicken fingers and french fries were favourite orders.) Usually the whole house would want to come, although one evening Helen came with us but took a separate table and, all through the meal, pretended she didn't know us.

Generally, the days were pleasant, even though at times some mediation might be called for between house members. There were Church Street members who might sabotage a carefully planned outing by declaring at the last minute that they were not going. This was often because someone else in the house had done something that annoyed them. If the reluctant individual didn't come, one of us on the team would need to stay back or the plan would need to be scuttled entirely. When there was dissension, Gord would be distressed. He understood the dynamics of the house – that Anne Marie and Helen did not like each other, and that George and Helen could bait each other. Gord usually got along with everyone. He was soft-spoken and a peacemaker, and he had an intuitive sense of how to be present when someone was upset. He often found a way of bringing around the reluctant individual. The other three core members would express anger directly, but I think Gord tended to bottle up his anger, expressing it aloud to himself in his room at night or perhaps overindulging in chocolate bars.

One of our more successful house outings was a late August day trip downtown to the Canadian National Exhibition. After looking at exhibits of some new products, we strolled along the midway, stopping to try some of the games, and we considered the rides. I discovered that, while Anne Marie liked some rides that catered to children, such as the merry-go-round, she also liked the adult Ferris wheel. She persuaded me to come on it with her, with just the two of us sharing a two-seater. When it stopped with us suspended in mid-air at the top, I was nervous, and, realizing this, Anne Marie deliberately rocked our flimsy carriage back and forth as much as she could, laughing and shouting out all the while, "I'm not scared!" It was fun for her, I guess, to make me suffer for a few minutes. We did not have the easiest relationship. For instance, tensions would arise between us around the size of food portions.

On Saturday mornings each of us had some chore to do as well as the responsibility to vacuum and tidy our own bedroom. Anne Marie vacuumed the hallways and stairs, pausing to talk to each person who passed her going up or down or coming in the front door. Helen helped with cleaning the kitchen. George and Gord looked after garbage, recycling, and lawn mowing or snow shovelling. Gord was especially faithful to shovelling, a task that could be required on any day of the week in the winter. He would sometimes shovel our neighbours' walk as well, a kindness they appreciated.

Gord had a girlfriend whom he'd met at an ARC dance. One Saturday when they were at the mall, she pushed Gord to shoplift a little novelty makeup pouch. He was caught by the security officers, threatened with arrest, and certainly given a good scare. Worse, he was banned from the mall for a year – something he took very seriously, and he did not return to the mall again all of that year. On another occasion, the same girlfriend demanded a ring from Gord. He obligingly printed out a bank withdrawal slip for the two hundred dollars that he had been saving for his vacation, signing it himself. However, his withdrawals required Julie's signature as well. Fortunately, the bank teller called our house, and the plan was foiled.

It fell to me to have a long and difficult talk with Gord about breaking off his relationship with this young woman, whose bossiness, manipulation, and deviousness made the relationship plainly unhealthy. It was a hard decision for Gord. They enjoyed the physicality of hugging and dancing close to each other. Gord has a generous heart, and he likes to please people, and I think he did also care about the woman. Even more perhaps, he so much wanted to be like his brothers, who had girlfriends. However, finally he decided to give her back her photo – a sign for him that it was over. She seemed to accept this and stopped calling him. He looked around for other women both at ARC dances and in Daybreak, and he did have other girlfriends over the years.

Gord had a strong spiritual sensibility and a way of knowing just which person might need some kindness or prayers when we were at dinner or gathered with the rest of the community for common prayer or a liturgy. I think he could read our slightest gestures – the sag of shoulders, the downward glance. "Open your heart" or "Keep your heart open," he would entreat over and over in his prayer, almost as a kind of mantra. Or he would pray, "Take care of . . ." (someone he loved, often his mother or his siblings, or his boss at the Woodery). But Gord was not an angel. He had a reputation for starting rumours about romantic relationships among the assistants, and he was periodically scolded by one or another assistant.

In his bedroom, Gord had created a prayer corner with a picture of Jesus, a cross, and a night light where he could sit quietly. He could enter deeply into retreats and would spend a long time in silence in the chapel. I was privileged to make the first L'Arche Covenant Companions retreat with Gord. I had been feeling poor in terms of patience and energy, and I was ready for a retreat. After five days of talks and prayer and sharing in small groups with pairs of "companions" from other L'Arche communities, we each announced the covenant – a commitment to live close to Jesus and the poor in L'Arche. (L'Arche people understand "the poor" as referring to anyone who is disadvantaged in some way or going through a difficult time.) Still today this remains the most profound L'Arche retreat I have made, because Gord and I made it together. On that retreat we often sang a little song whose refrain epitomizes the L'Arche experience: "By the hungry, I will feed you; by the poor, I'll make you rich; by the broken, I will mend you; tell me, which one is which?"[1]

Gord made short private retreats with his friend Father George Strohmeyer in Pennsylvania, where the L'Arche Erie community had a retreat centre. He would fly down and back alone, changing planes in Pittsburgh with assistance from an airline attendant, and be met at the Erie airport by a L'Arche assistant. As Gord's retreat director, George would meet with Gord and would give him cassette tapes of music and scripture to listen to. Gord would return home three days later "feeling peaceful," as he put it, and with a tape that Father George had made specially for him. He would play the tape over and over in his bedroom before going to sleep. After Father Henri Nouwen came to Daybreak, Gord would sometimes talk to Henri for spiritual direction and play tapes from him as well.

Gord received a lot of emotional support from his mother, Pat, and he gave her support. From Daybreak's earliest years she was a faithful volunteer, helping with fundraisers and in the office, and later in the community's Seniors Club. On days when she came to Daybreak, she would have lunch with Gord, and sometimes they would go shopping. He was short and stocky, and Pat made certain that Gord had nice shirts, pants, and a good suit, all altered to fit him.

George was deeply loyal and faithful to his family and friends and also to his sports teams. Most assistants were not big sports fans, but after three years, when Joanne followed Julie as house leader, she and George hit it off as she was interested in sports and, most important, was a Habs fan. George subscribed to the *Toronto Star,* but only for the Sports section, which he would pore over each day. He had attended elementary school and a technical high school, and he had learned to read. He took his time, mouthing each word to himself.

One Sunday morning at breakfast George and Gord were clearly making oblique references to the previous night, Gord saying under his breath, "Don't talk about it," to George, and George chuckling to himself and smirking. The rest of us were curious, and at first

George offered only one of his standard responses when he didn't want to talk about something: "Wouldn't ya like to know!" But he could not contain himself, and gradually he let on that the two of them had been over at the local hotel, a rather seedy establishment, for a pop or beer the previous evening and one of the patrons had invited them downstairs, where they had watched women engaged in mud wrestling. It had obviously been a titillating experience for both of them, but probably more enjoyed by George, who was older and perhaps had fewer inhibitions, having lived for many years in a small-town men's culture before coming to Daybreak. (Gord had moved to Daybreak from his family home at age eighteen, when he was still attending school. From his perspective, what they had seen was shocking and certainly not something he would be telling his mother about.) That hotel had been respectable at one time, but it was increasingly visited by the morality squad and was finally shut down. The owner re-opened in an empty building close to the edge of town, where the same bright pink neon bikini-clad girlie sign was lit up at night. I don't think George and Gord were aware of the new location.

We were blessed when Steve M., our bassoonist friend from the Green House, opted to associate himself with Church Street after the moves in the fall of 1984. For several years while he was still single, Steve would stay with us whenever the ballet was not on tour and when the performance schedule in Toronto was not too intense. Sometimes, he would bring along his bassoon if he needed to practise a new piece. Besides helping out in other ways, he would watch sports with the men and sometimes go out with them, and he would take George and often, Lloyd, to the weekly games of the Gustav Mahlers, the hockey team on which he played.

In the baseball season, Steve would invite George on weekend road trips to see games in other cities. Sometimes Lloyd and Peggy, the other two most ardent sports fans in Daybreak, went along with them, and one time a group of five – George, Lloyd, Steve, and two male assistants – took a train to Houston to see a Texas Rangers game. When Lloyd developed a heart condition, Steve and George would still include him in the Mahlers' games if he was feeling up to going. Steve got along well with everyone, but it was with George that he developed an especially strong bond of friendship.

∽∾∾

There was vulnerability in Daybreak's rapid growth and the busy schedules that everyone kept. With more assistants living a different rhythm because they were in daytime roles in the Woodery and Day Program, it was no longer possible for all the assistants to come together, as we had done previously at the Tuesday Morning Meetings. The feeling of intimacy among assistants and the sense that they were getting back more than they were giving became less strong. Meanwhile, when Sue M. had completed two terms as international coordinator, Joe Egan was asked by L'Arche International to take on the additional role of international vice-coordinator. [2] The Community Council had supported Joe to do this, but I am sure none of us, Joe included, fully grasped the implications of his carrying two roles and how often he would need to be away supporting other L'Arche communities. Joe and Gus, who constituted the Daybreak administrative team, no longer could keep their fingers on the pulse of the community.

Living in L'Arche requires significant sacrifices in terms of personal time as well as salary, and no one likes to feel taken for granted. Several assistants—more than the usual number—announced they would be leaving at the end of that summer. Other factors also contributed to discontent. The assistant body was changing with Gen Xers arriving. They brought more independent attitudes and New Age interests. One new assistant came with crystals and had training in how to use them to treat people's aches and pains. Another had massage training. One day when Gus was giving a tour to some visitors, he opened the kitchen door in the Big House to discover one of the male assistants lying virtually naked on the table receiving a massage. Gus was upset. Other assistants pointed out that they had little time and money for self-care or recreation. Then ill feeling arose when word got out that one summer assistant, albeit someone with previous L'Arche experience supporting a core

117

member who could be volatile, was being paid extra so he could cover his student loan payments.

In March 1985, it appeared we would not have enough assistants to cover the homes come September, and there was a sense of looming crisis. We were all asked to pray, and I was asked to take on the newly created role of assistants' coordinator, and Julie, to become our house leader. My work would be to care for the current assistants and to recruit others. I would work in the Daybreak office during the day but would be home for dinner and would help in the house two evenings a week and on some weekends. Nick would continue on a similar schedule. As soon as possible, another assistant would be added to the Church Street team. By October we did have our usual quota of assistants. Julie had the qualities of a good house leader, and the switch worked out well. I liked the rhythm of leaving the house in the morning and arriving home with the core members after work. I think it gave us a sense of solidarity as a household.

Sue M., as a much-loved and respected Daybreak elder, came to explain the house leadership change to everyone at Church Street. After dinner, at our usual prayer time, she produced two symbols – figures made in the metallurgy workshop of L'Arche Trosly in France. Julie received a shepherd, representing her care for the well-being of each person in the house. (Indeed, Julie did display this care for all of us over the ensuing years, until she returned to England.) I received a horn player, because an important part of my new role was to "announce L'Arche." This meant to make L'Arche better known, especially on campuses of colleges and universities, where young people might be interested in becoming assistants.

I began to meet with all the assistants regularly, to listen and try to ensure that their needs were met and they were well. At decision-making points, I would offer the wisdom I had received: Stay if you are growing as a person and are happy. I did try just once, unsuccessfully, to twist someone's arm. Like Jean Vanier and others, I had to learn to trust that the people we needed would come. Until that time, L'Arche had relied on word of mouth and prayer to bring the assistants we needed. One afternoon, a brainstorming session with three or four assistants in the Church Street living room yielded the wording for our first recruitment poster. "Change the World One Heart at a Time," it challenged, in very large print, and just below in parentheses, "The first may be your own,"[3] and some pictures of core members and assistants together. The new role was a good fit for me. From my teaching days, I had been interested in the well-being of young people and tried to encourage them in their quest to live their lives meaningfully.

∽o∽

Julie and I switched bedrooms when our roles changed, Julie taking the downstairs bedroom behind the kitchen and I moving up to one of the two third-floor bedrooms. Having the downstairs bedroom permitted the house leader to better keep tabs on the movement of people in and out of the house, and to hear any untoward disturbances.

One night around 3:00 a.m., I was aroused from a deep sleep by Julie calling out my name as she panted up the steep stairs to the third floor. She had been awakened by a sound that she thought was likely Helen, who was a nighthawk, coming down to check on her. When she switched on her bed lamp, a burglar had lunged at her from the foot of her bed. Fortunately, she had screamed and he had fled. Of course, we immediately called the police, and they checked around the house and found a kitchen knife outside the side door. We were never certain whether a door had been left unlocked or whether the burglar jimmied the side door or front door lock. The house had only press-in doorknob locks on the outside doors. They had seemed safe enough, since crime was rare in Richmond Hill.

At breakfast the next morning, we described the incident in the night to the other house members. "You should have called me," George said. "I would have hit him with the broom!" That day Joe Egan made sure deadbolt locks were installed on both doors, and Julie was offered trauma counselling. I think she went once. I admit that I was grateful not to have been sleeping in that back bedroom.

∽o∽

During most of the nine years that I lived at Church Street, the core members had family whom they would visit on long weekends. Unless Helen was going to the Newroths', her sister Lillian and her husband, Don, would pick her up. Besides a small suitcase, Helen always had additional bags containing her rug hooking, camera, photo albums, and other essentials – far more than anyone could manage on public transit, even were she to have learned the complicated route to their home. However, the others each knew their particular routes. George would head south to York Mills subway station, where he would take a bus to his hometown. Anne Marie would travel to her mother's, taking a bus, then the subway, and finally another bus. Gord's route to visit his family home was the most difficult. It involved three major vehicle changes and negotiating busy transit stations.

It was not until Gord had flown back from Australia alone in 1982,[4] after a visit he made with Sue M., that he was able to persuade Joe Egan that he could learn the route. Matthew (or Matthuse, as Gord called him) was sympathetic to Gord's desire, and, as he was one of the assistants living with Gord in the Big House at that time, he undertook the transit training. Gord learned to take the bus to the top of the subway line, travel south by subway to Union Station, find his way past the VIA Rail area to the ticket booths for the GO trains (GO being the regional transportation network), buy a ticket to Mississauga, and find the right westbound platform for his train. He had to be careful not to fall asleep, because he needed to count the stops to Union Station. He didn't read, but as an added check he knew the colours of the Union subway station wall tiles. (Each station had a different colour combination.) At Union, a large board displayed the destinations of all the GO trains, their departure times, and the platform from which they were leaving. Figuring out this display would have been impossible for Gord. The first time he went alone, he took the eastbound rather than the westbound train. But at the end of the line he realized his mistake and retraced the route, arriving home safely, albeit late. Gord had already made the trip several times when I came to live with him.

When John Guido came to live at Church Street, he wondered how Gord managed to find the right GO train platform given that he was not able to read, so he shadowed Gord one time. His small stature, quiet voice, and a bit of a speech impediment meant that Gord did not easily get people's attention. However, he persisted in approaching fellow travellers, showing them his ticket, and asking what platform he should be on until he got a clear response. He asked four different individuals on that occasion.

Gord could also recognize the stop for Maple Leaf Gardens, Toronto's large sports arena. One Sunday evening he did not return at the expected time from a weekend visit to his family. We waited, anticipating he might have gone in the wrong direction on the subway or perhaps got on the wrong bus and had to backtrack. Eventually, he turned up, just as we were about to notify the police. On his way home on the subway, he had got wind of a wrestling match at the Gardens and had decided to make a detour.

∽∘∾

On some weekday evenings and Saturdays, house members were involved in classes or programs. Gord was in a Saturday afternoon bowling league, played ball hockey, and took swimming lessons. In the summer, he would take his bike out for a spin around the neighbourhood, often dropping in on the Vorstermans family. George usually spent time at the arena or the ballpark, both of which were just a block to the south of us. Helen went to weekly Weight Watchers meetings for many years; and one year, Gord joined Weight Watchers and attended with his friend Brother Pat, a Franciscan friar from Ireland. For a time, Julie accompanied Anne Marie and Helen to an evening pottery course at a local high school. Anne Marie also took swimming lessons. Even in the pool she would try to engage people in conversation, but, when encouraged, she could swim the length of the pool without stopping.

Other evenings in our house were probably not very different from those of any other family. People who had not cooked would help with the dishes, and everyone would make their lunch for the next day. Then, Helen would settle into her needlework in the living room, and, in the winter, if they didn't have something on, Gord and George would spend the rest of the evening in the second-floor TV room watching hockey. If Steve was visiting, he would join them, and often Lloyd would walk over from Mill Street. Sometimes Lloyd would bring donuts for his host friends and a plain chocolate bar for me, since he knew I could not eat flour. Like George, Lloyd and Gord had favourite teams – Lloyd's the Boston Bruins because Bobby Orr had played Junior A hockey for Lloyd's hometown Oshawa Generals, and Gord's the Toronto Maple Leafs. As a result, during hockey season we could sometimes hear raucous sounds from upstairs. On weekends, the TV was similarly claimed by George and Gord to watch professional wrestling.

If she didn't have something on in the evening, Anne Marie would tend to go to her bedroom early. She had her own small TV and liked to watch *Little House on the Prairie* and *The Waltons,* and she would sit in her rocking chair reviewing aloud her day as well as anything else on her mind, or she would listen to her radio. She was probably the only person in the house who regularly listened to the news.[5] In 1990, it was Anne Marie who heard that the first Gulf War had started, and she rushed downstairs to share this news. We had been speaking about its likelihood at dinner and wondering whether it would affect the little L'Arche community in Bethany, near Jerusalem.[6] Still today, Anne Marie takes an interest in the news.

Four weeks before Christmas, at the beginning of Advent, the whole house moved into a somewhat different mode as our practice of Kris Kringle (sometimes called "Secret Santa") got under way. We each drew the name of someone else in the house. One assistant was asked to organize this, and only she or he knew who had whose name. Then each of us assistants, in addition to having a name ourselves, was assigned to help one or two of the core members with carrying out their Kris Kringle activities. The idea was to pray silently for the person whose name we had and also to do secret kindnesses for their person and make or purchase a modest Christmas gift for them. Kindnesses might range from polishing their person's winter boots to placing a cookie on their pillow or adding a treat to their lunch bag. Lighting the candles on our Advent wreath at our prayer times leading up to Christmas would add to our anticipation. Just before Christmas, we would have a special dinner and exchange of gifts and learn who our Kris Kringle had been. I believe this practice did increase the loving-kindness among us, putting us more in the spirit of Christmas.

The Church Street house tended to be a magnet for assistants on their free time, I think largely because of Julie's outgoing and welcoming personality but also because often the Church Street core members, who needed less personal care in the evenings than those in some other houses, could join in the gatherings. Gord and George might stay upstairs watching TV, but Anne Marie and Helen enjoyed the social atmosphere in the living room.

Our house was also good at creating celebrations. One that was especially memorable was an All Saints' dance on a November first evening – a substitute for a Halloween party. It still gave us opportunity to dress up and celebrate, and it was on a better night because a group of L'Arche Le Printemps friends could be with us. We invited the other Daybreak houses also, and we rolled up the living room carpet so that there was a good space for dancing. Anne Marie came dressed in red and white, as Saint Valentine. George was Saint George, who slew the dragon. Francis came as Saint Francis, with pictures of animals pinned to his shirt and a "tail" to his pants. Julie was Saint Winifred, from Holywell in Wales. According to legend, Saint Winifred's suitor had chopped off her head when she decided to become a nun, but her uncle, who was another saint, Saint Beuno, put it back on and she lived. Julie drew a line of red lipstick around her neck to show where her head had been cut off. Mike C., who was a Church Street assistant that year, came as Saint Joan of Arc with pieces of charred wood attached to his waist. There were at least two Mary Magdalenes, one being from L'Arche Le Printemps. I was the elderly Saint Elizabeth, with a baby doll John the Baptist. Daybreak kept a very large bag of old articles of clothing – exotic looking shirts and dresses, scarves, shoes and wigs – to be ransacked for such occasions.

For Julie's twenty-fourth birthday, her assistant friend Sharon Mayne organized us around a *Coronation Street* theme, as this was Julie's favourite television program. While Julie was out, Sharon drew Union Jacks on plain paper and George and Anne Marie helped us colour them. One of these was fixed to the front door, along with a Coronation Street sign. Red, white, and blue bunting

123

and streamers were hung inside and out. When Julie came home, Gord tried to imitate Julie's accent, and Helen teased her. For dinner, we ate English fare – fish and chips with vinegar, and mushy peas, and of course, a birthday cake decorated to look like a Union Jack.

∾ᴏ∾

Thanks to a Jesuit who had spent time at Daybreak and was now a university chaplain, we began to welcome students from Marquette University in Milwaukee for their reading week. Invariably, some of the students would fall in love with L'Arche, and almost always we would recruit one or two fine assistants from these groups. Other universities established similar programs. In addition, Marquette students launched a campus enrichment week called Communities That Care, to which they invited Daybreak and other nearby L'Arche communities to send pairs of buddies. The L'Arche people lived in the dorms and student houses, demonstrating what it could be like for people of widely differing abilities to share friendships. Together they re-created the fun that is characteristic of L'Arche life. The core members interacted with and became teachers of the students, and the pairs of buddies gave workshops about L'Arche. Some also shared stories about living in institutions before they came to L'Arche.

For one of the earliest Marquette trips, Michael, my Arctic Adventure companion, and Mike Bromhead from the Green House, were chosen, and also Anne Marie and Julie from Church Street. The two Mikes charmed the young female students, and Anne Marie's habit of asking many questions helped to bring the quieter students out of themselves. Anne Marie gave a very good presentation about having CP and what she can do in spite of this condition, and she answered the students' questions. The two women enjoyed staying in a student house. Anne Marie was greatly amused when an air bed that Julie slept on deflated during the night, and she laughingly told that story several times when they returned. Their time together on that trip remains a favourite memory for both of them. Later, Julie and Anne Marie, or sometimes Julie and Gord, became a speaking team sent to local high schools and colleges where people wanted to learn about L'Arche. Both core members had slide shows about their lives in community. Julie told me that, typically, the students would be much more interested in hearing from Anne Marie or Gord than from her.

Anne Marie enjoys demonstrating an unusual skill that I don't think relates to having CP: she is able to read upside down, and only upside down. This proves handy when she is sitting opposite a person sharing a menu in a restaurant or playing a card game. When I lived with her, Crazy Eights was her favourite. Today, it is Sequence or Skip-Bo. She will play such games over and over with a willing opponent.

My bedroom was over Anne Marie's, and the soundproofing was poor. If something was on Anne Marie's mind I often had some sense of this, so I was not surprised when she approached me one day after I had been at Church Street for some time, to say that she would like to find a boyfriend. Anne Marie knew that she could not have an assistant as a boyfriend, and she had not met any core member she was interested in at Daybreak in Richmond Hill so far, nor at ARC, where she worked. However, there were three men of similar age and ability to Anne Marie in the downtown houses of the community. These men were all able to travel to Richmond Hill independently. This was important, since she did not know the route to the downtown homes.

Finding and keeping genuine friends is often the biggest challenge for people with intellectual disabilities. I was eager to help and to coach her a bit on how she might make such a relationship work. Anne Marie already had identified the first man whom she wanted to invite on a date, and she had decided on the Swiss Chalet restaurant as where she wanted to go. Anne Marie loves to eat out and can tend to order extravagantly. My strongest suggestion was that they "go Dutch," so as not to put a financial burden on either of them, a suggestion she accepted, albeit it a little reluctantly. My second suggestion was that she ask her date where he would like to go. She could propose Swiss Chalet, but they should work this out together. I made a number of alternative suggestion – a less expensive restaurant, a movie, bowling. None interested her.

Anne Marie called the first of the young men, and they went out twice, both times to Anne Marie's choice of restaurant. However, the second time, Anne Marie ordered something expensive, for which she did not have enough money. The young man, a kind and diffident fellow, paid the difference. When they got back to Church Street, I helped Anne Marie reimburse him, but the next time she called him, he was not interested in going out. She tried another man. He had been dating a woman on and off, and although he and Anne Marie did go out once, he decided he did not want a different girlfriend. She tried the third man. Again, he was not interested after one date. She concluded that he was gay. However, they did continue to enjoy talking on the phone.

Looking back, I wonder if we could have helped Anne Marie more with this quest. We did try the social evenings of another social service in our area, but those present either had much higher needs than Anne Marie or already had a partner. At the time, I felt frustrated that Anne Marie seemed unwilling or unable to choose to grow in the skill of sharing decisions, such an important part of friendship, and I was discouraged.[7] However, the pool of options for meeting someone suitable is much smaller for a person who has a disability. Successful long-term mildly romantic relationships such as Francis and Linda shared, or marriages such as Joanne and Allan shared, are rare.

I could not seem to get close to Anne Marie. Carmen had won her trust when Anne Marie moved to Church Street. Carmen was strict in a motherly way, and perhaps this was helpful to Anne Marie. She still telephones Carmen weekly. Anne Marie had found it very difficult to leave her family and move to Daybreak. She was still in her early twenties, and she knew that her mother had cancer. In fact, her mother survived a number of bouts of cancer, but, understandably, cancer is a disease that Anne Marie has long feared, and she has feared becoming "skinny" because she associates weight loss with cancer. Over the years, what has helped Anne Marie to be less lonely is that she has had strong bonds with her family, as well as with Carmen. Anne Marie and Ellen had lived together at the New House. They both enjoyed amusement parks, and for years they would spend a summer day together at Canada's Wonderland.

Both women are less agile now, but Anne Marie nevertheless takes her walker and goes out weekly for a donut and tea with a woman core member friend from a nearby Daybreak house.

Anne Marie is one of the most intellectually able Daybreak core members. In the early 2000s she had a part-time job helping with mailings at the Henri Nouwen Literary Centre. I was working in the same office then. Anne Marie often had interesting questions or comments to contribute during our tea breaks. It was not surprising that she was one of the first core members elected to the Daybreak Council when the decision was made to include core members. She was paired with Kathy Kelly, who was also on the Council. Kathy's role was to go over the agenda with Anne Marie before the biweekly meetings and, at the meetings, to remind Anne Marie of opinions she had expressed. This Council role and the preparation over tea with Kathy called forth the best side of Anne Marie. She did not need to compete with anyone, as could be the case when she was with other core members, and she was able to contribute worthwhile ideas and have them considered.

9. "Just gig-nore him": About Helen

Love doesn't mean doing extraordinary or heroic things. It means knowing how to do ordinary things with tenderness. Jean Vanier

When Steve and Ann Newroth founded L'Arche Daybreak, in 1969, they surely had in mind that it might become a permanent home for Helen, who was Ann's aunt. The first few core members they welcomed to Daybreak were men. One other young woman came but did not stay. Then Helen came in 1971. She was very attached to Ann and to Sue M., who also arrived in 1971. All her life, Helen had a dramatic flair. In those early days she could be found sometimes in the wee hours asleep on the floor outside Sue's door. When Daybreak opened the Church Street house, Helen moved there. Around that time, 1977, Steve and Ann took a sabbatical and then went on to do other groundbreaking work in the social services. At Church Street, Helen was known to have no use for men (or to convey that attitude at least) and to attach herself passionately to one or another young female assistant – Tina, Marie, Colleen, now Julie and later Joanne. Helen was fiercely loyal to each one. I was her favourite person only occasionally, when no younger woman was available.

As well as visiting Lillian and Don, Helen would visit Ann and Steve and their children. I think Helen revered Ann and Steve. To us assistants, she always called them Mr. and Mrs. Newroth. When Steve accepted a job with the Ontario government, with a mandate to close down an institution another hour's drive north of the one where Greg had lived, and to find homes in the community for the residents, we had to look for opportunities for Helen to travel up to visit them.

One Friday afternoon when Steve was working in Toronto, I drove Helen downtown to meet him at the Mowat Block, an impressive government building in the heart of the financial district. She had carefully packed her suitcase and just one tote bag with her needs for the weekend, including some large towels, with which she liked to cover the entire bathroom floor when she took a bath. She knew that meeting "Mr. Newroth" at his office was not a time to look like a bag lady. She had had her hair done, and she wore her best dress and coat.

We found a parking space, threaded our way among the tall buildings, and walked together up the wide granite steps of the block and through the glass doors, with Helen carrying only her handbag and me carrying her suitcase and tote bag. Helen had a well-developed sense of the "occasion." In another life, I am sure she would have been onstage or a prominent socialite. She enjoyed playing a part. In fact, sometimes it could be difficult to tell who the real Helen was. With a fine display of dignity, she approached the concierge at the reception desk and made her request, "Mr. Newroth, please." The concierge looked Helen up and down, glanced at me, and then obliged by calling Steve's number. (Helen did often seem unusual to people who did not know her, not only because she was quite small of stature and had the features of someone with Down syndrome but also because by then she was getting older and a bit wizened.) After a short time, the elevator door opened, and Steve emerged in formal business attire and carrying his briefcase. Helen was hardly more than half Steve's height. I was taken by the look of surprise on the face of the concierge as Steve approached Helen and, with a slight gracious bow, took her hand, kissed her on the cheek, and said warmly, "Helen, how grand it is to see you again!"

Soon after I moved into Church Street, Helen arrived home one warm September day with her arms wrapped around two dripping Wendy's bags. She had taken some money from the grocery pouch that she found on the kitchen counter and purchased Frosties (a kind of extra-thick chocolate ice-cream shake) for all six of us who were at home that afternoon. She'd carefully carried them the fifteen-minute walk from the fast-food outlet. On another occasion, close to Christmas, when we again had neglected to put away the grocery money, she took a bus to the mall and purchased Christmas gifts of pyjamas and games for children in the community whom she enjoyed babysitting (with an assistant) when occasions arose.

Helen would take money unrepentantly if, to her mind, she needed it for some good purpose. As Julie later remarked to me, "Helen's moral compass was entirely her own. Putting money in the church collection or buying me a present when I'd been away for week easily justified helping herself to money if it was left about." The same apparently applied to items that she regarded as necessary for her personal care if they had been missed in our weekly supermarket trip. Toothpaste was one. She liked Julie's brand, and Julie might discover her toothpaste in Helen's bathroom cupboard.

Nivea was Helen's preferred hand and face cream. One evening I noticed my fairly new jar of Nivea had disappeared from my bedroom. Suspecting the only other person in the house who used the brand, I peeked into Helen's room. Sure enough – I could see a new-looking blue Nivea jar sitting on her dressing table, and in the bathroom wastebasket there was an empty Nivea jar. I confronted Helen, but she was not about to have a conversation with me about the Nivea. "Just gig-nore her," she muttered, walking away from me. (Helen had lots of her own pronunciations: "Cacklic secretary" for Catholic cemetery; "pescetti" for spaghetti, "calackulations," for congratulations.) I had already seen her "gig-noring" tactic in use with others, especially George.

I knew that Helen was guilty, but she was not going to admit this or return my Nivea, and anyway, at the rate she used it, the jar was likely to be half empty by now. I abandoned the issue after trying to get a response from her several times, but I continued to hold a bit of a grudge. During evenings at home, Helen would do her needlework in the living room and at an appropriate time would break off to have her nighttime Diet Coke and cigarette (in those days several people smoked in L'Arche homes). She liked to be the last person to go up to her room. Two or three days later, in the late evening, I left Helen in the living room to finish her cigarette while I said good night to Anne Marie. Helen and I had not been talking much, and she certainly knew I was still upset with her. In a cabinet in the living room, we kept a house bottle of sherry and some sherry glasses for celebrating at special house meetings such as Christmas and the New Year. When the house was settled that night, and I finally retired to my bedroom, I was surprised to discover on my bedside table a glass of sherry and a torn piece of paper with "LOVE HELEN" printed in pencil in her characteristic hand. Of course, I was appeased.

Helen had many unusual likes and dislikes. Early in my time at Church Street, I had a minor showdown with her one evening when I discovered she had again put the house's entire brand-new container of cottage cheese in her lunch bag. I brought my hand down hard on the kitchen counter for emphasis as I said, "Helen, you cannot take the whole container!" She could tell I had hurt my hand and she laughed and then I had to laugh also. Very often she did get her way, taking only a few slices of bologna – the only cold meat she liked – and an ample amount of cottage cheese along with a can of Diet Coke for lunch. I think her visits to Weight Watchers had persuaded her that bread was bad, and for some time she did not make a sandwich, such as the others took for lunch. Besides the Diet Coke in her lunch, she had another before she went to bed. After a few years, we helped her buy Diet Coke by the case, and she kept it in her closet, divvying out two cans each day.

When I moved into the house, there was a long-standing spat between George and Helen. Helen liked to use makeup. Some days she would come to the breakfast table wearing an excess of rouge (or "blush," as it is called today). George would fix his eyes on her from the other end of the table and say, "Got your war paint on, eh!" Furious, Helen would "gig-nore him," as she put it to the rest of us, loud enough for George to hear. Then she'd get her own back later by muttering under her breath at some other opportune time when George was nearby, "Phew! He smells!" Carmen suggested that George and Helen actually liked each other. This may have been true. They seemed to share a kind of Beatrice and Benedict relationship of one-upmanship, although Helen certainly put more effort into annoying George.

Helen could be outright mean to men. George was a target as, at night and in the mornings, he used the same bathroom as Helen and Anne Marie. Helen did not think men and women should share a bathroom, but there was only one bathroom on the second floor, where the three large bedrooms were occupied by Helen, Anne Marie, and George. Helen would remove the night light from the hall — something George needed as he often got up in the night — or she would hide the soap or the toilet paper or George's razor and shaving cream, and sometimes after she had finished in the bathroom she would lock the door so that no one could use it. An assistant would need to find a skewer to open it. On one occasion, Helen was reported to have smeared Vaseline on the door handle so it could not be turned. Carmen told us of an incident when a priest was staying on the second floor at Church Street: Helen had covered the toilet with plastic wrap to cause him an embarrassing accident. At a gathering at the new Daybreak Meeting Hall, Helen noted that there were Women's and Men's signs on the bathroom doors there. She carefully copied out these two words and, with an abundance of Scotch tape, taped the Women's sign on the second-floor bathroom door and the Men's sign on the first-floor bathroom door.

Helen had a well-established reputation for being cleverly mischievous. She was good at "losing" her bus money and getting free bus rides. She was also known to spin stories about the meanness of Church Street assistants. She had gleaned a free meal by telling the new owners of the local diner that the assistants beat her and did not feed her. Carmen learned this only when she and Helen went together to the diner for a meal. The owner began to scold Carmen for not feeding Helen. Helen's response was a hearty laugh.

I think that of the various core members I came to know well, Helen was the most self-possessed, but her sister described an occasion when she seemed to doubt herself. Something prompted her to ask, "Lillian, what's wrong with me?" Lillian chose not to enter into a description of Down syndrome. She responded, "Helen, there is absolutely nothing wrong with you. You are a wonderful person, and I love you very much." All true. Helen's niece Ann had similar experiences with Helen and noted that after her initial query, Helen did not seem interested in pursuing the subject.

A mosaic chromosome pattern is associated with greater intellectual ability among people who have Down syndrome. Helen was thought to have such a pattern. She was certainly very creative in the games she played and the ways she was idiosyncratic. A different aspect of Helen's cleverness showed in her ability to do crafts. She had good fine motor control. Nearly every female assistant who lived with Helen received the gift of a coaster (which she called a "toaster,") or a hot mat or rug-hooked hanging or cushion cover made by her. (She would snub the men and not give them gifts.)

Helen would travel alone by bus down Yonge Street to Hillcrest Mall to shop for sewing supplies and, sometimes, camera film, and would eat her dinner out on Fridays, the days she got paid at ARC. She loved to shop, and, if she had money left, on Saturdays she might travel farther south, to another mall at Steeles Avenue. Helen had a Polaroid camera that gave her a great deal of pleasure. One day a clerk called us to say that Helen had chosen two packages of film but did not have enough money to pay for them. (Helen had provided her with our phone number.) Helen had already put the two packets in her tote bag and was not about to take either one out. She had placed some money on the counter for the clerk and clearly thought what she was offering should be enough. (In fact, Helen had more money in her purse, but she was not going to let that on to the clerk.) In the end, I went to the mall to persuade Helen to pay in full or put back one film packet. I think she reluctantly chose former.

If we were attending a special event, Helen was sure to have her camera in one of her tote bags or on a strap around her neck. She enjoyed lining people up for a photo, and, of course, everyone enjoyed seeing the photos that the camera immediately printed. At home, Helen would place a strip of masking tape across the bottom of each photo and carefully, if unevenly, print identifying information on it, sometimes asking one of us assistants to spell names for her. Then she would insert the photos in her album. When others had a camera, we would try to tell Helen to save her film, as it was expensive, but Helen liked to be the photographer. If someone else was taking the picture she tended to be annoyed, would wear a grumpy expression, and would refuse to smile for the photo.

Helen loved to be in the kitchen. She was always ready to make dinner on Mondays, her cooking night. Her favourite recipe was salmon loaf with scalloped potatoes, and her preferred cooking partner was Julie. On some Saturdays, after chores, Helen might do some baking with one of us assistants. Also on Saturdays she would walk to the local public library to borrow music tapes. (She had a cassette player in her bedroom.) Sometimes Helen came across as irreverent — she could produce a few swear words when annoyed — but she liked hymns, especially "Amazing Grace," and would get the librarians to look for every version they could find.

Except for Fridays, when most people ate out, and Sundays, when we had a house meeting in the living room, we followed the L'Arche tradition of taking a few minutes for prayer around the table after dinner. As in the Green House, each person had their night to cook, and it was the cook who led the prayer. At Church Street, this person got to choose the reading from *I Meet Jesus*, a simple catechism that was in use in some of our homes. The book had a few lines of large print and a drawing on each page. George almost always chose the reading on the page with the picture of the Virgin Mary. Anne Marie liked the picture of a little child walking along a road holding hands with Jesus. George and Anne Marie could read the accompanying short texts. Gord chose various pictures and would repeat the phrases line by line as someone read with him. Helen's favourite page had this text:

> One day I meet Jesus
> he smiles at me,
> he touches me.
> I can tell he loves me
> just as I am with my difficulties
> my heart rejoices
> a new source of life flows within me
> a small light burns in my heart. [1]

She liked Julie to read the text for her. She would not repeat it out loud herself.

Helen came from a musical family, and we had heard she could play the piano. However, she would not play in front of an audience. One day when I was upstairs and Helen was the only other person home, I heard the strains of "Oh! Susanna" drifting upward from the living room. Delighted, I crept down to listen, but once she realized I was near, she stopped playing. At one of the Daybreak coffee houses where various community members contributed short performances, Julie offered to set up a screen – a large bedsheet – between the piano and the audience, so that no one could see her, and under this condition, Helen agreed to play. She got enthusiastic applause for her duet of "Chopsticks" with Julie and her one-hand rendition of "Frère Jacques." I think she was quite pleased and proud, though she would not come out from behind the bedsheet to take a bow.

People were impressed by Helen's cleverness, and they often went along with what she wanted. One day she persuaded the bus driver to divert for a block from his route down Yonge Street and drop her in front of our house, because she couldn't walk, she explained. And the librarians would look the other way when she borrowed more than the allotted number of music tapes or returned them long overdue. When Helen went to the hairdresser, Julie would give her a couple of two-dollar bills. (Yes, two-dollar bills existed in the 1980s.) She would hand over one, and when the hairdresser, who knew her well, told her that was not enough for her standard wash and set, she would produce the second bill with a flourish and say, "Oh well, I guess I won't eat tonight!"

Helen avoided calling men by name, instead using pronouns, making up names for them, or addressing them as "dear" or "dah-ling." She could flirt, and she enjoyed doing so with the men she liked – especially her brother-in-law Don, whom she always referred to as "my sister's husband." When Don was near enough to hear, she would mutter, "Get rid of him!" to Lillian under her breath, just as she did sometimes with George in our house. When she talked to Julie or to me about Gord, she referred to him as "your son"; George was "him" or "you know." When she was speaking to Julie, she referred to Mike Coffey, our male assistant one year, as "your husband" and his fiancée, Maggie, who was house leader at the Big House, as "your husband's wife."

Helen and Lillian both loved to sing, and they knew the favourite oldies. When Helen was visiting, they would burst into song while doing the washing up. The longer Helen sang, the louder she would get. One day, Don heard the strains of the Judy Garland song "For Me and My Gal" wafting up from the basement, where they were folding the laundry. He managed to videotape them. They put on quite a show for him, twirling and flipping their aprons and tea towels around as they sang at the tops of their voices, belting out the last lines again in a reprise – "The bells are ringin…in Loveland, for me and my gal!" (John Guido, who came to Church Street in 1989, and I visited Lillian and Don a few months after Helen died. We shared many Helen stories, but I think the high point for all of us was viewing that video again.)

Helen's immediate family were United Church people. However, the idea of confining her attendance to this one denomination did not make sense to Helen. Both the United and the Catholic churches were a short walk from our house. She attended the Sunday morning service at the United Church and then would make her way up the block to attend the noon Mass at the Catholic church. She liked to receive communion. She would sit at the front, and in the course of the distribution of communion she would manage to join a second line and so receive communion twice. The parish priest indulged her. He seemed even rather delighted that Helen so much wanted communion. At our annual Daybreak Community Weekend, everyone received an award. The awards were often send-ups of some aspect of the person, but they might also acknowledge an achievement. One year Helen received the Ecumenical Award for her dual church attendance. She accepted the award with great dignity. It was difficult to tell whether she got the joke. If she did, she probably would have had no intention of letting this on.

Helen liked giving gifts and would put little items on the bed of her favourite female assistant – a cookie, a coaster that she had made. However, she did not like receiving gifts and would sometimes refuse to open them. If she did, she would usually find a way of regifting them or she would put them in the garbage. Ann,

Helen's niece, told me about a gift that a loving relative carefully prepared for Helen, a photo tree with small pictures of Helen's family members. Although the tree was probably from Bowring or some other high-end shop, Helen dismissed it as "tancy." Ann surmised that she applied this word to things that she felt were both fancy and tacky.

It was not unusual for Helen to give a Deepest Sympathy or Get Well Soon card with a nice picture of flowers or a cat to someone celebrating a birthday. She liked to shop for cards alone at the local drugstore. She chose them for the pictures and did not ask anyone to read them to her. When she herself received cards for Christmas or her birthday, she always checked inside to see if the sender had enclosed any money. If there wasn't any, she would refuse even to hear who the card was from.

When Julie left Daybreak, at the end of the summer of 1987, she took with her a supply of two-dollar bills to enclose in cards to Helen. Julie deeply missed the people who had had a great impact on her life. The very next summer, Joanne, who replaced Julie as house leader, took Helen and Gord and Janet, one of the core members from downtown, to visit Julie in England. Julie recalls, "At dinner at my sister's, Helen refused the cake because she was on a diet, she said, and Dr. Prasad (her beloved family doctor) would be angry. In Helen's presence, I 'phoned' Dr. Prasad, and, in my mock call, I explained the situation so that the doctor could confirm that it was okay for Helen to eat the cake since she was on holiday." Helen went along, probably knowing that it was a ruse but enjoying the attention, and also knowing that Julie would find a way for her to enjoy the cake. Helen loved this sort of elaborate charade.

Joanne was totally new to L'Arche, but she brought years of experience working with people with intellectual disabilities. She did not want the responsibility of house leader, but we had no one else who could take the role. Although she was a good leader, and the core members in the house embraced her, she left after a year. I reluctantly took back the role in the fall of 1988. Carl had come for a visit in June 1988, and I nabbed him as more mature and experienced than some of the other prospective new assistants. I felt he would be able to take over when I would be away for several weeks, something I foresaw that autumn as my mother was moving from our family home.

Carl managed the house leader role during the time I was away, but when I returned he confessed that the house was more of a challenge than he had expected. Everyone pushed the boundaries a bit, but Helen took full advantage of his newness and his being a man. As an example, Carl described arriving home one Friday evening after dinner out with Anne Marie and Gord, to find George anxiously waiting on the front steps. "You need to call the Kmart manager right away," he said. "It's about Helen. I got the number." When Carl had the manager on the phone, he asked to speak to Helen. There was a pause, and then the manager came back to say, in a cool tone, "She won't talk to you." Carl's response was "Please tell her just to take the bus home." "She has no money for the bus," the manager retorted. "She wants you to come and pick her up."

Carl knew that not having bus money did not stop Helen from getting on a bus, but he could not tell the manager this. When he arrived to get Helen, she was seated outside the manager's office and greeted him gleefully with "Hello, dah–ling!" and a triumphant smile. He was about to leave with Helen when the manager insisted he come into her office for a private conversation. "Helen tells me you lock her in her room and never give her any money," the manager said in a confrontational voice. Aghast, Carl pointed out that Helen had hardly seemed angry with him when he arrived, but it nevertheless took a few minutes to reassure the manager that Helen was not being abused. Helen, of course, was delighted with the whole scenario.

In the summer of 1989, before Carl left Church Street, he saw a police car drive up to the house one Saturday afternoon. An officer helped Helen out of the vehicle. As she headed into the house, she warned Carl, "Don't tell my sister!" (On the other hand, if Helen felt one of us assistants was blocking her in some way, she would threaten us with "I'll tell my sister!") Helen had planned to go to a sewing supply store. She knew her way there by bus, but she had fallen asleep, missed her stop, and awakened to find everyone exiting the bus at the top end of the subway line. Realizing she didn't know how to get home, she followed the protocol she knew and approached a man in uniform. The police came and willingly drove her home.

When John Guido came to Church Street at the end of that summer, Helen needed to get used to another male house leader. She thoroughly ignored him for his first few weeks. Especially in public, she would make no acknowledgement of him at all. But then, to his relief and delight, one evening at a Daybreak dance she wanted a partner for the chicken dance and the hokey-pokey, and she grabbed John and pulled him onto the dance floor. As the years unfolded, John and Helen became very precious to each other. She would address him as "my boy."

In the fall of 1989, Helen developed hyperglycemia. In retrospect, I thought perhaps her succumbing to sleep on the bus was an indication of its beginnings. Helen loved Baskin-Robbins ice cream, and on her way home from work she would sometimes get off the bus at the plaza a few blocks north of us to indulge herself. But then, she might fall asleep for a little while on the bench outside the store. When Helen was late home, it took a little while for us to discover where she was, and then to learn what was making her so sleepy. Before Helen had the diagnosis of hyperglycemia, John got a call from a security guard at the local mall on another Friday evening, asking him to pick up Helen. She was asleep and he could not rouse her, but he had located her ID in her handbag, the guard explained. After her usual Friday meal in the food court, Helen evidently had sat down on a display platform and drifted off. When John arrived, he found her still fast asleep, sprawled across a window display with her assorted tote bags at the feet of mannequins sporting the latest women's clothing.

When Helen started falling asleep so unpredictably, we needed to hold on to her cigarettes for fear she would set herself and the house alight. She had usually kept her pack of duMauriers in her handbag. To her great annoyance, they were now locked up in the desk with the grocery money, and an assistant divvied out one or two each evening when someone could be with her while she smoked. Helen was accustomed to going directly to the mall with her pay on Fridays. Now, one of us needed to go with her when she was out around the town. To ensure she would come home

1. Big House, 1971. Helen second from left; Steve with
Frederick, right; Ann Newroth fourth from right.

2. Entrance to the L'Arche
Daybreak farm property, through
the 1970s and 1980s, late winter.

3. Green House members, 1981. Back:
Phil, Peggy, Michael, Lloyd, Francis;
Front: Peter, Annette, and me.

4. George helping Gord find a phone number in Church Street kitchen.

5. Maurice making muffins. He and Jim were often baking partners.

6. Peter enjoyed teasing us. Here, he is out for the men's breakfast at a local diner.

7. Lloyd had great loyalty to Holstein cows. Here, he is visiting a Holstein farm.

8. John S. holding a young lamb. John was Len, the farm manager's right-hand man.

9. George grading Daybreak eggs. He would chew on a piece of dowel as he worked.

10. Helen and Theresa baked bread and pies during our 1983 cottage vacation.

11. Gord and Helen in the Church Street kitchen.

12. George was a Los Angeles Dodgers baseball fan and a Montreal Canadiens hockey fan.

13. John played the spoons with Lou Moore's band at the King Henry's Arms, Aurora, Ontario.

14. Henri twirling one of the Daybreak children during a community weekend gathering.

15. Henri celebrating mass on his sixtieth birthday. Bill, at Henri's right, and Francis are serving.

16. Michael with his brother, Adam.

17. Henri invited Thelus (pictured here) and Wendy and Sue to accompany him to Detroit.

18. Ellen and Michael in 1981. Ellen thought Michael looked like one of the Beatles.

19. Henri was on a roster to help Adam get up and ready for the day.

20. Ellen with her friend Fred Rogers in the Cedars. ("Mister Rogers" of TV fame.)

21. The new Dayspring chapel building viewed from Daybreak pond. The Big House is in the background.

22. In Dayspring chapel, Clara and Lorenzo hang an Advent banner made by the Day Program.

23. Together, Mike and I post on Mike's Facebook page and look at his friends' pages.

24. Julie and Anne Marie at her mother's home on Anne Marie's birthday.

25. Daybreak seniors Annie and Roy enjoy a Blue Jays baseball game at Toronto's domed stadium.

26. Roy holds baby Miryam while Mary Bee, her mother, takes a picture.

27. Jean Vanier (left) and Francis were featured in a book of photos of active octogenarians.

28. Ellen holding the Torah at her Bat Mitzvah celebration.

29. Mel blessing the challah and wine before Shabbat dinner in his L'Arche home.

30. Steve Newroth and Peggy at Daybreak's first Silver Anniversary Tea, October 1997.

31. Surrounded by Thelus's nephew and Daybreak friends, Wendy and Mary Anne bless Thelus's gravestone.

32. Jean Vanier and I review the schedule at a 2008 youth forum.

first and we could accompany her to the mall, we spoke to the ARC supervisor and asked that Peggy bring Helen's pay home to us. When Helen found out that Peggy had her pay, she was furious and marched over to the Centre Street house, barged into Peggy's room, and demanded her money. It was clear that we should not ask this of Peggy again.

Helen's descent into Alzheimer's disease began not very long after her hyperglycemia diagnosis. This decline was heartbreaking for us in the house. I think the core members, all of whom had been familiar with the Alzheimer's of Bill Rous and Frank Sutton (an early core member who died before Bill), probably took the situation more in stride than did we assistants. We made small adjustments for a while. We were worried about her wandering as her confusion and her night-owl habit grew more pronounced, and, with the agreement of the others in the house, we installed various alarm devices on the front door. (Helen could not easily open the bolt on the side door.)

Helen was at a loss at ARC and gradually stopped going to work. She would spend quite a lot of time in the living room, where she might sort through her stacks of Polaroid photos or still attempt to do some needlework or just sit and drift off. She was often there with George, who had retired and would sit with a TV table in front of him doing artwork, his new hobby. He kept a caring eye on her, calling one of us if she seemed to need us. Gord had always loved Helen and would try to look out for her. Anne Marie's compassion was awakened when she saw Helen's neediness. I think the turning point for Anne Marie came when Helen came downstairs one day wearing her half-slip over her dress. Anne Marie offered to help Helen – something I think Anne Marie previously had never imagined doing. Clearly, from now on, one of us female assistants needed to assist Helen with dressing in the mornings.

Helen's vision or perception was affected so that she would sometimes mistake what she was seeing. I was filling in with her only occasionally, as, by then, I was studying full-time. On evenings when I sat with her in the living room, she would comment on the cute doggy in the window opposite us. I finally concluded that she was looking at a plant, but it did not seem to me to resemble a dog at all. Helen began to have difficulty with stairs, and one weekend when I was away and John was out, Gord offered to change rooms with her as he had a first-floor bedroom. It was a generous offer, as he himself had some difficulty descending stairs. [2] When John returned, Helen's and Gord's furniture and personal items had been moved by the two assistants who were home, and Helen and Gord were settled in their new rooms.

That year, Helen started to have seizures and became very shaky. She became bedridden and needed much more medical attention. A hospital bed was brought in, and Daybreak began to hire nurses to care for her. This changed the dynamic in the house, as the nurses often needed to access the kitchen, where we not only cooked but also ate at our large dining table. A meeting was held of those close to Helen to discuss whether she should be hospitalized. It was an anguishing decision, one I certainly struggled with, knowing that Bill Rous and Frank Sutton had been looked after at home until they died. The New House had a separate wing where Bill had his bedroom, and this had helped. In the spring of 1993, with her sister's agreement, Helen moved to a long-term-care ward in our local hospital. This marked a new direction for Daybreak. Subsequently, most Daybreak members have died in a hospital or nursing home.

In the late summer of 1993, I moved downtown to house-sit while finishing my theology degree. I had lived continuously in L'Arche homes for nearly thirteen years. These years had been rewarding but also all-absorbing, and I was longing for time to write and to pursue my growing involvement in interfaith dialogue groups. The house I looked after was lovely, and I was able to maintain my Daybreak and university connections as the owners didn't mind my inviting friends for dinner. I connected with one of the downtown L'Arche houses and helped out there one evening a week, but I saw much less of Helen and the other Church Street members.

Helen spent nearly two years in hospital – much longer than anyone expected. However, she did have many visitors. George and Gord and John Guido were regulars. Helen was quite shaky, but she would tightly grip one of George's very large fingers, and he would remain close to allow her to hold on to him. Gord had a job at the hospital for a while, dusting and polishing in the hallways. He was not permitted to enter patients' rooms, but he would spend an extra-long time polishing the nameplate outside Helen's door. Julie came back from England to see Helen the year before she died. When she walked into Helen's hospital room, Helen cried out, *"Oh my God!"* It seemed Helen recognized her!

While here on that trip, Julie bought a journal to be kept in Helen's hospital room so that those who visited could write some of their memories of Helen. Julie herself wrote: "My favourite memories of Helen are the simple ones, like Friday evening dinner out together, and shopping for clothes at Hillcrest Mall. But the main one is evenings walking to the store to buy a tin of Diet Coke, and then sitting together on the sofa while she drank her Coke and had her cigarette, and then put everything away before bedtime." Julie continued, "Other than my children, Helen is the person who has loved me the most unconditionally in my life. Her love and acceptance was pure and fierce; once you were her friend – and I was privileged to be a special friend for a few years – she was loyal and protective. She has influenced me more than most people I've met. The fact that there are people around the world who still tell Helen stories with a big smile is a testament to her character and love."

Helen certainly drove me to the brink at times. It was impossible to reason with her. But I also found her a tremendous inspiration, because, in spite of her limitations, she embraced life to the full and lived it with remarkable creativity and her own unique sense of humour. I was not often a recipient of Helen's special favour, but I think she knew that I was always there for her over our years together at Church Street, and when she acknowledged me I was quite touched. I have a picture of Helen and myself taken in front of the Church Street mantel, her arm around my waist and mine around her shoulder. (She barely reached my chin.) She has a look of triumph that says, "See, she is mine!" (On that occasion, at least.) Helen's legacy is huge and, though now it is over twenty years ago that she died, people still remember her. She lived her life to the full, loved passionately, and profoundly touched our lives. I was most struck to see the impact of her life on assistants considerably younger than I, and the love and delight she called forth from them.

John had been deeply helped by the fact of his relationship with Helen during a time of severe depression. He would say sometimes, "Helen saved my life," by which he meant Helen's love and the strong bond that developed between them over the three years he was at Church Street had saved him. In her hospital room, sitting beside her on her bed as she lay dying, John sang to her the oldies that she had loved – "In the Good Old Summertime," "You Are My Sunshine," "For Me and My Gal," and, of course, "Amazing Grace." At Helen's funeral, John delivered the eulogy.

10. "Hey! Hello!": George and his friends

In every human being there is a thirst for communion with another, a cry to be loved and understood—not judged or condemned; there is a yearning to be called forth as special and unique. Jean Vanier

George sometimes surprised us with his initiative and his knowledge. Once, we were with a small group on a Daybreak vacation, staying in one of the L'Arche homes in Gatineau, Quebec, across the river from Ottawa. The house received a local French newspaper. George examined the sports section even though he didn't read French. He somehow figured out that the famous Montreal Canadiens centre Elmer Lach was playing golf that day at a course in the area. He showed the paper to Steve M., who had come along as the other assistant on that trip. We agreed as a group to drive over to the golf course so George could try to intercept Elmer Lach and get his autograph. The remaining four of us waited with the air-conditioning running in our comfortable, fairly new Chevrolet station wagon, while Steve went with George to the eighteenth green. As it happened they ran right into Mr. Lach, who shook George's hand and obligingly wrote his signature on the back of an envelope. George was thrilled. He was standing on the grass with Steve, still staring at the signature, when a bird flew over and crapped on the envelope. George wiped it off, which smeared the signature. Steve was distressed, but George did not care. He had shaken hands with Elmer Lach!

Later that day we visited the Byward Market and then went out to celebrate Steve's birthday at an upscale Ottawa restaurant, and over the rest of the trip we cruised the Ottawa River and visited museums and the Royal Canadian Mint – a place George especially wanted to see – but this brief encounter with Mr. Lach remained the high point for him.

When I asked Steve once what brought him to Church Street, he said he "just really liked being with George," and then added, "Being a freelance musician or a freelance anything means that there are bursts of intense, sometimes stressful work, and I think that George introduces a calmness to me. Just sitting with someone can help to refocus on what's important and make life easier."

Though George was much older and their lives were very different in so many ways, he and Steve seemed like brothers as they talked over the latest sports scores and stories. Of course, Steve needed to look out for George when they were out together, and he did. George and Steve shared a love for hockey and baseball and football. The Mahlers hockey games were in the east end of Toronto and late at night. Nevertheless, even during ballet season, when he was working, Steve would drive to Richmond Hill, pick up George and, when Lloyd was well enough, Lloyd as well, drive to the arena, and play, and, after they had gone out to the team's favourite bar (where he and George drank pop), Steve would deliver the two men to their homes in Richmond Hill before heading downtown. On some occasions, he would have two performances the next day. These outings were a high point of the week for George, but I sensed this was true for Steve also. George would stay home to rest in the afternoons so that he could manage to be out late. Even if there was a Habs game on TV, he would still opt to go with Steve.

The Mahlers team came to know and love George through Steve. They welcomed him each week as he clambered out of the car and limped into the arena, defying the pain of his arthritis. He joined in the locker-room banter, calling them Dreamboat and Loverboy. The team called him Coach and would seek his advice, and he would toss out encouragement: "Put the biscuit in the basket!" "Stay out of the sin bin!" George loved both the hockey and the male company.[1]

In the baseball season, George and Steve would head off together in Steve's car for a few days and see as many baseball teams play as they could. They especially enjoyed getting to famous old stadiums – Busch Stadium in St. Louis, Fenway Park in Boston, Shea Stadium in New York before it closed, and, briefly, Yankee Stadium. More often they went to minor league parks, like the Hamilton Redbirds or the Niagara Falls White Sox at Sal Maglie Stadium in Niagara Falls, New York. George admired Sal Maglie, who had pitched for the Brooklyn Dodgers, and he liked to go to the stadium named in Maglie's honour. On another trip they visited the Football Hall of Fame in Canton, Ohio, but were rained out of Thurman Munson Stadium. (George knew that Thurman Munson was a New York Yankee who died in a plane crash.)

When Steve and Alida got married, George was impressed by the Italian wedding banquet, especially the spaghetti and meatballs, and he let everyone know that he went back for five helpings. Steve did not allow being married to interfere with their friendship. The only change was that Steve no longer moved into the Church Street house when he was not working. Some months later, the Mahlers disbanded after they finished fifth in their league and missed the playoffs. By this time George was using a walker and was no longer able to get in and out of cars such as Steve's. He needed a van with higher seats, like the Dodge Caravans that Church Street and the Seniors Club had begun to use.

In 1987, I was responsible for a small vacation group traveling by car to the East Coast of the United States. We had arranged to stay overnight with L'Arche Syracuse and visit L'Arche Boston and some other friends. George and Peggy were the only core members on the trip, and they were good friends. Ruth, a visiting American pastor, came with us. It was a gentle little group. Our first night we stayed in L'Arche Stratford to visit Mary Bastedo, who was serving as its community leader. While there, I received a call to say that George's mother, who had become frail, had passed away suddenly of a heart attack. George did not seem overly surprised, and he handled the news stoically. His mother was caring and had wonderful gifts both in baking and in crafts – she was a silversmith and a weaver, even weaving the Harris tweed from which she made jackets for George and his father and brother. Nevertheless, I think George relied most deeply on his father and, especially, his father's approval. He went home to attend his mother's funeral, where he had good support from other family members including his sister, who had come from California. Then, after three days, he flew down to Boston and rejoined our group. He was sad, but he coped well and seemed to enjoy the trip.

Our vacation was pleasant and low-key, and perhaps aspects of it were healing for George. For instance, we had brunch with Father John Sutton, who had spent a year as an assistant in the New House, where he and George had lived together. He was now a pastor in Boston. He too had lost his mother, not so long before. We also visited two of Henri Nouwen's friends. Jutta hosted us in her lovely house in a seaside town just north of Boston and took us to a concert and a polo match, the first that any of us had attended. We had great seats along the front of the wooden bleachers, where the horses pounded past only four or five metres away. Jutta brought along a wonderful picnic and champagne, since the day happened to be a special birthday for her.

Farther south, on Cape Cod, another of Henri's friends put us up in her beautiful summer home. We could pass in that upscale neighbourhood. On that trip George wore a flat British-style cap and a new light beige jacket and polo shirts. Peggy, as was ever her custom, wore dresses and cardigans. Our hostess took us on a walk over the dunes and along the shore for a short distance. I could see the difficulty both Peggy and George were having walking on the loose sand, George because of his deteriorating hip and Peggy because of her weak ankle. God help us, I thought, if either of them falls!

While in the area, we took in a summer stock performance of the musical *Nunsense*. We all had many laughs, but what I most enjoyed was seeing the laughter and sheer delight of George and Peggy. George had an aisle seat, and when the "nuns" came up the aisle, he reached out his hand and one of them took it briefly. I think George thought the actresses were real nuns. Afterwards he chuckled over and over as he told our hostess, "The nun took my hand!"

We drove back to Ontario at a leisurely pace, stopping at Cooperstown, New York, to see the Baseball Hall of Fame, and, when we felt like it, pulling off the road in other towns to watch a neighbourhood ball game or tennis match for a few minutes.

During those years at Church Street, George certainly experienced some trying moments with Helen, who seemed to have no lack of ideas for inconveniencing him. One day Helen had hidden George's razor and shaving cream so thoroughly that neither he nor I could find it before he needed to leave for work. Later in the morning, having checked all other possible hiding places, I climbed on the bathroom vanity and felt to the very back of the highest cupboard, where I retrieved the two items. Helen would have had to have made the same climb and then have thrown the items up into the top shelf as she could not have reached nearly that far.

Standing with Helen and George in the front hall when they both arrived home from work, I confronted Helen, telling her that what she had done was totally unacceptable and that she must apologize to George. Verbal apologies were not in Helen's repertoire, and she remained mute in front of George – apparently ignoring what I'd said, but I think he was somewhat mollified to hear me speak strongly to her. I believe at some level George understood that Helen's annoying ways were at least partly an expression of her desire for his attention. He used to call her Murk McTurk. I have no idea how he came up with this.

That evening, as we began dinner, Helen inconspicuously slipped a can of Coke from the tote bag at her feet, glared at George, who was seated at the other end of the table, and flung the can at him with full force, saying, "Here you are!" There was a collective gasp as it whizzed past the other four of us, but George put up his hand and picked the can out of the air as casually and competently as Yogi Berra might have done. It could have hurt him or landed on the table and smashed dishes and glasses. George set the Coke down in front of him and smirked at her, as though saying, "Who's smarter now!" It was like a scene from a movie. I exploded at Helen that what she had just done was very dangerous. I believe she knew well that she had overstepped that time. She was silent.

I think we were all impressed by George's quick catch. His walking was becoming increasingly slow and awkward, but obviously his eye-hand coordination was working well. I recalled that he had been goaltender for his small town's industrial league hockey team many years earlier. Clearly, it was not just because of his bulk that he could limit the other team's goals.

When George moved to Daybreak in his mid-forties, he had already worked for twenty-five years in his uncle's feed and flour mill. He had a reputation there too as a good and reliable worker, and there was no doubt George was strong. This must have won him additional respect. He would enjoy lifting a one-hundred-pound sack of flour onto each shoulder. "Strong, eh?" he would say. Two of his nephews, adults with grown children today, remember George simultaneously lifting them each onto a shoulder, to their grandmother's alarm.

George liked women and took delight in children. He saw his brother and sister marry and have children, but marriage was not in the works for him, deeply as he longed for this. He continued to live at home with his parents and often was out and about in the town, which was much smaller than Richmond Hill. Everyone knew everyone else. George may have seemed a little rough around the edges — to get someone's attention he might call out "Hey! Hello!" even if they were across the road or driving by, at the same time always with his characteristic wave, huge hand held high and fingers spread wide.

He continued this practice in Richmond Hill. At times he could be a little overwhelmingly friendly. If someone didn't respond he would call out again, "Hey, Hello!" until finally acknowledged. Even though he was naturally soft-spoken, he could make himself heard. As Richmond Hill burgeoned throughout the seventies and eighties and nineties, he brought a small-town ethos to the strip of five or six blocks of Yonge Street that he regularly walked. For certain, some people regarded him as strange and ignored or slighted him, but his default was to assume others' goodwill, and many came to accept and even appreciate him for his friendly ways.

At the Woodery and working on the Daybreak farm, George looked the part of a farmer in his coveralls and work boots, and with the wooden plug that he perpetually chewed on — a piece of dowel that seemed at first sight to be the end of a cigar. Before walking about town he would change to ordinary clothes and shoes, often sporting his beloved Montreal Canadiens hockey sweater and cap. Sometimes he may have looked a bit unkempt, his hair standing on end when he pulled off his cap, but he was accustomed to turning out in a suit and white shirt and tie for special occasions. His father was a prominent figure in their town and his family well respected. They made sure he had nice clothes, and the male assistants continued to do so, accompanying him to the Big and Tall shop. No doubt from his youth he had been expected to represent his family well and not embarrass them or "let them down." For one thing, he would never swear, and he would be upset when others did so.

George would go back home each year for his town's fall fair. When he became less mobile and could no longer take the bus, an assistant would drive and spend the day with him. He still knew many of the people who would come to the fair. When he later joined the Seniors Club and, like the other seniors, was working on his life story book, Keith, a Seniors Club assistant, and I managed to track down Hal, the man who had been George's closest boyhood friend, and Keith recorded George and Hal reminiscing about their younger days. One day, Hal's father took his son and George to a neighbouring town to see a wrestling match between Whipper Billy Watson and Angelo Mosca. This was an occasion George remembered all his life. Whipper Billy Watson was a hero to George, not only because he was fair to his opponents in the ring but also because he took an interest in disabled children and raised funds to help them.

When George particularly enjoyed an event, it would become larger in his memory with the telling and retelling. John Guido took George to Whipper Billy's funeral at St. James Cathedral in downtown Toronto. Coming out of the church, George saw Angelo Mosca and Sweet Daddy Siki. George was on cloud nine and walked up to greet these heroes as old friends. Sweet Daddy was a bit confused by George's overture at first, evidently thinking he should know George – not surprisingly, since George looked like he could have been a former wrestler. However, George's conversation, with its vague allusions, must have seemed a bit bizarre, and the two men kept their distance after a few minutes. George had bouts of fantasy when he might imagine that he had been Whipper Billy's coach or that he was himself some other famous wrestler. At such times he could speak and act strangely. From time to time he went into hospital for short stays to regain his balance.

George liked English-style meals of meat and potatoes. I learned early on not to serve him fish or rice. He liked Chinese restaurants not because of any preference for rice but because they often offered all-you-can-eat buffets. On Sundays, it was his turn to cook dinner. On Saturday evening, he would carefully wash the right number of potatoes for baking and check to see we had everything on hand for his meal, including sour cream and butter. For the meat, he would choose steak if available (while the Daybreak farm still had beef cattle, there was rarely a shortage) or pork chops with applesauce. When he set the table, he would be careful to put out all the accoutrements, including the HP sauce, which he placed at the end of the table near where he sat.

George's mother made all sorts of delicious baked goods, and he loved sweets. He struggled with this, knowing well that being overweight added to the pain in his hip. Sometimes he would pick up a litre of ice cream at the grocery store and quietly slip up to the TV room and eat the whole container, leaving the evidence in the wastebasket. One of his frequent after-dinner walks took him to a restaurant in the plaza where he would order his favourite dessert – apple pie with chocolate ice cream. He also enjoyed their french fries and hot roast beef sandwiches smothered in gravy. He liked to eat on his own on Friday evenings, when everyone at Church Street either ate out or fended for themselves at home, and he might eat out on other evenings, especially if there was a guest coming for dinner at Church Street. Though he was a friendly person, George did not like having to welcome people he didn't know to the dinner table.

One evening I found him waiting for me in the kitchen when he would normally have been out for a walk or upstairs watching TV. He held a slip of paper, which turned out to be a tab of about eighty dollars that he had run up at his favourite restaurant. He needed to ask me to go with him to the restaurant, he said, to pay it and to talk with the manager. This was a humiliating situation for George, and I felt bad for him. I helped him get the money from his bank account to pay off the debt, and he agreed that it would be best if he told the manager not to run a tab for him in the future. (George, like other core members, used his weekly pay for small day-to-day expenses and spending money. The government disability cheque went into the bank and was for larger expenses – room and board, clothing and footwear, vacations, and special events.)

I think another aspect of the appeal of certain restaurants – George had more than one favourite over the years – was the friendliness of the waitresses, with whom he liked to flirt. Some seemed to understand George and had just the right way with him, making him feel attractive and maybe even allowing him a hug, but not compromising themselves. George knew how to be a faithful friend. His disability was believed to have come from his having had whooping cough and then contracting meningitis as an infant. Were it not for his difficulty assessing some social situations and catching some subtleties in interactions, a long-term intimate relationship might have been possible for him. He had the habit of teasing any man – Steve included – who got married by calling him a sucker, but I always sensed behind this teasing a profound loneliness and longing.

George liked to show off his strength to men who seemed likely equals, and he was not always a good judge of who these might be. One evening we welcomed one of the Daybreak Board members and his wife for dinner. George reached out his hand to greet the man but then squeezed tighter and tighter. "Strong, eh?" George queried. Our guest was wincing. One of us assistants had to urge George to let go. In other situations, George was a gentle and compassionate person. With anyone in a wheelchair, he would look for ways to be helpful, and he was likely to stop them to shake hands even if he did not know them. If I briefly lost track of him when out shopping, it was usually because he had paused to hold a door for someone and at the same time to engage them in conversation.

George came from a traditional family, where his mother looked after the men. I am sure that he never had to make his own lunch when he lived at home. Over the years I sometimes had George's name for Kris Kringle or I helped another house member who had his name. It was easy to find kindnesses to do for him. One possibility was making his queen-size bed properly. He generally just pulled his bedspread up over the rumpled linens and blanket. Another secret kindness was to remake his lunch. After dinner, he would put a chunk of cheddar cheese – he disdained processed cheese – between two slices of unbuttered bread and stick this and an apple in a brown paper bag in the fridge to take with him in the morning. The bread would dry out overnight, but he didn't seem to care. We would secretly slice the chunk of cheese for him and add other items we knew he liked, some butter or mayo, tomato slices, and perhaps some cold cuts, then seal the sandwich into plastic wrap to keep fresh. We might then slip in a baggie of carrot or celery sticks (he actually liked these veggies), a dill pickle, and maybe a cookie.

George loved to be with men whom he thought of as like himself, such as those who played baseball or hockey. Once baseball season started, he would spend a couple of evenings a week down the street at the local baseball diamond. One of the men's softball teams welcomed him as a friendly fan and later as an assistant who looked after their bats, and they folded him into their comradery. He would enjoy going out for a pop or beer with them after the game. One year they won the championship, and he was included in the banquet where they received their trophy. Everyone on the team, including George, was presented with a small replica trophy.

When Carl visited in June 1988, he set about trying to get a glimpse into the world of the Church Street members. He later wrote about a couple of evenings he spent with George:

> Early in my visit I had watched a baseball game on television with George. He observed the game knowledgeably, knowing the players' names and catching even subtle details of play. After dinner on Thursday, George had to leave in some haste. He explained that he was going to the neighborhood baseball field where he served as bat man for a local men's team. I asked George if I could come with him and he quickly agreed.
>
> When we arrived at the baseball diamond, all the members of the team greeted George with great warmth and respect.

As we sat on the bench watching the game, George looked Buddha-like. I asked George, "What do you prefer – watching a pro game on TV or coming to the park and watching in person like this?" George, who, I had discovered, was not generous with words, was unhesitating. "Here," he paused, "you can see everything." There were no camera close-ups or instant replays on this little ball field. More important, the people were absolutely real and he actually knew them. They were there for each other and they were there for George. There was no mistaking that George would choose for them.[2]

∽∘∾

The year after Carl was with us, John Guido became house leader. He stayed for three years and gave George a lot of support during significant health problems and surgeries in those years and for some time after. George and I picked John up from the airport. He had been home in New Jersey as his father had died. Only three years earlier, while John was living in one of our downtown houses, his sister had died. John was aware that almost all George's interests centered on sports, and he wondered how he was going to connect with George, given that he himself knew nothing about sports. George supplied the answer when they were walking into the house, saying, "My mother and my brother died. Your father and your sister died." (George's brother had died a few years earlier.) These common losses proved a key to the strong and trusting relationship they developed.

Between 1989 and 1993, George had three major operations. The third was a second hip replacement that left him with extreme pain. Before he came home from that surgery, he broke his femur and had an additional time in rehab. Doctors marvelled that he could still walk, albeit with a walker. He suffered a lot as he became less mobile and his body began to give out on him. At times his bodily functions became a cause of embarrassment and humiliation, and even social isolation. Proud and sensitive, he would sometimes refuse help with his personal care even from the male assistants he especially liked. He surely had a very high pain threshold as well as an intense determination to maintain his independence and live as fully as he still could.

When George became less mobile, he relied more heavily on the telephone for social contact. He had a personal phone book, and he would call people himself, frequently checking his book as he punched in each number carefully. There were various people he would call regularly after dinner. First would be his father. For a while after his mother died, his father lived on in the family home with the support of a housekeeper. Later, when his father moved into an extended care home, George was relieved to discover that he could still reach him by telephone. If I was in the kitchen, where George would sit to make calls, I would invariably hear him say to his father before the conversation ended, "I didn't let you down, eh?" And he would wait for his father's reassuring response. Then he might call one of his nephews or a favourite female assistant and, periodically, his sister in California.

George worked all his adult life as a labourer, doing demanding work of which he was proud. He worked with care and dedication. George loved his job at the Woodery. Before that, on the farm, he had borne with the chicken and egg work, even though he did not like this job with its hundreds of clucking hens running about in the smelly chicken coops. Coming into the egg room to pick up eggs for the Green House, I would see George candling the eggs, holding each to the light so gingerly in his huge hand and then placing it gently into one of the cardboard crates where the graded eggs were stored. Those with blood spots or cracks were separated and not sold. (There were always some cracked eggs available to the homes.)

One bonus of the egg work was going on the weekly egg delivery with one of the farm assistants or with Len. George would have a chance to say hello to all the customers, and when they had completed the route, he and Len would stop for a coffee and donut. George also worked for a time in Daybreak's small recycling business. He and Lloyd or Bill V. would ride around the town in an old truck, picking up newspapers at the curbside. The business folded when there was insufficient market for the newspapers. It was a few years later that Richmond Hill got on board with recycling.

For certain George's work, and the praise he received for it, gave him a sense of self-worth. Joe V., the first Woodery manager, said George was his best worker. Altogether, Joe said, George must have put about three hundred thousand three-and-a-half-inch nails into the skids that the Woodery made during each of the years when they had that contract. George would carefully line up each nail before using the nail gun.

A while later, the Woodery had a contract to make the wooden reels or spools that are used to hold hydroelectric wire. By that time, it was occupying the whole of the downstairs of the barn. There were two sizes of reels, one about three feet across and one about six feet and very heavy. George was proud that he was the one who could help Joe Child move them out to the yard to be picked up. If George was sick for a few days and needed to miss work, he worried about not being there to help with the reels.

For a long time, George had four anchors keeping his life stable and rooted in reality – his work; his family home, where he spent long weekends and Christmas; his relationship with his father; and the knowledge that he had a strong, flexible body. Throughout his sixties, these were slipping away. When facing the stress of great loss, George could tip over emotionally.

After his father moved, George was still able to have short visits with him fairly often. In fact, George liked the facility his father had entered and announced that if, in the future, he needed to move to such a place, he would choose this one. Its appeal was threefold – the ensuite bathrooms, the absence of stairs, and the presence of friendly and attractive female attendants. By far the more difficult aspect of his father's move was that the family home had to be sold. George loved that house, an elegant old red-brick mansion located on a corner lot with a large, grassy yard around it. It was a landmark in the town and, in 1991, had received a centenary plaque at a ceremony George had attended with his father and sister.

Those of us close to George were aware that this would be a difficult loss for him. He knew that I had had to help clear and prepare my family home for sale a couple of years earlier. To try to help him normalize his situation, I shared with him my own feelings of loss and how I had chosen a few things that I wanted to keep. I suggested that he could do the same. We made a trip to take pictures of the interior of the house while it was still fully furnished. It had molded ceilings and a beautiful chandelier, an abundance of polished wood, a stained-glass window, very nice furniture, and tasteful art. We retrieved some of his pennants and hockey souvenirs from his bedroom, and we arranged with his niece and nephew that he would make a second such trip when his sister arrived from California, so that he could choose some special items that had belonged to their parents.

John took George for his final visit to the house. His sister ensured he was able to choose things he wanted – besides other sports memorabilia, two small paintings done by an aunt, silver candlesticks created by his mother, and two chairs, one that was comfortable for him and where he subsequently often sat in the Church Street living room, and a small chair with a petit point cover made by his mother. This was a painful time for George and must have brought back many memories. Before he and John left, he punched a hole in the dining room wall.

What brought George the most anguish was the prospect of reaching retirement age. By then he had missed a lot of work because of his surgeries and he was having more and more problems with mobility. George did not *have* to retire, and in fact he continued to work for a couple of years after his sixty-fifth birthday, but as this birthday approached, he grew very anxious and crashed, falling into a world of unreality. His eyes would glaze over and he would think he was Hulk Hogan or some other famous wrestler. Then his judgment would be impaired and he might push past others, knocking them into a doorframe or wall, or act in other ways that could endanger himself or other people. It was difficult to persuade him at such times that he needed help. I walked into the house one day to hear George stomping up the stairs followed by John shouting after him, "George, it's because I care so much about you that I want you to go to the hospital."

George had a very good doctor, with whom he hit it off – they could talk together about wrestling and hockey – and the doctor responded quickly each time George needed help, finding a place for him to get his bearings. The nurses liked George and would compete to be assigned to him. After two or three weeks, he would return home to normal life. Of course his absence would concern everyone at Church Street; he would be prayed for each evening, and we would visit him when possible. On the day of his sixty-fifth birthday, John and Gord and I picked George up from the hospital to take him for lunch at a Chinese restaurant. He was confused and very drowsy, and we were sad to see him this way. However, a couple of weeks later he had recovered his equilibrium and was ready to come home. We celebrated his return with his favourite chocolate birthday cake and ice cream. He went back to work. Less than three months after his sixty-fifth birthday, George was well enough to fly with John to California, where they visited George's sister, took in the Dodgers home opener, and attended the christening of John's godchild.

Later still, George, having come to terms with the idea of retirement and finding unexpected pleasure in simply being at home doing artwork and looking out for Helen, we had two retirement parties for him. One was an intimate party, of the Woodery workers at a pizza restaurant. Joe C. gave him a box of dowels cut just the right length for George to use as plugs. The other party was a large, celebratory retirement lunch at his favourite Chinese buffet restaurant. Steve had taken him out for some errands that morning, and they were "just stopping in for a bite of lunch." George was totally surprised and very touched. He stood at the entrance for a couple of minutes, his eyes tearing. There were many balloons, a big "Congratulations George!" banner, and more than one rousing rendition of "For He's a Jolly Good Fellow" and "Three cheers for George!" He received other gifts – a mug signed by everybody at the Woodery, a package of art supplies, and many congratulatory cards – but it was the box of dowels that most delighted him.

After George's father moved to the extended care home, George, unlike the other Church Street members, could no longer go to his family home for long weekends and Christmas. He was sad and anxious about this loss, but he managed to keep his balance. The team tried to be proactive in planning so that he could look forward to these times. Well ahead of the weekend, one of the male assistants – John and later Jeff, Tomek, and others – would discuss with George what day outings he would enjoy: a trip to the McMichael gallery to see the Group of Seven paintings and First Nations art and to eat a gourmet lunch, a stop at Mr. McGregor's tea room in Kleinburg, a visit to the Mennonite market at St. Jacobs, an afternoon visit to family members, a sports event, Thanksgiving at Jeff's mother's home.

On Christmas morning, they would rise well before dawn and drive to his hometown, where they would visit George's nephews and his niece and their families. They would be on time to see the children open their presents, and they would stay for a family Christmas dinner. Sometime during Christmas Day, George would have a telephone call with his sister and her family in California. After he got over the sadness of the loss of his family home, George loved these Christmas visits, and his family loved to have him and his assistant friends. Often it seemed that if George were to hit a low point, it would be in January, near his birthday, but, on the whole, he coped better as he got into his later sixties.

After George's first hip replacement, in 1989, he had become Steve's alarm clock, watching the time carefully and faithfully dialing Steve's number. They would talk briefly about sports news as, by then, George would have checked the scores in the morning paper, and Steve would let George know the time that he would like him to call the next morning. This alarm clock idea was brilliant on Steve's part, as it gave structure to George's mornings, when he was recuperating from his surgeries and when he did finally retire, and to Steve it was much more desirable than some electronic wake-up alarm. George took the responsibility seriously, even after Steve was married. Steve's wife, Alida, being a teacher, left home early, and George knew that Steve would not stir in the mornings until the phone rang. For nine years, unless one of them was away, he never failed to call Steve at the appointed time – usually eight or eight-thirty or, if Steve had worked late the night before, nine.

In 1992, John Guido moved and assumed a new role, and Church Street welcomed two new young team members. The next year, the downstairs bedroom behind the kitchen was renovated and a bathroom installed in its large walk-in closet, and George was able to move into this bedroom. This arrangement pleased him greatly as it saved him having to struggle up the stairs to the second floor. At the same time, a ramp was built to the side door of the house. Helen's main-floor bedroom became the TV room. Later, Annie moved into Church Street. She and George could joke with each other and got along very well. She called him Bugs in recognition of his love for the Looney Tunes Bugs Bunny cartoons. When greeting people, he would sometimes offer a goofy grin and quote Bugs Bunny, "What's up, Doc?"

When George was back on an even keel after one of his hospitalizations, his doctor friend, whom George and all of us on the team knew as Ralph, broke the traditional taboo about socializing with patients and came to dinner with his wife at Church Street. This gave great pleasure to George as well as to the rest of us, who knew how important this man was to George's well-being. I am sure the doctor appreciated the life we lived together in our homes, and that it mattered a great deal to all of us, not just to George, that he was well.

❧

George died of a sudden massive heart attack on the late evening of October 24, 1998. He had had a good evening, making his way with his walker up Yonge Street and stopping at the CoffeeTime donut shop. Now he was sitting at the table in the kitchen. Gord was in the kitchen too, and George told Gord that he was feeling dizzy and asked him to get an assistant. Markus and Anjali both responded. Markus, who had EMR training, managed to get George onto the floor and began CPR while Anjali called 911. The ambulance crew said George was already dead when they arrived, and, though they took the appropriate measures, the doctor at the hospital in Richmond Hill where they took George confirmed this. The assistants called Carmen and Joe V., who had followed Father Henri as Daybreak's pastor, and Joe called me to come to the hospital to see George's body.

While I lived with George we were not especially close. At times when I was house leader and I tried to encourage him to watch his weight and pocketbook, he would become edgy with me. However, during the last couple of years of his life, a close bond developed between us, I think largely the result of working together on his life story album in the Seniors Club. On days when he had not seen much of me, he would phone me after he had finished dinner, always to ask me how my day was, and of course after answering I would ask him the same, to which he would usually offer a two-word answer – "All right." There may have been some romantic element in our relationship for him, but I think it was more like that of a fond brother and sister.

Ralph came to George's funeral. Later he wrote about George in a Toronto newspaper, describing him as having "a gift for people." "Almost everything about him was massive, his size, his enthusiasms, his greetings, his loyalties," wrote the doctor. George was one of his "favourite people."[3]

11. "*Mistah* Henri": The contributions of Henri Nouwen

We cannot remain faithful unless we are nourished spiritually and intellectually. Jean Vanier

Before he came to us at L'Arche Daybreak, Henri Nouwen was famous as a best-selling writer and a teacher of pastoral theology at Yale and then Harvard Divinity School. His spirituality, as expressed in his books, especially *The Wounded Healer*, resonated with L'Arche assistants. We had experienced the unconditional welcome and love of the person who has been wounded by exclusion and failure and has come to a place of acceptance. We recognized that this welcome and love could be healing for assistants, who come with their own wounds, often of self-doubt and fear of failure.

Henri had an instinct for creating community. During his time at Harvard, he made his campus home, the Carriage House, a sanctuary for his students. Former assistant John O. describes it as "a true godsend. For Roman Catholics like myself his home was the stable locus for our common spiritual life." John adds, "I remember well the day that Henri told me he had decided to leave Harvard and to move to L'Arche. There was a calmness and serenity about him that day unlike anything I had ever seen in him before."

Henri had wanted to move on from the academy and find a real home. In 1985, Jean Vanier had invited him to L'Arche in France to discern his future. During his months there, Henri travelled to Canada and visited Daybreak, where we had been praying for an open-minded spiritual leader who could bring us together in spite of our diversity. The Daybreak Community Council and other long-term assistants met with Henri to discuss the possibility of his coming to live at Daybreak as our pastor. I remember sitting beside him on the old couch in the Green House living room, where we met. He seemed nervous, constantly crossing and uncrossing his legs. He talked of the numerous visitors he was likely to have, saying that his presence would change our community. We were somewhat insular in the mid-eighties still, and we did not encourage many visitors, some of whom were likely to see people with disabilities more as curiosities than as fellow human beings. However, it quickly became obvious to us that Henri was the answer to our prayers. Early in his week at Daybreak, a core member was struck by a car and seriously injured trying to cross Yonge Street. The community was in crisis, and Henri came to our rescue, bringing his pastoral gifts to all of us and especially to the core member's family. (Fortunately, the member recovered from his injuries.)

Henri was not, however, an easy community member. Unaccustomed to community life, he could have unrealistic expectations about our ability to accommodate guests. Also, he was often anxious and in need of reassurance, worrying about how a talk had gone or whether someone liked him. In spite of his ability to gather in a breath and become focused and able to listen very well, he tended to be easily distracted. As soon as he arrived at Daybreak, he bought a car and then, the same day, crashed it while engaged in a conversation with an assistant who was riding with him. Fortunately, neither of them was injured, but the car had to be replaced.

Soon after Henri arrived at Daybreak, in the summer of 1986, he asked to be invited to each home for dinner, so that he could meet everyone in the community. At Henri's first dinner at Church Street, Helen faced a dilemma. How to address him? Or even to speak about him? He asked that we call him Henri, pronouncing his name like the English Henry, not the French "On-ree," which the spelling suggested. But Helen never used the first names of men. She generally did not have difficulty finding amusing alternatives, often ones that suggested a subtle put-down, but Henri had a different status. He was not just any priest. He was particularly welcoming and kind to her when our Church Street group came to community worship, and he held the congregation of the packed Catholic parish church up the street from us in rapt attention during his homilies at the main Sunday morning service. (The pastor of the parish invited

Henri to speak at or celebrate this Mass regularly.) Though it was out of character for her, Helen seemed even a bit shy with Henri. She decided he would be *Mistah* Henri, with a strong emphasis on the Mistah.

Henri insisted on informality with him. He did not wear a clerical collar at Daybreak and rarely wore a suit. Nevertheless, he always vested to celebrate the Eucharist, and he celebrated with dignity and decorum. He loved to create beautiful worship spaces, drawing on his well-developed aesthetic sense. He had brought with him many icons, other pieces of art from Europe, and colourful altar cloths and vestments from Latin America. He always ordered fresh flowers. And he encouraged those with musical gifts to bring their leadership.

Recognizing immediately that many core members had difficulty standing and that the effort to stand was more distracting than it was an aid to worship, he did away with this expectation except for the reading of the Gospel and the distribution of communion, when all who were able would stand. Since most people sat on the chapel floor, Henri soon realized that the small table that served as an altar was too high. From Joe C. at the Woodery, he commissioned a low altar and some stools for himself and the servers. Using many pieces of highly polished cherrywood, Joe, with John B. as his assistant, built a splendid altar in the shape of a boat – conjuring the idea of the ark.

After several weeks of getting to know people, Henri called together a pastoral team and a committee of individuals who had a particular commitment to the community's spiritual life. He trained interested core members to serve at Mass and ordered vestments to fit them, and he chose others to be eucharistic ministers. He invited some assistants to give reflections on the readings and urged those with musical gifts to use them.

Henri encouraged us to appreciate the rhythm of the Church year, to prepare mimes and readings for Advent and Lent, and to find ways that everyone in the community could join in marking these seasons nightly in our homes. The pastoral team created kits with thematic readings, often written by community members, posters, and the pictures of the key figures of a biblical text or shapes such as hearts to cut out and write our prayers on and then paste onto the poster in each house. His intent was that, when the time arrived, we would all be ready to fully celebrate Christmas and Easter.

When a community member was dying, Henri would call us all to come to their home or the hospital for a final visit and, after they died, to gather to share our memories of the person and to remember their life and what they loved by looking at their photo albums and mementoes. People spoke through tears but also through laughter. Thus, we learned to recognize and claim the unrepeatable grace of each person's life and friendship with us, not just to grieve their loss. Our funerals became truly celebrations of the life of the individual. At the graveside, Henri ensured that all who had lived with the individual and as many others of us as wished could be present and that the shovel was passed around to each one, so that we could all participate in burying the dead. He also helped us to remember the anniversaries of the Daybreak people who had died – the Daybreak saints, as we continue to call them.

Henri was aware of what Sue M. had described as our "loosey-goosey" ecumenism and the New Age mix among the newer, Gen X assistants, and he could see the potential gift in all of this. He requested that the community survey its members to learn who had faith affiliations. Then he suggested that people who were unclear about what church or faith they belonged to consider choosing a faith identity, and those who were clear consider formally joining a faith community. Those who did not wish to embrace a faith group were not expected to, but for those who wished, if they had not had these rituals in their youth, this could mean being baptized, being confirmed, declaring their desire for membership, and committing to Sunday attendance at their local church.

Francis, who was living at the Mill Street house, asked me to accompany him to adult confirmation classes at the Catholic parish. When he was a boy, he had watched all his brothers be confirmed, and two of them later become priests. Francis was considered ineligible for confirmation because he could neither read nor memorize the catechism. Now, rules had relaxed, and Francis could certainly qualify as a faithful Catholic. His church was important to him, and he was already an usher and attended the Knights of

Columbus men's group. He was very proud on the Sunday he was confirmed. It seemed to give him a new sense of self-worth.

Bill V., Daybreak's first core member, approached Henri about becoming a Roman Catholic. At Henri's direction, Bill attended classes at the Catholic parish, along with an assistant. Henri explained to Bill that it was important that he be in the class so that others in the parish would get to know him. Bill was baptized by Henri the following Easter. Over time, Bill and Henri became close friends, and Bill became Henri's faithful server when Henri celebrated Mass in the parish. Henri always ensured that Bill was included in the pastor's invitation to breakfast in the rectory after the service.

Most people in our Church Street house had loose United Church or Catholic connections. Although she attended the United Church with her sister and brother-in-law Lillian and Don when she was visiting them, pinning herself down to one denomination was of no interest to Helen. Anne Marie's family was Catholic, but she did not attend church and had no desire to do so. George's family were United Church adherents, and George liked the idea of joining Richmond Hill United Church. He learned from his father that, because he had been very ill as an infant, he had not been christened at the planned time. For Gord, the decision was more complicated. Gord's mother was an active Anglican. His father, who had passed away, had been a United Church member, and Gord was accustomed to serving at Mass whenever a priest was staying with us. To discern this question, Gord made a retreat with Father George in L'Arche Erie. When he returned, he announced that he had decided to join the United Church.

Most of our household attended Richmond Hill United on the Sunday that George was baptized and he and Gord were confirmed and welcomed into the United Church, along with Lloyd from Mill Street and Thelus, who lived at the Centre Street house. The men wore suits and Thelus, a lovely dress. Henri was there to accompany the minister and give them a blessing. Sue M. came, and Gord's mother and his brother and sister-in-law from out of town. There was a luncheon reception afterwards in the church hall, followed by a gathering at Church Street. All four of the Daybreak folks who joined the United Church that day became regular attendees on Sunday mornings. I think they had a strong sense of belonging there. As the years unfolded, the church's minister was an important pastoral presence in George's life, and the lay pastoral ministers faithfully visited Lloyd and Thelus and Gord as they grew older and became infirm.

∾∘∾

Early each weekday morning, Henri said Mass for a small group of people. He was always in a rush, usually coming from a series of phone calls. The chapel door on the lower level of the Dayspring would fly open, and Henri would quickly cross the room to the tiny sacristy next to the furnace, then reappear a moment later, still adjusting his robes. He would close his eyes, draw in one deep breath, and become centred. Henri's welcome and care for all of us and his pastorally-focused reflections meant that morning attendance grew rapidly. Often, most of the Woodery would come before they started the day's work. By this time, Ellen had moved from ARC to work at the Woodery. She liked to attend these small services, where she would see friends and could pray aloud for those she cared about. The fact that she was Jewish did not seem an issue to her, or to her parents, who had chosen Daybreak for its family-like atmosphere. Ellen sometimes declared, "Jesus was Jewish too, you know," a fact that Henri would affirm. Instead of the consecrated bread and wine, Ellen would receive a blessing as a daughter of Sarah and Abraham.

At one memorable post-Easter service, probably in 1990, as a dozen of us stood silent around the altar listening to the scripture reading about the early disciples having locked the doors of the house where they were staying, "for fear of the Jews," Ellen suddenly blurted out, "I am a Jew, and I didn't kill Jesus!" I think all of us were a bit stunned. Henri hastened to reassure her that she was quite right. But Ellen's words that morning pierced through my (and our) obliviousness to the anti-Jewish polemic in the scripture reading and, over time, brought changes in our community.

Henri had a keen sensitivity to people's struggles and to interpersonal dynamics. He maintained a huge network of friends, for many of whom he was also a counsellor at times. When I would spend a night away in one of the Dayspring retreatant bedrooms, I could hear Henri through the heating ducts making calls to California late at night, taking advantage of the three-hour time difference. Sometimes I would awaken at five in the morning to hear him again speaking on the phone in Dutch or German to someone in Europe. He gave spiritual direction to those in the community who sought it, and he was also gifted at listening and feeding back to us during discussions at community meetings. He would hone in on the nub of what seemed a complex issue and gently and succinctly summarize what he had heard.

A couple of years into his time at Daybreak, Henri went through a profound spiritual crisis. He had been giving much thought to the roles of the younger and older sons in Rembrandt's painting *Return of the Prodigal Son,* both of whom he could identify with. He emerged from the crisis when, after having long thought of himself as the younger son, who needed forgiveness, he realized that his calling was to assume the role of the father – the one who blessed and forgave. In time, he wrote a beautiful book about this painting and the biblical parable, and how it helped him to understand his vocation at last.[1]

Henri was in great demand as a speaker, and he travelled frequently to various Christian churches and academies across North America. Also, L'Arche Canada asked him to speak at national meetings and to lead retreats. I think that early on Henri recognized we were sitting on a treasure at L'Arche, in the form of the deep relationships, the fun, and the gifts we shared as such a diverse community.

He soon began inviting one of the core members (and usually an assistant), to accompany him wherever he was travelling to speak. He found the core member's presence helped him to relax and stay centred. And for the audience, hearing the often-surprising interventions of the core members was an important learning experience. Bill V. was Henri's favourite travelling companion. Bill, who could create community on an elevator ride, would tell one of his jokes and loosen up the audience. Then he would usually sit close to Henri on the podium and, from time to time, interrupt him with a wisecrack or an amusing and often disarming comment. The fondness of Bill for Henri and of Henri for Bill was obvious to all and, quite incidentally, served to demonstrate what L'Arche was about. After giving a talk, Henri would comment that the audience might not remember what he said, but they would always remember Bill and that he and Bill were together.

When Henri was to speak at a national convention of the Episcopal Church in Indianapolis, he invited Thelus and Wendy, as well as Sue M., to accompany him. Thelus was thrilled with the trip, and she called home to her friends from the limo in which they were riding. (In those days, phones in cars were a novelty.) Wendy, who was Thelus's good friend as well as assistant, is a gentle and sensitive Anglican priest who came to Daybreak in 1992. After respecting her desire to rest from ministry for several months, Henri sometimes asked her to share pastoral ministry with him. (Wendy became Daybreak's pastor in 2001 and continued in this part-time role until she retired in 2013.)

∽∞∽

At Henri's suggestion, we had moved our community worship from Tuesday evening to Friday evening and added a small common worship or eucharistic gathering after work and before dinner on Tuesdays in one of Daybreak's Richmond Hill homes. After the Corner House was established, this worship time was always held there because three of its four teenage core members used wheelchairs. Henri would also travel into Toronto to say a midweek evening Mass at one of the downtown Daybreak homes. The Friday evening community worship continued to alternate in denominational leadership, with Henri warmly welcoming local clergy and sometimes leading Taizé prayer.

Henri's celebrations of the Eucharist were inclusive and very welcoming, and more people were now clear about their faith identity and could ask for a blessing instead of the Eucharist if they wished. Henri always distributed communion in both species, so that all could partake of the consecrated wine as well as the bread. On Friday evenings, the chapel in the lower level of the bungalow

170

would be bursting with people as the community grew and, under Henri's leadership, interest in our spiritual life increased among both assistants and core members. Also, more visitors came – often people who had read Henri's books and people from local churches.

A cosmopolitan, Henri opened us to the wider world, not only transforming our spiritual life but also enriching our intellectual life, and encouraging us to adopt a new, broader vision of the role of L'Arche in our world. He had grown up and been ordained in Holland, had studied pastoral counselling at the renowned Menninger Institute in Kansas, had joined Dr. Martin Luther King, Jr., and others on the famous Selma to Montgomery march in 1965, had taught at the best universities, and had friends in the peace movement and in Dorothy Day's Catholic Worker, a pacifist social justice movement. Not long before he came to L'Arche, he had spent several months in Central and South America, where he saw first-hand the extent of the suffering and injustice experienced by those who were poor. And immediately prior to his arrival at Daybreak, he had taken part in a speaking tour across the United States, challenging the American government's interference in Latin America. When he arrived, he was nearly finished writing a book about Father Stan Rother, a murdered priest from Oklahoma who had lived among poor rural farmers in Guatemala.[2] (In September 2017, Stanley Rother was beatified as a martyr in a ceremony in Oklahoma City.)

Henri worked with us gently to bring more to our consciousness the pressing issues in our society. Because of his presence, we had an influx of visitors of all kinds – peace activists, social justice advocates, pastoral leaders, and gay and straight friends who were ministering to people dying of AIDS, an epidemic then at crisis point. Henri would often invite groups of us assistants to meet these visitors and listen to their stories. One who made a strong impression on me was John Vesey, a Maryknoll priest from Guatemala whose predecessor had been Stan Rother. John's own life was then being threatened. We listened intently as he narrated his experiences and described the extreme brutality of the government soldiers. The danger and fear with which he had been living became palpable. He had come to North America hoping the situation in Guatemala might cool off in his absence. Stories such as his and those of Catholic Worker members and AIDS nurses and pastoral workers from New York and California contributed to awakening my desire to be more in touch again with what was happening beyond our immediate, almost all-absorbing life in Daybreak homes.

In the early 1990s, Marcie, an assistant who had been a member of a dance company, brought together a group of Daybreak assistants and core members, some in wheelchairs, to form a sacred dance group that came to be called the Spirit Movers. Delighted with them, when he was speaking at events in the Toronto area, Henri would often ask the troupe to accompany him and perform. (At first, the Spirit Movers rehearsed in their free time, but for many years now they have been a one-day-a-week day program, meeting and developing new dances in the Dayspring on Fridays and performing for various events in the city from time to time. The program is unique in its inclusivity. To develop a new dance the group listens together to a piece of music, each dancer suggests movements, and they work together to incorporate the suggestions into a coherent whole. They wear simple costumes and use diaphanous scarves to contribute to the grace of their movements. Those in wheelchairs and their partners seem to flow together as one. One of their most memorable performances was for Pope John Paul II, when World Youth Day was held in Toronto.)

Loved and "softened" by those who welcomed him unreservedly, Henri, like all of us assistants, grew more deeply into his own gifts. For one thing, he discovered the delight of being included in skits. One of the high points of Daybreak's One Heart at a Time twenty-fifth anniversary gala theatre presentation was a duet that he and Sue M. sang, dressed as old "cow-pokes" and "riding" makeshift steeds.

౷౿

Debbie was the inspiration behind a Daybreak home for children with multiple disabilities. Zenia, Liska, and others inspired by Rose, were also keen on this idea. A house at the end of our block of Church Street was purchased and renovated. In 1988, Nathan Ball moved into Church Street, bringing three years of experience as an assistant in a L'Arche *foyer* for people with multiple disabilities in Trosly, France. He was to help out part-time with the establishment of the children's house, soon known as the Corner House. It welcomed four young teenagers. Each brought particular gifts that we discovered as we came to know them, but they also faced limitations that were new to us. For example, Hsi-Fu (pronounced "See-fu") was blind. When Nathan returned to Church Street one evening, he described an alarming experience during Hsi-Fu's first meal at the house. Nathan had been holding a glass for Hsi-Fu to take a drink. Evidently thinking he was being offered food, Hsi-Fu bit down hard on the glass. It broke, and he got a chunk of glass in his mouth. Hsi-Fu's need for a plastic cup was duly noted by all the assistants.

With Henri's encouragement, Nathan was working on a theology degree at the University of Toronto. He and I had the two third-floor bedrooms at Church Street. He often left one or other of his textbooks sitting out in our little lounge area, and I dove into them, hungry for the intellectual nourishment. One book, Paul Knitter's *No Other Name?* especially attracted my attention. For some time I had been questioning Christian triumphalism and the early disciples' apparently narrow view of who is eligible for salvation. Ellen's and Mel's and Roy's presence in our community as Jews and now Alia's as a Muslim teenager at the Corner House, only heightened my questioning. Here was a theologian who evidently had thought about the same matter and whose work was now a textbook in a well-regarded theology school. Nathan encouraged my interest.[3] The next semester, I registered to audit an introductory course at Regis, the Jesuit college at the University of Toronto's School of Theology, where Nathan was studying.

The following autumn, I was given some sabbatical time, and, with Henri's support, I registered in the master of divinity program. Between 1989 and 1993, besides being a part-time and then full-time student, I helped out at Church Street. I also returned to the University of Guelph for a semester, to teach one section of English, commuting three days a week. It seemed wise to check out teaching again after ten years at L'Arche. It was much as I remembered it. I enjoyed the students, but I did not sense any call to leave

L'Arche. I was still growing as a person, had precious relationships, a strong sense of belonging, and opportunities to contribute to the life of Daybreak as well as to be involved outside the community. Meanwhile, L'Arche, influenced by Henri, was moving out more and more into "the world," seeking opportunities to make the gifts of people with intellectual disabilities known.

Henri supported my interest in Jewish–Christian relations. He was familiar with what I was learning and told me of having accompanied his priest mentor uncle to the Second Vatican Council in Rome, where his uncle (Monsignor Anton Ramselaar from the Archdiocese of Utrecht) had assisted Cardinal Bea with the writing of *Nostra Aetate*, the document that changed the Catholic Church's teaching about Jews especially and also opened it to see truth in other religions. He pointed me to books in his library by Abraham Joshua Heschel and Elie Wiesel.

Henri was my adviser for my practicum, which focused on discovering God's presence in the simple interactions of our life in Daybreak. He suggested I write a paragraph or two each week looking at something or someone in Daybreak through a theological lens and also that I call together a group of Daybreak assistants, of which he would be one, to reflect on these with me. This worked very well, as everyone seemed to look forward to the time together and there was a good "unpacking" of my short theological reflections. Later, two of the assistants in this group pursued theology studies themselves.

Nathan moved to a downtown L'Arche home for his final year of studies, and we welcomed a new Church Street assistant to take his third-floor bedroom. Regina W., who was from Austria, had come for a year at L'Arche while she considered further studies in counselling or pastoral work. Once George grasped where Regina came from, he always called her Sound of Music. Serendipitously it seemed, Regina was also reading Jewish authors. She introduced me to the stories of Isaac Bashevis Singer and to the beautiful novel *Job*, by Joseph Roth. We would have conversations about our reading and about how best to support the core members in our house. Today, Regina is married, has a teenage daughter, and gives pastoral care in a seniors' home. Over nearly thirty years, we have stayed in touch. I have visited her in Austria, and she has returned here to visit us. She faithfully sends Christmas greetings to Gord and Anne Marie. Julie's and Regina's are examples of the unexpected lasting friendships that can spring up at L'Arche.

During my studies, I was able to take courses at all the mainstream denominational colleges. Regis, as a Jesuit college, has an emphasis on systematic theology, and before graduating I wrote a substantial paper for the required oral exam showing how, for justice's sake, our understanding of the Catholic teaching on revelation needs to grow so that we do not regard righteous non-Christians in a condescending manner, as secretly saved by Jesus Christ. I made a solid argument, supporting it with references to the respected Jesuit theologian Bernard Lonergan. It satisfied the examiners and also satisfied me, allowing me to feel more at ease again within the Catholic fold.

Shedding ancient Christian stereotypes and learning about modern Judaism helped all of us to better support Daybreak's Jewish members. The opening of the Corner House brought the arrival of Alia. She did not speak but the house assistants had frequent contact with her gracious Muslim family. We would periodically invite Alia's father, Mr. Qureshi, or Khalida, who had come to work in the Daybreak office, to teach us about Islamic traditions, especially with regard to prayer. For one of our Lenten services, Henri suggested Mr. Qureshi tell us about Muslim customs of fasting. At nearby York University's Muslim students' centre, I met a young musician named Dawud. He willingly came with his drum and taught us simple songs, most in English, celebrating Allah. We were able to obtain a tape of these songs from him for Alia. Daybreak assistants were and are still predominantly Christian, and a few were not comfortable using the word Allah to refer to God. They felt better when they learned that Arabic-speaking Christians also call God Allah.

Around 1993, Henri asked me to bring together a Daybreak interfaith committee. By this time Nathan had become the community leader. I had begun to write articles about our community life and about core members who especially touched me. He encouraged me to write, to represent Daybreak at Christian-Jewish Dialogue meetings and on an interfaith committee of the

Archdiocese of Toronto, and to coordinate Holocaust Education Week events at Daybreak and other sites. By then, in our liturgies we had adopted the habit of substituting inclusive language whenever possible and modifying anti-Jewish language.

One late November day when Henri and I and Mary Bastedo, who was on the Spiritual Life Committee, were sitting at the same table eating lunch at the Day Program, I mentioned the problem with some of the wording of the beautiful, ancient Advent hymn "O Come, O Come, Emmanuel," which refers to the Church as Israel. (Of course, the reference is to the Church as the "New Israel," but the problem is that for centuries the Church taught that it and the New Covenant *superseded* God's ancient covenant with the Jewish people, and that some people still tended to assume this in spite of the Vatican II teaching.) Mary and Henri were both musical, and we needed only a few minutes to come up with alternative wording. We sing these alternative words during Advent to this day.[4]

Meanwhile, with the community's growth and more and more people attending worship services, Henri began raising funds to replace the bungalow Dayspring. It was decided that the land just west of the pond and south of the Big House would be the site of a large and beautiful new Dayspring chapel building.[5]

Then, in September 1996, we learned that Henri had died suddenly of a heart attack while he was in Holland. We were in shock, but Henri had taught us not to shut down in the face of death but to truly celebrate the life of the person who had died, and we did this. There were two huge funerals, the first in the cathedral in Utrecht and the other organized by Daybreak and held in the partially completed Eastern Rite cathedral just a ten-minute drive from us. For the latter, Daybreak welcomed the world, it seemed. Henri's family came from Holland, and his friends flooded here from all over North America. He would have turned sixty-five the following January, and he had been looking forward to partially retiring and mentoring Joe V. to become Daybreak's lay pastor. (Joe was suddenly thrown into the pastoral role.) Henri had been with us for ten years.

Henri left us a rich legacy in terms of our spiritual life as a community, in the ways he called core members and assistants to lead, in how he listened and helped us find unity, in showing us how to celebrate funerals and remember those who had died, in his welcome of diversity in our faith life, and in how we saw the contribution of L'Arche to the wider world. We benefited from his wisdom, counsel, and friendship, and from his generosity. Whenever he published a new book, he would sign and give copies to each one of us who expressed interest. Always generous with all his resources, he also helped various individuals financially when they faced unexpected needs. In concrete terms, besides his many books, his legacy was to be the Dayspring chapel building, which he had envisioned and was fundraising for when he died.

Following Henri's inclusive manner of leadership, before a design for the new Dayspring was created, the entire community was canvassed to determine the key features that people wanted. For this, Carl and a core member visited every Daybreak home, taking notes. The old Dayspring had only benches around the walls for those who could not sit on the floor. Peggy stressed the need for chairs with arms, and an accessible washroom. Others wanted a large foyer that would allow us to visit together before and after services, lots of natural light, a modern kitchen, a meeting room, and, as well as a large chapel, a space for private prayer. We hoped that the building would reflect our identity by including the art of core members, and also that it would convey a sense of being close to nature. The meeting room should have a fireplace and a deck opening onto the pond. The idea of a bell tower was also very popular. I think we all loved the final design, which was by well-known Toronto architect Joe Lobko.

The inclusive consultation gave everyone a sense of ownership and pride in the new building. When the construction was complete, those who wanted to help with the move met at the old Dayspring and processed with the religious objects and vestments and altar along the Daybreak lane, past the Green and New houses, the Meeting Hall and barn, over the creek and around past the woods and the edge of the pond to the new Dayspring, as the bell rang out continuously from the bell tower. Jean Vanier came for the official opening in 1999, and many guests were there as well as all of the community. The new building was dedicated to Henri and to Adam,

Henri's friend and mentor, who had died only six months before him. Near the chapel entrance hangs a framed picture of these two men and a brief write-up about each.

Henri would have loved the building, with its use of much natural wood, high ceilings and large picture window in the chapel looking out to birch and weeping willow trees and across the pond to the evergreen woodland. From the brightly coloured flowers and rainbows and animals and people and angels and swirls made by core members, especially those in the Daybreak Seniors Club, Carolyn, who had worked with the seniors, had used her artistic talents to paint striking door panels for the chapel. There were no permanent symbols, such as a cross, that could have limited the chapel's use for interfaith gatherings. We had decided to commission a painting of a mosque with the opening words of the Qu'ran in Arabic calligraphy. It would be hung on one wall of the chapel, as a way to honour Alia and other Muslim members who would come in the future, and we had purchased Shabbat candlesticks in honour of our Jewish members.

After coping with the tiny furnace-room sacristy, Henri would especially have approved of the good-size sacristy, where the celebrant and core member servers can vest, and where the accoutrements for the Eucharist and vases and icons and art that he loved are still kept. He would have been pleased with the small adoration chapel, with its Road to Emmaus-themed tabernacle and high stained-glass window of the sun at daybreak. And he would have been happy that the original art of Daybreak members is displayed along the hallway and that many community members made the ceramic tiles that are placed here and there in the kitchen and washrooms and around the fireplace in the Pond Room. When the Daybreak Craft Studio opened, in 1998, Mary Bee, its founding leader, had scoured the Daybreak property, gathering seeds, leaves, nuts, stems of dried berries, and other tiny items from nature. She made molds from these and then invited all of us, assistants and core members, to come to the studio and make one or two tiles each, which she then fired in the new kiln.

Most of all, Henri would have been pleased that the new Dayspring has become truly a community-building centre as well as a place of prayer and worship. L'Arche people come from across the region and beyond for meetings and formation. Local churches use the Dayspring for Saturday retreats, and, by now, many thousands of high school students have spent a retreat day there. It has been the venue for pre-Passover Seders and interfaith events and weddings of Daybreak members, and social times, and for many meetings of the Daybreak Council, the Board, and the long-term assistants group. For several years, it housed a small bookstore selling books on spirituality, especially those by Henri and Jean. Steve Ellis ran it with help from volunteers including various core members.

When I first came to Daybreak, we could swim in the pond, but it has suffered from the development around us. With a grant from the Ministry of Natural Resources, it was renewed; native plants, shrubs, and trees were introduced along its marges; and students from an alternative high school constructed an ecologically sensitive wooden walkway around it. It is a lovely place for meditative strolls. There are water lilies and fish and a muskrat in the pond; every year some mallards and a pair of Canada geese return; and sometimes a blue heron alights on the deck railing to scan the water for its lunch. Near the Dayspring building and under the largest weeping willow, there is a bench made by the Woodery and dedicated to Adam, a place to sit and meditate or simply to look out across the pond. Sometimes our neighbours in the subdivision discover this quiet oasis. Henri's spirit of welcome and his love of beauty surely nourish them also.

12. *"Mazel Tov!"*: Celebrating Ellen and Mel

*Each community member is encouraged to discover and deepen his or her
spiritual life and live it according to his or her particular faith and tradition.*
Charter of L'Arche (v. 1993)

I first met Ellen when I was a new assistant at the Green House
and she lived nearby, at the New House. I was on a roster of drivers
who would take a van load of Daybreak people to ARC Industries
in the morning and bring them home at the end of their workday.
Ellen was among these folks. For a while, Ellen, who was in her
mid-twenties, was attracted to Michael, who was about her age,
and whom she identified as looking like one of the Beatles. She
would call him Ringo. Mike did not relate to the Beatles. He was
into Superman, so her overtures were not much noticed, but I
do have a picture of the two of them side by side, Mike smiling,
with his arm around Ellen, and Ellen apparently giggling with
happiness. It was my first glimpse of the longing for romance and
the sometimes seemingly adolescent ways – papering the walls of
their bedrooms with teen idol posters, for instance – in which some
younger adults who have intellectual disabilities express this. But
L'Arche community life was full of friendships and activities, and
people did not seem to pine away in the same way that teenagers
sometimes do in the face of unrequited attractions.

Like many people who have an intellectual disability, Ellen
cannot easily articulate her feelings, and responding to questions or
expressing preferences can be difficult for her. She makes allusions
or oblique references. In fact, hers is a manner of communication
similar to Michael's in some respects. Often, I can understand the

reference only if I have some awareness of what has been going on in her or his life lately.

One summer day, Ellen came over to the Green House to wait to be picked up by the small group she would join for a cottage vacation. She was sitting silent at the table in shorts and T-shirt and baseball hat, and she seemed both nervous and excited to be going away. I did not know her well, but, wanting to break the ice and put her at ease, I was searching for a subject to make conversation. I asked her what she was looking forward to on the trip, and after a pause, to my surprise and delight, she launched into a recitation of lines from the Walrus and the Carpenter poem in Lewis Carroll's *Through the Looking-Glass*: " 'The time has come,'" the Walrus said, "'To talk of many things: Of shoes – and ships – and sealing wax, – Of cabbages – and kings...' " I surmised that she was anticipating seeing the movie or listening to some favourite stories or poems being read aloud. Sitting with Ellen those few minutes, I learned not only that she loved rhymes and could create them herself but also that I needed to be mindful of physical boundaries with her. Her baseball hat was askew. I said something like "May I help you with your hat?" and reached out to straighten it (something I would never do today without getting clear permission). She scowled and clenched her fist. "Do you want this?" she asked. Over time, I came to understand that to simply say *"No!"* or "Don't touch my hat!" was beyond Ellen. Part of her disability is that sentences giving information are almost impossible for her to formulate. And yet she has many abilities.

When, at the early morning post-Easter Mass, Ellen drew our attention to the anti-Jewish content of the Gospel reading, I was already beginning to study theology. By her simple comment, she had called us to really hear what was being read. This text is in the Catholic lectionary, I thought to myself. How can the Church be giving us such a potentially harmful text to read without any context? Especially in the light of the Holocaust and the recognized complicity of many Christians in it. Ellen's comment marked the beginning of what became a growing sense in the Daybreak community that we needed to comment publicly on – or adjust the reading of – such texts, and also to recognize and celebrate our interfaith dimension.[1]

I heard Ellen's comment not only as a communal challenge but also as a personal challenge, and I resolved to do what I could to help her feel affirmed in her own faith tradition. What came to me was to try to take her to a synagogue service. With her parents' permission – I learned that they had attended services as a family when Ellen was young – I began to inquire about local synagogues, knowing that I would need to find an egalitarian one, as Ellen would not be content with what would seem arbitrary boundaries between what she and men could do in a service. As it turned out, there was one within a short drive. I called the synagogue office to ask if Ellen and I could attend.

On our first visit, as we entered the sanctuary the congregation was on their feet singing loudly in Hebrew. I was not at all familiar with synagogue services, but this was clearly familiar territory to Ellen. She seemed to grow several inches as she stood beside me and someone handed us prayer books and kippot, the small Jewish head coverings worn by women as well as men in egalitarian congregations. The congregation was chanting the *Shema,* "Hear, O Israel . . ." (the Jewish declaration of faith), and Ellen seemed spellbound. Then, suddenly transformed, she took the lead: all her body language announced that she belonged; I was the visitor. Proudly, she walked up the aisle and chose our seats – in the front row, certainly not where I wanted to sit.

Ellen can be quite impulsive. There were some amusing and (for me) uncomfortable moments when, almost immediately, she slipped out of her seat and joined the Torah procession. She stopped opposite the rabbi on the bimah (the raised Torah-reading platform), eager to help lift the beautiful cover off the Torah scroll.[2] Nonplussed, the rabbi smiled and discreetly acknowledged Ellen, but other members celebrating a special occasion had joined the rabbi on the *bimah,* and what she was doing was clearly not part of the plan for the morning. I overheard a woman behind me whispering to her husband, "Who is that woman?" At that moment I had no idea what I could do that would not create an added disruption.

I was thankful when the rabbi indicated to Ellen his appreciation for her help and let her know that now she could resume her seat.

After Ellen had attended the Shabbat services alternate weeks for several months, and been present when some young people celebrated their Bat or Bar Mitzvot, the Jewish coming- of-age ceremonies that mark young people's public assumption of responsibility to live their faith lives as adult Jews, she began to make allusions to having such a celebration herself. We asked the rabbi if we might meet with him. Seated across from him at his desk, Ellen opened: "I never had one of those . . . You know, with everyone throwing candies at you and saying *Mazel Tov* and everything." Behind those words I knew there was a world of longing to be "normal" and like others, and also, sometimes, to be really special.

The biggest obstacle, to my mind, was that Ellen could barely read a few words of English and would not be able to learn Hebrew and to read the Torah, as I had noted young people doing during their Bar or Bat Mitzvot. The rabbi grasped this and went on to say that if Ellen could memorize the blessings for before and after the Torah reading, that was actually all that was necessary for the service. She could have a proxy reader for the Torah portion itself. However, she must also try to learn about Jewish traditions, and she must commit herself to some act of *tikkun olam* (literally, the mending of the world) – some kindness that would contribute to goodness in the world.

The rabbi gave us the name of a congregant who was a teacher. He was sure she would be willing to make a tape for Ellen so that she could practice the blessings and commit them to memory. The tape turned out to be beautifully personalized. The teacher, Ruth, spoke directly to Ellen, using her name, introducing the two Torah blessings, and saying them slowly in Hebrew and then chanting them, so that Ellen could choose whichever form she preferred. Ruth included also the blessings for bread and for wine, said before meals, and the blessing said with the lighting of candles on Shabbat evenings, setting aside the seventh day as a day of rest. The candle lighting is an act normally carried out by the woman of the house. Ellen had often heard her mother and father say these blessings.

The first words of the blessings are the same, and she already knew these words in Hebrew.

Ellen and I scheduled a short meeting with Henri, as Daybreak's pastor, to tell him about her plan to celebrate her Bat Mitzvah. I foresaw it as a small event to be celebrated with her family and a few close friends, but I was sure he would be pleased for her. However, Henri immediately declared that Ellen's Bat Mitzvah would be a gift for the whole community. He laid out a plan for periodic announcements in the printed weekly newsletter that went to all the houses. These would let everyone know that Ellen was preparing for her Bat Mitzvah. Then there would be two preparatory common worship services shortly before the actual event, one for the Toronto homes and one for the Richmond Hill homes. At these Ellen, with help, would describe her preparation and the meaning of having a Bat Mitzvah celebration and would practise the blessings she had learned. Not everyone would be able to attend the synagogue service, but in this way everyone would understand the significance of this event for Ellen – that her Jewish identity was being celebrated, even as some of them had chosen to formally join a particular church. At one of these worship times, Ellen would be presented with a tallit (prayer shawl), a gift from the Daybreak community. She would wear this when she was called up to the Torah for the first time.

Ellen needed to decide what she would do to meet the requirement of *tikkun olam*. She and I had already occasionally been visiting the mother of a Daybreak member who was in a nursing home. Ellen is a kind and empathetic visitor with those who are not well. She agreed that we should make our visits more regular so that she was fulfilling this "mitzvah."

In the ensuing months, our local synagogue was forced to close for financial reasons, but the rabbi put us in touch with a small lay-led congregation that he suggested would be ideal for Ellen. It was indeed. It turned out that Ruth, who had made the tape for Ellen, also attended services there, as did others who seemed to understand exactly how to support Ellen. She would move about during the service, so as to sit beside various members whom she was getting to know. She listened to the commentary on the reading of the day – the *d'var Torah* (the word about the Torah) – and, as in our Dayspring services, she sometimes interrupted with a surprisingly relevant comment. This smaller and more informal congregation was aptly named the Kehillah Ahavat Hesed – the Loving Kindness Congregation.

Meanwhile, Ellen's closest friends came together in a little support group. We met with her every two or three weeks to encourage her and learn about her progress and to help with some of the planning for her celebration. Ellen learned the essential blessings as we played them over and over whenever we were out in my car, especially on our trips to Shabbat services, and I made copies of the tape for other friends to help her. Together we also learned more about Jewish holidays and their traditions, including certain foods, such as the potato latkes (a kind of pancake) associated with Hanukkah. Some traditions were familiar to Ellen from her childhood.

Reena, Daybreak's counterpart Jewish organization, invited us to send assistants to the classes on Jewish practices that they provide for their staff. Mel's house leader, Julie M.-S.; Jane P., who was an assistant friend of Mel; and I attended. Reena provided us with helpful resources, including a simple plastic-coated picture guide to lighting the candles and blessing the bread and the wine at the beginning of the Shabbat meal. Mel used this on Friday evenings for many years. Meanwhile, with her friend Toni, Ellen made a Star of David candle holder to celebrate her Jewish identity. At Hanukkah, the assistants in her home learned how to help her light the Hanukkah menorah and say the nightly blessing.

At Passover, her father had long celebrated a Seder supper for Ellen's Daybreak home. For this, we used a booklet (a Haggadah) intended for interfaith Seders that was co-written by a rabbi associated with the Anti-Defamation League in New York and a Christian liturgist. That spring, we planned a very large pre-Passover Seder, asking friends from the Kehillah to attend and teach us about the meaning of this feast of the ancient Israelites being brought from slavery to freedom. It is a story that can have contemporary symbolic relevance for all. We set up a head table and eight round tables in the Meeting Hall, each seating eight or nine people, and borrowed the Seder plates, kiddush cups, candle holders, and all we would need for each table, bought the matzah and other traditional foods, and ordered kosher meals. Ellen's mother, Claire, brought most of the symbolic foods for the Seder plates, and Ellen and Toni made the *haroset* (a blend of apples, nuts, and honey), which represents the mortar between the bricks that the Hebrew slaves were forced to make before Moses led them out of Egypt. Doug Wiebe, who had been Ellen's house leader, coordinated the kitchen.

We made a seating plan ensuring that the many Daybreak members who wanted to attend could do so, and that each table would have one or two Jewish friends who could explain the tradition as the story unfolded. We were able to borrow enough booklets for everyone from a local church where the same Haggadah was used to teach catechumens about the Jewish roots of Christianity. At the head table, Ellen's father led the Seder with Ellen and her mother next to him, and Ellen's closest Daybreak friends, David and Joe C. from the Woodery. Henri was also at that table. The story of the Exodus is told before the meal is served, and the telling, with symbolic foods and songs and special readings, takes quite some time. David quipped, "I'm so hungry, I could eat a rabbi!"[3]

∽ᴏᴏ∽

As the September 1994 date for Ellen's Bat Mitzvah celebration drew near, all was not smooth sailing. Two days before, the work of planning having been completed at a special dinner at the home of Lieba and David Lesk (Lieba was the synagogue leader), the guests chosen by Ellen and her parents, invitations sent out, programs printed, the feast ordered, and a beautiful prayer shawl presented to Ellen by the Daybreak community for her to wear on the big day, Ellen fell into a nervous funk. Sitting in the car outside her house as I was dropping her off after a final meeting, she was scowling and clenching her fist and refusing to talk.

At that point, this was as much a crisis for me as for Ellen; I realized I had become very invested in her Bat Mitzvah. With great effort, I found the courage to say, "You know, Ellen, this is *your* event, not mine, nor anyone else's. You don't have to go through with it.

We can call it off and just go on with life as usual and I will still be your friend and so will Toni and Joe and Mary Bee and Susan and Paula and Lieba and all the people at the synagogue, and you know that your parents will certainly stand with you, whatever you decide." We sat in silence for a few minutes. There was a letting go happening inside me that was quite palpable. Then, breathing with a new freedom, I posed the question, "Shall we call it off?" A pause, and I knew Ellen was still thinking deeply. Then a one-word answer: "No."

Ellen's Bat Mitzvah was the grand celebration that she and all of us, her friends, had hoped for. After the Torah reading and Ellen's saying the final words of the second blessing, she was indeed showered with candies, and all present joined hands in a huge, joyful circle and danced around her, singing *"Mazel Tov."* Ellen stood still on the *bimah,* looking like she would burst with happiness. As we resumed our seats, at the back of the room Mel, who was sitting with his house leader, Julie M.-S., turned to her and said, "I can do that! I want to have a Bar Mitzvah!" After the dancing and candies, Ellen gave her *d'var Torah,* for which she had chosen Shel Silverstein's *The Giving Tree,* reading it aloud with her friend Mary Bee, and before the service concluded, Henri spoke.

Ellen's celebration continued with a wonderful feast and more dancing. Many of the Kehillah members recalled afterwards Henri's gracious words thanking the Kehillah for welcoming so many guests from Daybreak and stressing the gift that Ellen's Jewish identity was for us, making an occasion for our two communities to come together in friendship and for us to learn more about Judaism. This was certainly part of what I had hoped for – a kind of crossing over into each other's worlds. The father of one of the young men in the Kehillah declared, "I thought my son's Bar Mitzvah was the most joyful day of my life, but this celebration exceeds that!" Ellen's parents had been careful not to put any pressure on her with regard to her Bat Mitzvah, and they did not get involved in her preparation, but they were very proud of her success. Ellen's father commented that since it was unlikely he would ever be able to give his daughter a wedding celebration, he wanted her Bat Mitzvah to be a grand affair, and indeed it was.

When Harold, Ellen's father, heard that Mel wanted to celebrate his Bar Mitzvah, he offered to help Mel prepare. Mel began attending the Kehillah Shabbat services regularly and became known there. He had a heart for the poor and the homeless, and he was already volunteering at the Daily Bread Food Bank and with the Good Shepherd mission, so doing *tikkun olam* was no problem for him. Ruth made another tape, specifically for Mel. Harold would go to Mel's L'Arche Toronto home once a week after they had both finished work and they would go to the basement, play the tape, and sing the blessings at the tops of their voices. One of the male assistants, a young man from Holland, also helped Mel practice and learned along with him.

Meanwhile, in the months that followed her Bat Mitzvah, Ellen descended into a time of depression that sometimes manifested as anger. I wondered if it was a kind of mid-life crisis. Or could she have expected that her world would magically change after her Bat Mitzvah? Perhaps she had expected that, with becoming a Jewish adult, her disability would fall away and she would enter a new life more like those of women who did not have a disability.

Her troubled moods seemed to appear mainly when she was at home in her L'Arche house, and not often when she was at the Woodery. She worked mainly among men, and she clearly felt well loved and supported by her co-workers. David would give her a hug from time to time, and Joe Child, as the manager, would set her up with tasks that she would feel proud of doing. Joe appreciated Ellen for who she was – "a neat person," as he often said – and he had been part of the little group who supported her during her Bat Mitzvah preparation. At home, Ellen had watched broken-hearted as a fine male assistant whom she had loved deeply left her house and got married, and then another and another had come and gone over several months. Also, at that time there was a house assistant who, it was recognized later, seemed unable to relate well to Ellen.

During Ellen's troubled period, some assistants began to say that she needed to be in a more institutional place, and they were starting to get the ear of the community leader. A meeting was called, and Ellen's friends turned out in full force to defend her place at Daybreak. We knew that she loved Daybreak and helped to build the community. If people were invading her personal space or provoking her, she did not respond well, but she had never actually harmed anyone, and she often expressed her care for others. We could attest that Ellen had a tender and sensitive heart and strong gifts of relationship and faithfulness. People needed to see past her anxiety and rough edges. Joe C. made the point that he did not find Ellen a problem at the Woodery. Problems seemed to arise with others who perhaps did not know how to be with her. It was one of those, fortunately rare, moments when it was very important for all of a core member's friends to stand up.

Meanwhile, Ellen spent some weeks in a hospital for an assessment. It was a miserable experience for her, but good came of it, in that the professionals there were able to teach her house team how to be more supportive of Ellen, especially when she was feeling sad and upset. Gradually she came out of this period, and at the same time the community embraced more fully the value of professional training. Ellen settled back into her home and was happier, and she returned to her job in the Woodery, welcomed back by her co-workers. She and I resumed attending Shabbat services on alternate Saturdays. She would often be invited to open the Ark where the Torah scrolls are kept and, sometimes, to hold one of the scrolls or be invited to share in an *aliyah* (being called up to the *bimah* during the Torah reading) – something that she was qualified to do as a Bat Mitzvah.

One of the people who could really *see* Ellen for who she was, was Henri's friend Fred Rogers of the *Mister Rogers' Neighborhood* children's television show. When he visited Henri at Daybreak, Henri introduced him at our Friday evening community worship, and Ellen, locking eyes with him from across the room, started to sing, "It's a Beautiful Day in the Neighbourhood." They sang the song right through together for all of us. Fred chatted a little with Ellen after the service, and they discovered that they shared a birthday. This was the beginning of a connection between Ellen and Fred that continued for some years. They exchanged birthday cards, Ellen sending them with help from her friends. This heart connection and the missives from Fred were very precious to Ellen.

Sometimes when an envelope from him arrived, she would hide it in her room immediately, not letting anyone even read it to her. She saw Fred again at Henri's funeral, and, for a time after Henri died, Fred returned on occasional visits. On one of these, Sue M. arranged tea with Fred at the Cedars for a few invited guests. Ellen and I were among them. We all sat around the dining table, with Fred at the far end. As Ellen sat down, she placed a small replica of a dachshund at her place. (Her family always had a dachshund, and she was particularly fond of them.) Fred immediately recognized the dog and engaged Ellen in conversation about dachshunds. It turned out to be a lovely visit for all, especially for Ellen and for a Daybreak parent and his children. After that, I helped Ellen write a letter to Fred, and soon she received a *Mister Rogers' Neighborhood* postcard back with a handwritten message from him:

Dear Ellen, Thank you for your fine letter. I liked eating cake and singing songs with you too. I am glad to hear that you're helping out at the Woodery. I think of the beautiful coffin that was made there for Henri. Please give my greetings to Beth. Love from your friend, Fred

In 1999, at the opening of the new Dayspring, Ellen and Baruch, one of the leaders at the synagogue, were asked to carry up the Bible and set it for the first time on the new pinewood lectern. When she turned around, she spotted Fred in the row just behind her, and she erupted in a joyful *"Fred!"*

∞

Sometimes, Ellen and Mel and a little group of us, their Daybreak and closest synagogue friends – Baruch, David, Bonnie – would go out for lunch after the service. Mel's father was nervous about Mel wanting to have a Bar Mitzvah, fearing he would freeze and the event would be a disaster. When he called me about his concern, I was able to persuade him that if Ellen could do this, his son could too. Mel's father began attending the Kehillah services and could better understand the warmth and sense of safety in this little congregation. As the date of Mel's Bar Mitzvah approached, Baruch helped Mel prepare a short *d'var Torah*. Baruch suggested that it be a

191

dialogue between them, so that Mel would not have to speak alone. Mel's text was about Abraham.

For his Bar Mitzvah, in November 1996, many of Mel's friends from L'Arche Toronto and his old friends from Daybreak in Richmond Hill, as well as family members from as far away as the West Coast, came to celebrate with him. Henri had died just two months earlier, but it felt as though his spirit was with us, and Mel's celebration was as joyful as Ellen's had been two years earlier. As soon as Mel finished reciting the blessing after the Torah reading, Ellen rushed up to hug him, declaring, *"Mel, you did it!"* A *Toronto Star* photographer caught this moment. The next day, Leslie Scrivener's article about Mel's Bar Mitzvah appeared with this photo and the title "Man Celebrates Bar Mitzvah." She had asked Mel, who was fifty-four, why it was important to him to have a Bar Mitzvah. What he said captured the poignancy of the day: "When I was thirteen, the other boys had one and they became adult Jews, but I never had one."

Three years later, Mel was invited to travel to France as one of the core member delegates at the International Federation of L'Arche Assembly in Paray-le-Monial. The trip, which Mel would make with his friends John Guido and Paul Kennedy, a Board member, would include a preliminary visit to L'Arche Poland. After the international assembly, John had suggested they travel on to Israel. Mel's father, then eighty-four and quite ill, was very pleased that Mel would visit Poland and Israel, places close to his own heart that he himself had never visited, and he urged Mel to go. John helped Mel make a final visit to his father in the hospital. His father gave Mel his blessing, and they said goodbye knowing they might not see each other again.

Mel's ancestors had lived in Kraków, and, with the help of a Board member from the local L'Arche community, they were able to find the graves of his grandparents in the old Jewish cemetery. While in Poland they also visited Auschwitz. Although his family had come to Canada earlier to escape the pogroms, Mel was well aware of the history of the Holocaust. John told me that Mel was very quiet as they walked through the death camp. Later, Mel spoke sometimes of "all the shoes – the children's shoes" that he had seen in a huge glass case.

Mel got word that his father had died soon after arriving at the international assembly. He and John flew home for the funeral and held a short *shiva* in Mel's L'Arche home with the assistance of Lieba from the Kehillah and other friends. As it happened, former assistant Sharon R. had been a palliative care nursing advisor for Mel's father, and they drew some comfort from this. Mel and John flew back to France just before the end of the assembly. Then their threesome travelled on to Israel.

Mel knew that he was fulfilling his father's dream for him, and he had a wonderful trip. They visited Jerusalem, where they had an invitation for Shabbat dinner from friends whom Mel had met at the Kehillah, and of course they went to the Kotel, what Mel used to call the Wailing Wall (in fact, the Western Wall of the Temple Mount – a holy place for Jews), and they crossed into the Palestinian Territories and visited with Kathy B., their good friend from L'Arche Toronto, and met people in the workshop she was helping with in Bethlehem.

∽∽∽

Many years after her Bat Mitzvah celebration, I stood in a hospital room with Ellen and her mother and sister and a few others as Ellen's father lay dying. Ellen sat at the head of her father's bed, closest to him, sometimes soothing his brow. The mood in the room was very quiet. Wendy asked if anyone would like to offer a prayer. Ellen started into a blessing which I recognized as the *sheheheyanu*, recited on the first day of Jewish festivals. It is a blessing she had often said with her father when he had come to help us mark Jewish celebrations. Ellen associated this blessing with momentous occasions, and it must have come to her for this reason.

Ellen had long worried about her father. Folded into their history were his paternal expectations and her desire to please him. I am not sure he could recognize her gifts as well as her Daybreak friends did, though he certainly loved her and was a faithful father and also a great supporter of Daybreak. Harold had been ill for many months, but Ellen had not wanted to speak about it or to have others raise the subject. She would tense up and show her fist and rebuff efforts that her friends made to help her prepare for this loss. However, she had clearly made this passage of acceptance by herself and was able to be lovingly present at her father's deathbed. That this moment was possible seemed a remarkable grace.

The next month, when Ellen came to my apartment for dinner, we spoke about her father's passing. "You were a loving and faithful daughter," I said. The pride on her face was evident through her sadness. Barely audibly, she responded, "I cried." And then, "Did you cry?" "Yes," I replied. (I had cried mostly because of the transformation I had seen in her.)

Ellen's sister and only sibling, Susan, was not well when Harold died, and she passed away only a few months later. After Susan died, Ellen announced to me, "I need to look after my mother now." They stay in touch on the phone and sometimes she welcomes her mother to her Daybreak home.

Sadly, Lieba, who was the primary leader of the Kehillah, passed away in 2003. There was an attempt to keep the services going, but some of the key families had moved away or no longer attended, and in 2005 the Kehillah finally folded, giving its Torah scrolls and the beautifully carved portable Ark that held the scrolls to another small congregation. I looked for an alternative synagogue to take Ellen to, but the best possibilities – egalitarian and most welcoming – were too far from Richmond Hill, and gradually we stopped attending. However, for three or four years, with the support of a wonderful woman rabbi and Joe C., Ellen and I and a small group of her Woodery co-workers did attend the Rosh Hashanah services held in a large gymnasium at the Jewish Community Centre. We would come just for an hour or so, trying to time our visit to be there for the Torah procession and reading and the *d'var Torah*, which was given in English by the rabbi. Some of the group would have forgotten the day and be wearing their work clothes and boots. We tried to enter and leave unobtrusively, but always Ellen led the way and sought out seats at the very front. I think our presence was welcome and actually brought another dimension to the worship for the accepting rabbi and people who followed her.

For a while, Mel and an assistant attended services led by the same rabbi at an adult learning centre in uptown Toronto, but they needed four subway and bus changes to get there. Mel also tried services at the university's Hillel House, and one time, I took him to an old Orthodox synagogue in the Beach neighbourhood of Toronto. However, the men and women sat in separate sections, and Mel could not see well enough to negotiate steps and aisles alone. That time, I entrusted him to one of the older men. After the service, this congregation served schnapps rather than wine or grape juice for the kiddush, and Mel approved of this. It was more like his grandfather's shul, he said, but he was not interested in returning. Perhaps this was because the service was entirely in Hebrew. Meanwhile, Mel's L'Arche Toronto community had also begun to invite a Jewish friend of their community to explain the significance of the High Holy Days, and they were hosting pre-Passover Seders and Holocaust Education events similar to those at Daybreak.

Judaism differs from Christianity in that many of its essential elements are performed at home. Most important is the weekly marking of Shabbat. While their Jewish heritage is important, among non-Orthodox Jews such as Mel's father and Ellen's parents, synagogue attendance is not so much emphasized. In their L'Arche homes, Mel and Ellen were each able to say the blessings over the Shabbat candles and the bread and wine on Friday evenings and, with the help of assistants, they persisted in doing this.

∽o∾

Ellen is nearly sixty now. Like Michael, she experiences the ill effects of the epilepsy medications she has needed, and her body is aging quickly, but her memory is fine. When she comes to dinner, we say the appropriate Hebrew blessings before our meal, and later, we look at pictures of old friends on my computer and then, putting the phone on speaker, we make one or two long-distance calls to Doug, to Mary Bee, to Jo – who have moved to other cities, but all of whom she lovingly remembers. When we talk to Jo, Ellen will remind her of Sam, the dog that Jo had when they lived together at the New House, and she will ask after Jo's cat.

Both Ellen and Mel were gifted from their early years with a sensitivity to and love for animals. Besides her family's dachshunds, Ellen's close friends Toni and Dave have a dog that she is very fond of. When I wanted to adopt a cat, I took Ellen with me to the Humane Society and watched which cat seemed to respond to her. We chose a little tuxedo female that continually rubbed against Ellen's ankles. We called her Hillary, after Sir Edmund Hillary, the mountaineer, because she liked to climb to the very highest places in my apartment. She lived with me for many years, but she belonged to Ellen also, who loved to visit and feed and stroke her. Ellen can imitate cat sounds in a way that would bring Hillary straight up to her. Before Hillary died, Ellen had one last visit. She sat down beside my computer table, where Hillary had chosen to make her bed during her last weeks, and she looked intently at the thin little cat. Hillary rose and walked to her, touching her nose to Ellen's. It was a precious moment. Today, I have a new cat, Gregory, with whom Ellen is forming a good relationship.[4]

∾⧂∾

For years, Mel rode horses at his stepsister Jennifer's stable, sometimes participating in dressage. More recently, when riding had become too much for him, he still spent a few hours each week grooming the horses. Mel eventually retired from the food bank and then even from the stable. He was approaching his mid–seventies and enjoyed being at home. He had moved to a small basement apartment in his L'Arche house, where he could be away from some of the busyness. He enjoyed visits from Mercedes, a Labrador retriever therapy dog that came to the home, and he still liked going out occasionally for a beer with Steve.

In the late spring of 2016, John Guido visited a small inclusive shul on the Danforth, not far from Mel's L'Arche Toronto home. He had a good conversation with Rabbi Miriam Margles, who, he discovered, was involved in interfaith dialogue and was very pleased to learn that L'Arche was nearby. At the time, no one had any idea that Mel was very ill. John was hoping Mel might again want to attend services, and this would seem an ideal congregation.

Mel died in June 2016, of a cancer that had grown undetected and was inoperable. I visited him just a few hours after he received the diagnosis. John was with him. Mel understood his situation and seemed resigned and peaceful. He chose to go to the palliative care ward for his last few days. He was never alone, as his friends and stepfamily came to accompany him and to say goodbye. Steve and Alida split the hours of his first night in Palliative Care. They both needed to work the next day and had expected they would be able to sleep, but Mel stayed awake the entire night talking about the many people he remembered from his nearly fifty years at L'Arche, first at Daybreak in Richmond Hill and then as a founding member of L'Arche Toronto. A few hours before he passed away, he asked for Mercedes. She lay beside him on the hospital bed, his hand resting on the dog's curly brown head.

His friends John, Steve, and Raphael, who was the L'Arche Toronto community leader, and Mel's brother-in-law, Mark, washed Mel's body according to Jewish tradition and wrapped him in his prayer shawl. Mel had asked for "a respectful Jewish funeral," and for burial near his parents' grave. The L'Arche Toronto community held an initial community gathering that Ellen and I attended, and she spoke of her memories of Mel. Then followed a very large memorial service, where there were more loving tributes. John and Steve and Raphael each spoke about Mel. Rabbi Margles taught us a *niggun*, a Jewish melody, and she chanted the Kaddish, the prayer for the dead, explaining its meaning. We sang one of Mel's favourite songs, "How Great Thou Art," and repeated the Twenty-third Psalm, which had been beautifully painted by one of the assistants and hung in the dining room of Mel's L'Arche home. (Out of respect for Mel, who regarded the "Our Father" as a Christian prayer and would never say it, the members of his house had adopted this psalm to repeat aloud at the end of their dinnertime. They copied it from the funeral home memorial card when Mel's father died.) As the service ended, all our voices soared in *"Hava Nashira"* − Let us sing Alleluia − in gratitude for the gift of having known Mel. Beside me sat a deeply moved member of our Kehillah of former days.

Mel had lived in L'Arche since 1973, and he carried much history as a longtime community member. He had a good sense of humour, a compassionate heart, and quite a bit of common sense. He was an activist who cared for the poor, and he had loved well his parents and stepfamily and L'Arche friends. He valued his Jewish heritage and never betrayed it, and he also had a great sense of fun and liked a bit of irreverence. He enjoyed skits and somewhat off-colour jokes, and old songs such as the one about the down-and-outer who could afford only one meatball, and the waiter who loudly announced the poor fellow's humiliation to the other diners. Mel would belt out the refrain with his musician friend Robert Morgan while Robert strummed his guitar:

One meatball, one meatball
You gets no bread with one meatball! [5]

13. My "House of Belonging"

The people we have welcomed in L'Arche have a great gift of simplicity in relationship. They are not governed by social conventions . . . They are not interested in anyone's profession or rank, but they are perceptive about people's hearts. Jean Vanier

In the mid-1990s, Daybreak purchased two new homes in the subdivision built on the farmland it formerly leased. One house, on Brookwood Drive, to which Peggy and Thelus moved, had an elevator installed because stairs were becoming difficult for them. Both women now needed the support of live-in assistants. The other house was on Devonsleigh, a new street running along the north side of the Daybreak property. This house replaced the Mill Street house, which had proven too small. It was handy to the Day Program and Woodery, and the soon-to-be-established Craft Studio.

In June 1995, Francis and Michael and Mary Bastedo, who was house leader at Mill Street, moved to the Devonsleigh house, along with two women core members and other assistants. Mary and Francis had "house-hunted" together, and Lloyd had been looking forward to moving there too, but he had passed away. He gave the house its name, the Red House. Even though it is one of several red-brick houses on the street, Lloyd had argued that its bricks were slightly redder, but I think the deeper reason for his wanting this name was that there was a Red House at the Jesuit community in Guelph, where he had visited his dear friend Phil.

In time, as the number of long-term assistants and associate members of the community who did not have a role in the homes grew, the Community Council decided that it would be good for each of these people to have a formal connection with one of the homes. I was invited to count the Red House my "house of belonging." This arrangement made good sense as I had longtime friendships with Francis and Michael and Mary. I was involved daily with the seniors, but I felt immediately that belonging to a specific house where I was known and had a place would be both comforting and life-giving. Sharing meals together is a fundamental aspect of our community life, and, to this day, the Red House is the house where I have dinner once a week, as well as the house with which I am linked for community events. Sometimes I have some Red House members for dinner at my apartment.

Over the years stretching back to my time in L'Arche Le Printemps, I had discovered that, as the people with disabilities called me to be part of their lives, they revealed to me that I belonged — not just that I could do something worthwhile by relating to them or helping them. I am sure that, had I not found this meaningful sharing of life in L'Arche, I would have looked for belonging elsewhere. Now, with my Red House connection, Michael and Francis were calling me again. These two men were together in the Red House for fifteen years, until Francis died in 2010, and Michael still lives there. Mary was house leader until 1998, after which she carried other roles. When she moved out in 2006, the Red House became her house of belonging also.

In 1996, Michael suffered two profound losses: first his brother, Adam, and then, in September, Father Henri (Michael always used the honorific). Adam, who was never very strong, had died of pneumonia in February of that year. When Henri learned that Adam was gravely ill, he was on a much-needed sabbatical, but he returned immediately to be with Adam, and he welcomed each of us into Adam's hospital room to say a final goodbye. Michael was broken-hearted at Adam's death. He spread his arms wide as he stammered, "I loved him t-this much!!" And then he clung to Henri and wept. Michael trusted Henri deeply, and Henri was a great help to him at that time. While acknowledging Mike's profound grief, in time Henri gently suggested to him that he had many brothers and sisters in the community.

Somehow, Mike was able to take hold of this consoling idea, and to this day he continues to call people he especially likes his "brother" or his "*sees*-ter." (While some words are difficult for Mike to pronounce, he also enjoys giving different emphases to certain words.) When these special people have children, he declares himself to be the uncle, which he pronounces "wuncle." Michael was heartbroken again when Henri died, six months after Adam. He is convinced that Henri is "with Adam – wup in heaven."

∽∾∾

In 1999, Francis and I were invited to be part of the Daybreak delegation to the International Federation of L'Arche Assembly in France, the same meeting which Mel and John Guido had attended. Each assistant and core member pair was grouped with a third person, usually a Board member, to form a triad. Francis and I were happy to learn that the third person completing our triad was Father Bill Clarke, who was chaplain to L'Arche International. I had been with Francis both in the Green House and in the Seniors Club, and we knew each other fairly well, but preparing for the assembly brought us closer. At the assembly, there would be opportunity to present our own community and to meet others from well over a hundred L'Arche communities around the world.

Before the assembly, all the North American delegates were sent to L'Arche communities in Europe for a visit. Francis and I were warmly welcomed into L'Arche Liverpool. We stayed in one of the L'Arche homes, attended community events, and toured their workshop. On our one free day, we hoped to visit the Beatles Museum. Sadly, it was closed, so we had to content ourselves with purchasing some postcards and walking around the outside. Then we strolled along the dockyards. I told Francis about my father's having sailed from England for Canada as a young man after the First World War, and we speculated on which port his parents would have left Europe from when they crossed the ocean, probably in the same year, after the fall of the Austro-Hungarian Empire. During that time we also spent a lovely weekend with Julie Gittins and her family near Manchester.[1] She took us on a scenic drive through the textile mill country of Lancashire County, and in the evening we went to a pub. As we were leaving, Francis gathered up all the unused coasters on the tables to take home as souvenirs.

We travelled on to the assembly with the Liverpool delegates – a boon since they were familiar with the rail and subway systems. In his late sixties, Francis was still in excellent health, and he proved a fine traveller, managing his own suitcase as we climbed up and down stairs and moved through the London Underground to find the still fairly new 'Chunnel' train. In Paris, we made our way to the Gare de l'Est to catch the very fast train, a TGV, to Lyon, where a bus took us on to the medieval pilgrimage city of Paray-le-Monial in eastern France, where the assembly was held. There, we met up with Father Bill.

We stayed in simple hotels and hostels used by pilgrims. Francis shared a room with Bill, who helped him with his morning routine, while I shared with three women delegates. Each morning began with options for prayer – a Protestant service, a Catholic Mass, or prayer in the tradition of the people from Asha Niketan in India. To recognize that there were L'Arche people of other faiths present, an interfaith prayer space was set up as well. I was assigned to look after it and to choose readings from the sacred scriptures of the major world religions reflecting the theme for each day. This prayer space was in the sixteenth-century Saint Nicholas' Tower, in the heart of the old city. I was pleased to spend a little quiet time each day in this ancient edifice, with its cool, thick stone walls, which surely carried much history. Francis enjoyed serving Mass for Bill. One day, he reported excitedly that he had met the pope. In fact, he had met a friendly elderly monsignor who was wearing a red skullcap and bore some resemblance to Pope John Paul II.

The Federation meeting was a rich experience for both Francis and myself, giving us a new sense of the breadth of L'Arche in the world and how its basic ideology of a shared life of friendship and respect among people of differing abilities was adapted to different cultures. Each day a community from another region of the world presented its story. Usually, this was a narrated mime in the traditional costumes of their countries, with buddies performing in tandem. The costumes were often quite beautiful. I was especially struck by the colourful African costumes and the elegant traditional dress of the delegates from L'Arche Japan. One mime touched many of us. It was presented by a community that rescued and welcomed children who were viewed as curses by their families and were left in the desert to die.

There were also opportunities to do artwork and prepare music and skits in small groups. Francis, who had brought his mouth harp, joined a music group. One day several busloads of us went to Taizé, an ecumenical community in Burgundy. It was formed during the Second World War in an effort to work for peace. There we listened to an exchange between Brother Roger, its founder, and Jean Vanier, and we participated in the hauntingly beautiful chanted prayer of Taizé.

The assembly meetings were held in a tent that accommodated all six hundred delegates and had a large stage. We listened to talks by Jean and the leaders who were ending their terms, and we all voted for the new international leaders, expressing the collective will of the communities that had sent us. One afternoon there was a market with a multitude of stalls selling L'Arche products. These included mustard, honey, jam, ceramics, candles and many small crafts, such as leather key chains, and cards. Each booth offered free samples, which Francis especially enjoyed collecting. Some evenings, Francis and Bill and I joined others from around the world at one of the local brasseries or pubs.

By this time, rather than celebrating a Eucharist, which would exclude non-Catholics, L'Arche had adopted the custom of foot washing (or, if an individual wishes, hand washing) for large, diverse gatherings. This simple, inclusive liturgy is inspired by Jesus' example of service to his disciples at their last supper. It excludes no one and can be understood as a universal gesture of service and humility and of seeking reconciliation where this is needed. It is an expression of our fundamental equality and unity.

On our next to final day together, we held a foot-washing service for all six hundred of us in the town's massive Romanesque basilica. I thought it might be rather chaotic, with jugs of water and basins and towels all over the place, but it was well organized with people in small groups with others whom they knew, and it flowed very smoothly. Before the assembly ended, the former leaders of L'Arche International were thanked, the new leaders were announced and welcomed, and there was a celebratory fiesta on the theme of the circus. Cheryl, who established the drama and arts program at L'Arche Toronto, directed a short skit for our Ontario group. There were a couple of dancers, and two or three clowns. Carl and Bill V., who were among the Daybreak delegates, wore long wigs and were lions, and Francis and I were animal trainers.

∽o∾

Francis was the senior member of the Red House, and from its beginning he had claimed the place at the head of the dinner table. Mike continued to call Francis the Cowboy and to pronounce his name "Wanless." As Francis grew older, and his hair and beard turned white, he called himself Old Goat. When Francis died, Mike, who was by then greying and close to sixty, claimed Francis's place at the head of the table and declared, "Now, me am the Old Goat!" Francis's picture is on the mantel over the fireplace, and these days after dinner Mike usually sits opposite it in a chair similar to Francis's recliner. It has a lever to raise and lower it automatically. Lover of all things mechanical, Mike enjoys operating the lever. From time to time, looking at the picture on the mantel, he acknowledges Francis's former presence in the house as he settles into his chair. Most recently, he has been pleased to point out that he too has some signs of white hair.

Today, all of the original Red House members except Michael have died or moved on, and new people have come and gone. While I am a friend to each person, I make a point of spending time with Mike once a week after dinner. Recognizing that Mike and I share a long history, Steve K., when he was house leader, suggested that I focus on helping Mike stay in touch with other old friends. This has been meaningful for both of us. Mike has even less fine motor control than in earlier times, so I hold his iPad as we look at other people's posts and photos and update his Facebook page, and then, putting the phone on "speaker," I help him with at least one phone call. When he comes for dinner at my apartment, Mike may ask to sit for a few minutes in an ancient easy chair that was Lloyd's when he lived at the Mill Street house, more than twenty years ago. The chair reminds us both of Lloyd's kind friendship. (When the household moved, the chair was deemed not to be in good enough shape to keep.)

While Mike has many important, more recent friendships in Daybreak, the bond between us remains strong. Sometimes still today, when a new person arrives, if I am present Mike asks me to help him tell the blizzard story once again. "Tell him about th-those kids, th-that lady," he will say. But for both of us the story is more deeply about the beginning of our friendship and, for me, the discovery of the mutuality in relationships in L'Arche that so attracted me many years ago.

Mike continued to go daily to ARC for a number of years after I left the Green House. He would often say, "I want a real job." Because of his love for children, some of his assistant friends thought that Mike might be able to have a volunteer position in a preschool near Daybreak. He did a placement accompanied by an assistant. It went well and Mike was happy, but even though the assistant would have continued to accompany Mike, he did not get the position when the management realized he could have a grand mal seizure. The same thing happened when he tried out for a volunteer position pushing people in wheelchairs at a rehab centre. Michael is compassionate with those less able than he is, and he is very sociable. I think the people he would have been helping would have enjoyed meeting him, and his intellectual limitations might even have helped some of them put their own struggles in perspective.

Then an opportunity finally arose for him to join the Daybreak Day Program. This is a setting he likes because the assistants know what he enjoys and engage him in activities he can do. For some time now, he has had a job a half day a week answering the phone in the Daybreak office, where one of his friends, Tanya, works. "Yesss . . . Daybreak speaking," he will say with a big smile when the phone rings. And then, "H . . . hold the line," and he presses the speaker button so Tanya can hear the caller. He enjoys the status that the job accords him, and he is proud that, on the door, beside Tanya's name there is a much bigger sign reading "Mike's office." Mike loves inventing names for people and places that are special to him. He calls Tanya "Funny Mommy," and, of course, he is a "wuncle" to her children.

Mike spends similar time answering the phone and "hanging out" at the Cedars with his friend Steve K., whom he calls the "tiny cheese." Mike calls himself the "big cheese," although Steve is much taller than Mike. "Down the hill" is how Mike identifies the Cedars, because the Daybreak lane beyond the Green House dips down past the wetland before rising to the house, which is at street level. These days there is not much in his life that Michael can have control over, but creating his own names for special people and places is something he does well and with his own unique logic and sense of humour.

One of Mike's very special possessions is his father's World War II Royal Canadian Air Force hat. He has loved flying since he was a boy – perhaps inspired by knowing of his father's experience. He had not flown in a few years – not since the entire Red House flew to Germany for the wedding of former assistants Helen and Christian. For Mike's vacation one year, Steve K. suggested he and Mike could fly up to Sudbury to see a friend whom Mike had met at a L'Arche regional gathering. Mike was so excited that some of us feared he would have a seizure. Their visit together was good, Steve said, but the plane was all that Mike talked about afterwards. For the last two years he has wanted to spend some vacation time at Niagara Falls. The first year, he and his assistant friend, John M., took a helicopter ride over the falls, again a great hit with Mike, and the next year they had dinner in the restaurant at the top of the very high observation tower, from which they could look down over the falls.

In recent years, Mike has lived through one disappointment after another, but he still evidences the same courage and creativity and capacity to live in the moment that I discovered in him during my first few months at Daybreak. When his mother became ill and needed to use a wheelchair, he prayed every night for her to walk. One afternoon I arrived to learn from Michael that he wanted to go to school to become a doctor so that he could help his mother walk again. He seemed convinced he could do this. He prayed fervently for some weeks: "God . . . You help me . . . I w-want to get to sch-school . . . be a *d-doctor*! . . . I want to help my mother *walk*!"

Finally, his mother moved to a residential care facility in Richmond Hill and his father sold their family home – the "tiny castle," as Mike called it – and moved to be with her. Mike loved that house and grieved its loss. It was not an unusual house – a split-level two-storey, and almost identical to three or four others on the street, but it held many happy memories for him. After this transition, Mike could no longer go for nights or weekends away with his parents, but he began to discover a gift in their being closer to Daybreak, in that he can see them more often. Recently, he conceived a new idea: to have a job at the front desk at the facility where they now live. He would be the greeter for visitors while also visiting his parents. One of the house assistants mentioned this idea to the management, but so far, the "job" has not materialized.

Mike has slowed down a lot, and osteoporosis has led to his becoming quite bent. He uses a special wheelchair now, and he needs a lot of assistance to help him transfer. He has mobility in water that he no longer has on land. Until a couple of years ago, on hot summer afternoons he sometimes would go with a Day Program group to the outdoor pool of friends Rob and Namju. Anna, an assistant who was accompanying Mike to the pool for the first time, told me about his having headed for the deep end as soon as he got into the pool. She had called after him, "Michael, the water is deep at that end!" Mike yelled back over his shoulder, "I was *born* in the deep end!"

Although Mike tends to have more hesitations in his speech, when he is emotionally charged up, he can sometimes come out with full sentences with no pause, and he can completely surprise people with what he says. For a while, he had a fake flip cellphone that played a commonly used ring sound when he pressed a certain button, and it stopped playing when he flipped it open. His father told me of being out for lunch with Mike when the phone of the man sitting at the next table rang with the same ring as Mike's fake phone. Without missing a beat Mike whipped his phone out of his pocket, flipped it open, and said in an irritated voice, "I thought I told you not to call at lunchtime!" Just as smoothly, he closed the phone and put it back in his pocket.

Mike is easily distracted. At dinner, it can be difficult to persuade him to keep eating and then, during the prayer time after dinner, to focus on praying. Yet, for no apparent reason, at other times he can be remarkably centered, and he may home in on the needs of someone else at the table. Peter H., who came to the Red House after Francis died and who cannot talk, is someone for whom Mike has a special fondness. When Peter's turn to pray comes, others at the table may suggest names to him – his mother, his dad, his siblings, his friends, and David, with whom he works. Sometimes Peter makes his sign for "yes," bringing his closed fists together, but at other times he is hard to read. During a recent prayer time when there was no assistant who knew Peter's family, Michael suggested to Peter the names of those close to him. There were some long pauses as Peter did not make the yes sign and Michael waited. Then Michael said quite firmly, "I know Peter, y–you can't t–talk. I know that. But s–someday you *will* talk, Peter! Some*day*!" His words hung in the air for a minute. It was a striking eschatological statement, spoken with a kind of prophetic certainty. Michael believes firmly in a heaven where he will meet again his own beloved brother, Adam, who will also be able to talk.

On another occasion, Peter, who sometimes makes loud, seemingly uncontrollable cries at the dinner table, was drowning out the conversation. Mike, in irritation, shouted down the table, "Peter, shut *up*!" Peter was silent, as was everyone else for a minute. I was sitting next to Mike, and I said to him quietly, "Mike, that was not kind. Peter is your friend." Mike said nothing. I noticed a minute or two later that he had stopped eating and was staring up at the ceiling – the direction of heaven in his cosmology. In a subdued voice he said, "Adam's mad at me . . . Father Henri too."

Peter is a gentle, sensitive man. His not being able to speak does not keep him from communicating. Unless he is in pain, he will offer me a smile if I sit down beside him, and sometimes he takes my arm and wraps it around his shoulders – his custom with assistants he likes. Sharon K., one of Peter's favourite former Red House assistants, told me about taking him for a drive one evening after she had received some very upsetting news. Peter knew she was upset. He sat quietly for some time. Then, when they were nearly home, he reached over, took her hand, and held it against his cheek, and, for a moment, their eyes met. She later told me, "Peter's simple, spontaneous action cut through the chaos of my heart. It brought me a comfort that could never have been equally expressed with words. In the months to come, it sustained me. It helped me remember I was not alone."

∽∘∾

I love having dinner at the Red House, catching up on the news of each person, and sharing in the napkin "fights" and accompanying laughter which sometimes erupt at the end of the meal. Michael and Peter and Amanda and Nancy have been the stable group of core members in the house for ten years now. Recently, they have welcomed a new member, Dave. The house usually has an assistant team of five, of whom one or two will likely stay only a year or less.[2] John M., an American with twenty-five years of L'Arche experience, has been on the team for several years. This year he moved to one of the small assistants' apartments on the Daybreak property. John's apartment has become another special place for Michael to visit.

John is an excellent chef, and he usually cooks for house celebrations. All twelve of our birthdays are celebrated in the course of the year. Passing the candle around at the end of dinner, each person expresses some aspect of their appreciation for the birthday person. Nancy can be a good animator, calling the table to "Hip, hip, hoorays" for whoever is being celebrated.

Nancy cannot see well, but she loves music and has certain favourite female vocalists, including Adele whom she heard in concert, but outlasting them all is the East Coast singer Anne Murray, whose CDs Nancy often carries around. She would so much like to meet Anne Murray in person, and over several years we assistants have written letters with Nancy inviting her to the Red House, but so far, we have had no response beyond a standard fan club mailing. Anne is retired, we remind Nancy. Nevertheless, often, when I arrive at the house on Tuesdays, Nancy will ask me if I have heard from Anne yet. Before I leave, sometimes I help Nancy get ready for bed. When she is settled she likes to pray for her family and we sing the chorus, "Jesus loves me." She has a good musical sense and sings every note.

Each of us long-term assistants connected to the house – Mary, Steve K., and myself – has a different evening to have dinner and spend time with individuals in the house. Steve and his wife, Trish Glennon, and their children are linked to the house as a family and they all try to come for celebrations. (Trish, one of the Marquette students who came to Daybreak and stayed, and Mike have a warm friendship from the years when Trish headed the Day Program.) On special occasions such as Thanksgiving, John usually cooks the feast and we all eat at a very long table in the Meeting Hall, often with two or three parents or siblings of the core members joining us.

∽∘∾

In the past four years, Amanda has given us a great example of courage. A medical condition led to her no longer being able to walk. After many doctors' appointments and major back surgery, she spent months in a rehab centre learning to walk with a walker. Back home, motivated by having a second-floor bedroom, she learned to climb the stairs and to walk without any support.

Amanda has significant artistic gifts. In the Craft Studio, she works with clay and also paints, and during the months when she could not walk, she was able to occupy herself with painting. At the studio, Namju encouraged her to look at the work of some of the great artists, especially Van Gogh, for inspiration. She painted a beautiful rendering of *The Starry Night*. Mainly she does streetscapes of whimsical trees and buildings, but recently, when visiting me, she was taken by a painting I have of Georgian Bay and she asked me to photograph it so that she could attempt to copy it.

∽∘∾

Nearly four decades have passed since I first met Mike. As he and I both age, we have many shared memories, and he has memories of his parents' friends and of assistants from before my time whom I have come to know through him—Mary Jane, Jean G., Bernadette, the Halfertys. Mike is a bit of a flirt and gradually he has given the designation of "sister" more broadly to women he is taken with. "Yu–you are my "s-*sees*-teer!" he will declare with his charming smile, to the surprise of an attractive young female guest he has just met. When I am not his sister, I am simply "wold fwend."

Not long ago, after a mealtime in which everyone had seemed out of sorts and squabbles had arisen between Mike and a couple of other house members, I helped Mike call LJ. She is the daughter of Bernadette, an early former assistant, and both mother and daughter are quite special to him. Mike was still feeling grumpy, but as soon as he heard LJ's voice, his mood transformed. LJ is now married and a teacher, and they seldom see each other as she lives some distance away, but they spoke about her mother and her dogs and the horse she rides, and he asked her to bring the horse for him to see. "Maybe," she said. "Or maybe we can make the trip to see her and the horse sometime," I interjected. As Mike smiled into the speaker phone he reminded LJ that he was her "wuncle" and she his "*nee*ice," and, to his delight, she obliged by calling him "Uncle Mike." Before the call ended he commanded her to "Wait!" and he drew in a breath, puckered up his lips, and blew her the loudest kiss he could produce. "Did you get it?" he asked her. "Yes!" came the reply.

In spite of his deteriorating health and mobility, Michael still lives most days wholeheartedly and with imagination, and he has great wellsprings of enthusiasm for what he enjoys – a new Superhero or *Star Wars* movie, the Halloween Party fantasy of dressing up as Superman and choosing his favourite female assistant to accompany him as Lois Lane, the arrival of a friend's baby, or the promise of a trip to see an old friend. In addition to his capacity to love deeply and faithfully, he is creative in how he handles many situations, and he is persistent in what he thinks is important, especially his desire to care for the people he loves.

All his life, Michael has had great aspirations that could not be met. When he was young, he wanted to ride a motorcycle like the young man across the street; later he wanted a red sports car; he wanted a girlfriend whom he could marry; he wanted to be able to read and to go to university; he wanted to become a doctor to heal his mother. Over and over again he has shown remarkable resilience and found new interests and goals in the face of disappointments and setbacks. When I think of the choices Mike has made during his lifetime, a passage from the Hebrew Scriptures comes to mind: "This day I have set before you life and death, blessing and curse . . . Choose life, that you may live."[3] Michael has chosen well!

∽ око∽

Each week I look forward to my evening in the Red House. Its people serve as a kind of anchor for me, reminding me of the essentials of our life together – welcome and friendship and forgiveness and celebration. Nancy usually comes to the door and is the first to greet me, often with a CD in her hand. Amanda calls out her cheery "Hi Beth" and adds "Beth's here" for the benefit of others in the kitchen where she helps prepare the Tuesday meal. Sometimes I bring juice or some fruit for dessert, and I pass this on to Amanda. Then I usually find Mike and Peter in the living room with one of the assistants, Mike ensconced in his recliner chair and Peter in the rocker or on the settee. Other team members may stop to say hello, and Dave will emerge from his room to greet me. Francis smiles at us from the mantle.

14. *"How's That, Kathy Kelly?"*: The Daybreak Seniors Club

Before being Christians or Jews or Muslims, before being Americans or Russians or Africans, before being generals or priests, rabbis or imams, before having visible or invisible disabilities, we are all human beings with hearts capable of loving. Jean Vanier

Early in 1994 I was asked to join the team of the Daybreak Seniors Club. I was pleased because I already knew and was fond of the members of the club. On my first day, I walked into its meeting place, the Centre Street house, to the aroma of baking bread and the sound of laughter and of Peter R. playing "Daisy, Daisy, give me your answer, do . . ."[1] on the piano. Peter, who lived at Centre Street, was home that morning because he had a medical appointment. Normally, he would have been a few blocks up Yonge Street at a law office, where he had a job photocopying, delivering mail, and shredding paper. His mother, who died young, had been a concert pianist, and Peter could play by ear. He credited an early assistant with teaching him how to chord. Peter used to live at Church Street. Being independent with most tasks, in 1982 he had moved down the street and around the corner to the newly opened Centre Street house.

The significance of Peter's choice of song was not lost on me – Daisy was the nickname of Peggy, who was laughing with delight to hear her song – or on Annie, who was repeating quietly under her breath, "Your song, Daisy." Annie had in fact given Peggy this nickname some years earlier. The two women were seated with Lloyd and Francis in the living room, where the group gathered each Monday morning to plan their week. Meanwhile, in the kitchen, Kathy and Thelus were preparing the coffee and setting out a plate of cookies ready for the meeting. Roy came in behind me, stomping the snow off his boots. He burst into the living room, and everyone greeted him as he headed for the large recliner chair. As soon as he seated himself, he turned to Lloyd and said, "Lloyd, you're a jackass!" Lloyd took a moment, seemingly to gather his thoughts, and then, his face reddening, the words burst out of him: "And what are you?" To which Roy replied, "A bum." And then another pause, and Lloyd asked, "And what else?" "A jackass," Roy replied, breaking up with laughter, and Lloyd and everyone else laughed. I soon learned that Roy and Lloyd repeated this ritual greeting at the beginning of each day.

Doug Wiebe was taking from the oven the last of the forty loaves of bread he baked weekly, usually on Wednesdays, for Daybreak homes and families. Centre Street was ideal for Doug's enterprise as it was a duplex with another full kitchen upstairs. Over nearly ten years, he raised about $36,000 for L'Arche in Haiti and in India, by selling his loaves, mainly. One morning a week he would come to Centre Street very early, mix the dough, and leave it to rise while he napped. Then he would pack it into his pans, let it rise again, and use the ovens in both kitchens to bake it. As well, he baked and sold cookies. For a while Thelus assisted him with the cookies, but she found the schedule too demanding. Through trial and error, Doug developed a gluten-free bread recipe which I still use. (This was before it became easy to purchase gluten-free bread and baked goods in stores.)

After lunch on bread-baking day, Doug would return, and he and Roy would deliver the bread. His arms proudly wrapped around four or five fresh loaves, Roy would call out as he entered each Daybreak house, and usually an assistant would appear. If his boots were wet, he might remain on the mat at the door and toss the bread to the assistant. The Brookwood House had a black Labrador that belonged to Wendy. To Roy's surprise and chagrin, one day the dog leaped up and caught one of the loaves in mid-air. Roy enjoyed telling everyone about the "G-d dog" that caught the bread.

As a handful of Daybreak members had approached retirement a few years earlier, Susan Zimmerman, working with Carmen, had laid the groundwork for the Seniors Club. It was certainly the *crème de la crème* of programs for older people with intellectual disabilities. Susan was gifted at conceptualizing processes that people with disabilities could themselves own and give direction to. As she pointed out, the seniors had worked hard all their lives, whether at ARC Industries or in the Woodery or in other jobs, and now they deserved, like other retirees, to do things they had long wanted to do. The assistants were there to help them fulfill their wishes. Susan suggested they call themselves a club because the word "club" suggested shared ownership. The members of the club set the pattern of a relaxed schedule and shorter day. They did not want to have to rush off in the morning as they had done for so many years, but rather to sleep in a bit and then take their time getting up and having breakfast after others in their houses had left for work. Hence, the starting time of 10:00 a.m.

Importantly, Susan wrote down with each senior a list of activities that he or she wanted to pursue in retirement. Some activities interested the entire group, others perhaps mainly the men or the women, and some were activities to be done one-on-one with the help of an assistant or volunteer. When individuals could not decide on something they'd like to do, we would get out these lists and read them over together.

Susan's vision, whereby the six, and later seven, Daybreak elders would plan their own program, was possible because of their ability to choose and express their individual preferences. Almost all the Seniors Club members had come to Daybreak in its very early years, when neither their families nor social services considered apartment living an option for people with their abilities and when people with more complex needs were still being institutionalized. Roy, who came in the mid-eighties, after spending most of his life in an institution, was the exception, but like the other seniors he could clearly express what he wanted and didn't want to do. Today, most of these individuals might have been living alone or with one other individual in an apartment, with a worker coming in to give them limited support, but, sadly, in my experience, the people in such settings generally are rather lonely. They have little variety in their lives and few opportunities to develop friendships with people who do not have disabilities.[2] (In recent years, the club's members have mainly been people who are less able than the initial group. Several are in their fifties.)

By the end of the planning meeting on Monday morning, each person would have a copy of his or her schedule for the week. Activities might include entertaining a tea guest, baking (a Tuesday morning activity of Thelus and her friend Marion), an art class, walking dogs at the Humane Society kennels (something Lloyd enjoyed), fishing, a shopping trip, lawn bowling (which Francis liked), and playing bingo at the Richmond Hill Seniors Centre – which Peggy, Annie, and Francis regularly chose for Thursday afternoons. Most weeks, each person would have a time to work on their life story book, for which they would have a partner – someone who knew them well and could help them gather and preserve stories from over their lifetime. Susan herself had developed a methodology for doing this work.

A good cadre of volunteers made all this possible. The bingo players were accompanied by Pat (Gord's mom) and Mary Jane (a longtime friend and former assistant) and later Anne B. as well as one of us from the team. Besides the cards and banners made as a group, Ellen's mother, Claire, and Claire's friend Janet, taught an art class for Francis and Annie. Francis developed his rainbows in this class and discovered watercolours and that he could create interesting effects by tilting the paper and letting the paint run. He was suddenly receiving a lot of praise for his work. Latterly, he produced watercolour abstracts consisting of short lines and dots in pastel shades. I have one of these framed and often think of him when I see it. Later, Peggy made a new friend in Julia, who went swimming with her once a week. Both women were hockey fans and sometimes, as well, would take in NHL games together.

One day early in my time with the seniors, I was behind one of the ladies in the drugstore as she was about to hand over a twenty-dollar bill to pay for her purchase of a couple of dollars and some cents. When I noticed that she had a lot of small change, I suggested she could lighten her wallet by using some of her change, but she was adamant that she would use the twenty. Later, I learned from Kathy that she felt bad about not knowing how to count money, and, rather than show that she needed help, she preferred always to pay with a twenty. She would withdraw a couple of additional twenties at the bank each week even if she had a good supply of money left. Her handbag would become very heavy with all the change. Sometimes, she would let me buy some of her change, which, I explained, I needed for parking.

In a store with Francis on another occasion, the clerk referred to him as my father. At that moment it seemed a rather delightful misperception, and I decided to leave her with it. I was also aware that, if I corrected the clerk, we might be seen as in a hierarchal relationship of helper and helped – not what I wanted to convey. I soon learned that servers and clerks frequently mistook the seniors for our parents.

Most of the Daybreak seniors had known one another since the early 1970s. There were three women – Peggy, Thelus, and Annie – and three men – Lloyd, Francis, and Roy. Lloyd had retired in his late fifties, when, because of his heart condition, he could no longer do the work required at the Woodery. All the others had reached sixty-five before retiring and were receiving their Old Age Security cheques.

When I arrived, George had not yet come to the club because he didn't want to encounter Roy; nor Roy, George. The two men had become enemies soon after Roy arrived at Daybreak, in the mid-1980s. Roy had wandered into the barn during the Woodery lunch break one day, and, seeing George's coveralls hanging in the mud room and a pair of boots on the floor below them, and noting that both items were of a size that would fit him, Roy had put them on. George was furious when he discovered this new fellow wearing his clothes and boots. Roy, as was his habit, especially when frightened, let out a string of swear words that greatly exacerbated the situation because George hated swearing. They very nearly came to blows.

The Seniors Club assistants had been working on recruiting George into the club since he had retired. Everyone thought he would enjoy the activities and would fit in very well if only he and Roy could be reconciled. One of our assistants would go over to Church Street to spend an afternoon with George each week and let him know that his artwork would be appreciated by the other seniors and also that Lloyd and Peggy, with whom he already had a strong sports-based friendship, would especially enjoy having him at the club. Gradually, George listened to our explanation that Roy was unaccustomed to people having their own work clothes. When he was in the institution, the men wore whatever was available that fit. Roy had worked for many years on a team that hauled coal to the furnaces of the institution. No doubt he had worn coveralls and big work boots similar to George's. Also, no doubt Roy had learned many swear words in the institution without necessarily knowing their meanings.

Eventually, George decided to accept an invitation to tea at the club. The two men were cautious and even shy with each other, each just glancing toward the other occasionally and not addressing each other directly, but the visit was a good start, and George consented to join the club part-time. Before long, he was coming every day. He loved it that Annie called him Bugs and Georgie (as in Georgie Porgie, who kissed the girls and made them cry), and he would remind us of the rhyme, then chuckle that he made the girls cry. He enjoyed the drives and the all-day outings and doing the artwork on the banners that the club made.

Gradually, George and Roy discovered they were able to get along quite well. Besides both being tall and big of build and having done heavy work for years, they were similar in other ways. Both were kind and sensitive men, and they cared for those less physically able. When out and about, Roy was as likely as George to hold the door for an elderly person or to stop to greet and shake the hand of someone using a scooter or a wheelchair.

From the start, the seniors had wanted to be committed to at least one activity that served the wider community, and for many years they were faithful volunteers on a Friday delivery of Meals on Wheels to a semi-rural route around Oak Ridges, the village just north of Richmond Hill. Roy had taken on this delivery with an assistant, and, with Roy's approval, George joined them. In spite of his hip problems, George could climb into the second row of seats in the van, and, since he could read, he would hold on to the map and the list of addresses and would give the directions and the house numbers to the driver. Roy, though several years older than George, was more limber. He would clamber in and out at each stop and would delight in taking the meals to the doors of recipients, always with a hearty greeting. With women, he was shy and would often just laugh when they thanked him. With men, he would say loudly, "How are you, ya old bum?" Everyone on the route seemed to understand Roy and to like him.

We assistants were a team of three – Carolyn, Kathy, and myself. Carolyn, who had small children, was the leader when I came, with Carolyn's husband, Geoff, covering Fridays and doing the Meals on Wheels run. Later, the team was Kathy, myself, sometimes one other woman (Jean Lomas was one), and an experienced male assistant who changed each year or two. These men were often former house assistants who had married and were in transition. It helped that they already knew and were known by the seniors. Kathy and I were together on the Seniors team for the six years that I was with the club. I learned a lot from her as she was ever sensitive to the needs of the core members.[3]

∽๑∾

On Tuesday afternoons, almost all the seniors headed for the bowling alley. Bowling was a favourite activity of Roy, Annie, and Francis, who were very good at it, and of Peggy, whose foot and ankle problem would not allow her to bowl but who liked to keep score. (These were the days before automatic scorekeeping. Peggy was good at the required arithmetic.) At the alley, they could be a rather raucous group. There was little to absorb the sound when, each time he had a turn, Roy would shout out his triumphant or disgusted commentary with a salty sprinkling of curses. Joe Egan, who spent a few months with the seniors when he had a sabbatical, remembers Roy's loud *"F— it!"* when he failed to get a strike or a spare. A group of church ladies bowled two lanes down from them, and Roy's comments certainly turned their heads. I bowled with this group at first, but because George's painful hip prevented him from enjoying bowling, after he joined, he and I usually spent this time together.

On Wednesday mornings the seniors would often invite a tea guest. The guest might be a visitor to the Daybreak community or an old friend. Jean and Len, Daybreak's former farm manager, came after Len had a near-death experience during a routine surgery. He told us of the peace and light he experienced and wanted us to know that we should not be afraid of dying. Other guests were politicians, shopkeepers, clergy, and new Daybreak mothers with their babies.

Our activities included visits in small groups to friends and people in hospital or shut in. On one such visit the elderly mother of one of the other Daybreak core members was recovering from a miserable bout of shingles and asked us to shop for a couple of all-cotton undervests of a certain style for her. This little task occupied Peggy, Annie, Kathy, and me for most of an afternoon. We checked three or four shops before we finally found the exact vest she wanted.

Almost every week all of us women would find an afternoon when we could take a drive to a tea room in one of the nearby towns. Schomberg, Unionville, Kleinburg, King City, Aurora – we knew all the tea rooms within a forty-minute radius. Lloyd, who loved butter tarts, would sometimes come with us. Or he would choose a drive with the men along rural roads, to look for thoroughbred horses and Holstein cows. Francis was always happy to spot a horse with the same colouring as Trigger, Roy Rogers's horse. Fridays, an errand trip was planned for those who wished to do banking and personal shopping. A monthly essential of this trip was a stop at the local cable TV channel offices to allow Peggy to pay her bill. (Peggy had her own small TV and reading room in the finished basement of the Brookwood House.)

༄

As Daybreak's twenty-fifth anniversary approached, rehearsals began for the gala theatre presentation. Francis, who was thrilled to have a part in the play, was often absent. Besides her work in the club, Kathy was in the Spirit Movers dance troupe. They played a major role in the gala. Marcie was not only the troupe leader but also one of the lead singers. Thankfully Kathy was not often absent as the dancers rehearsed on Saturdays.[4]

The presentation, staged in February, 1994, in the beautiful Elgin Winter Garden theatre in downtown Toronto, and re-mounted in May in Markham Theatre, was a spectacular success. From the opening scene of tall Ben dancing and twirling with tiny Alia who, even though she was blind, was smiling out at the audience, all were held in rapt attention.

In the fall of that year, we gathered as a whole community for two days to remember and celebrate our graced history. John English, a Jesuit priest skilled in leading such community reflections, came, and Steve and Ann returned to help us "remember" the earliest days. This was a time to claim our "adulthood" as a community. Mary Egan and Mary Bastedo planned the meeting and Joe Egan and Nathan, who was then the community leader, facilitated. A huge time line was drawn across the front of the room. We were each given a brightly coloured scarf for the five-year period in which we arrived, and we were invited to cluster with our group.

In the course of our time together, the major community events were identified from the giving of the property by the nuns and the welcoming of the first members to building of the New and Green houses, the acquiring of the first houses in the Town of Richmond Hill and in downtown Toronto, the opening of the Woodery and the Day Program, the closing down of the farm, the conversion of the bungalow into the Dayspring, the Big House chapel fire, the moving of the household in the Big House to new homes and the conversion of the upstairs into offices, the establishing of the Spirit Movers dance troupe, the beginning of the Seniors Club, the opening and later closing of the Genesis Place apartments, and the emerging dream of L'Arche Toronto as a separate entity.[5] It was a wonderful overview. The gathering ended with Robert Morgan and Mel offering a rousing rendition of the *One meatball* song, a service of thanksgiving led by Henri, followed by, a formal dinner – a gift from the board.

∽०∾

At the club, an abundance of laughter often marked our days together. Besides the exchanges between Roy and Lloyd, there were Peggy's giggles when Annie would talk about her or other people's bloomers or make up unusual names; sometimes Thelus would put a rose, or a stick, between her lips and imitate Hoagy Carmichael at the piano; and when we were out driving, Annie might offer a commentary on the stores we were passing – No Thrills, and Pork Choppers, for instance, for No Frills, and Price Choppers. Sometimes we would sing the choruses of favourite old songs which Peggy and some of the others knew well – besides "Daisy, Daisy," we sang "Down by the Old Mill Stream," "Take Me Out to the Ball Game," "It's a Long Way to Tipperary" – a song Thelus loved – and others.

The seniors' longer outings required planning ahead to ensure we had vehicles that we could use into the late afternoon. All wanted to attend the Royal Agricultural Winter Fair, and there were many summer trips – to Edwards Gardens, strawberry or apple picking, to a Blue Jays game at the "Dome," our name for Toronto's still-new stadium with its retractable roof, and, for Roy and Annie, a fishing trip. Everyone also liked to take the ferry to Centre Island for a picnic, and to drive north to Tottenham to ride the old train pulled by the one remaining working steam locomotive in Ontario. On that trip, Peggy would invariably reminisce about taking a similar train as a child to Pointe au Baril, en route to her family's cottage.

The seniors were a popular group to entertain in spite of numbering nine or ten including us assistants. Each year we would have lunch invitations to homes of volunteers and friends. These were always a highlight, as were our tea visits to Mary Egan's parents.

The Seniors Club budget was small. In fact, in the days of harsh provincial government cuts to social programs, we all went down to the Ontario legislature at Queen's Park to join a protest. Peggy, who was recovering from surgery, sat in the wheelchair she was using at that time, and we set up our folding chairs beside her, under our large hand-printed sign declaring "No More Cuts!"

Henri, in those days, was encouraging us to adopt an expectation of abundance, not of scarcity, to trust, and to act out of this trust. When we needed art supplies, it was decided that I should approach the father of a Daybreak member to ask for a donation of large sheets of good-quality, heavy paper that we could use for banners.

We knew he had owned a stationery business, and we assumed this would be possible for him. He seemed surprised by my request, and I had the impression I might be putting him in an awkward position. However, a couple of weeks later he did bring us a big bundle of the kind of paper we needed. I hope we expressed our gratitude adequately.

The spacious first floor of Centre Street, with its big living room, comfortable furniture, and large dining room table, where we could do art, suited the club well. The entire group participated in the weekly art mornings, during which, as a service to the Daybreak community, we made many banners and cards with a variety of messages – congratulations on birthdays and anniversaries, get-well wishes, and messages to welcome new assistants and visitors to Daybreak and to thank assistants who were leaving. It could be painful to make farewell banners and cards for assistants whom we had come to love. Thelus had once asked Jean Vanier, "Why do assistants leave?" We would remind one another of Jean's answer: "God sent them to L'Arche for a time to learn about love, and our role was to help them with this and then to send them back into the wider world to live out their learning."

For the banners, there was a kind of assembly line, with everyone participating. Someone would have painted a pale wash on a number of very large pieces of paper the week before. Roy would work first, creating a swirl of paint across the centre. As we approached noon, Kathy was often in the kitchen preparing the tea for lunch. Every so often Roy would call out gleefully, *"How's that, Kathy Kelly?"* and Kathy would emerge to see his grand swirl. Thelus would add her sunflowers in various colours. Francis also had a distinctive flower, though more often he would create a rainbow using felt markers. Lloyd would draw a couple of Holstein cows, ensuring they had ballooning udders, or occasionally, with a glint in his eye, male anatomy. Annie would add her trademark whimsical angels with ragged wings. And George would make a border of tulips across the bottom. Finally, the banner would go to Peggy, who would write the message in her large cursive, using a bold-coloured marker. She prided herself on knowing a few French words, and if it was a welcome banner, she was likely to write *"Bienvenue."*

Then everyone would sign the banner. For a long time I had on my kitchen wall a framed banner given me when I returned from a trip to Winnipeg. It read, "*Bienvenue* back home, Beth!"

The seniors, like many other people with intellectual disabilities, tended to think about people's gifts and abilities very concretely. This was most obvious when we were naming the gifts of people being celebrated at their birthdays. The assistants might name abstract qualities: "You are kind, or considerate of others." The core members were likely to name something the person had done for them: "You took me to see my sister." And so it was that when George died, Francis focused on George's contribution to our banners, saying over and over, "Who will make George's flower borders now? I can't do them. I don't know who will do them!"

Visits or tea times with new Daybreak parents and their babies were high points for the club. There was not one of the seniors who did not love to hold a new baby. What struck me most was the gentleness of each person as she or he cuddled the infant for a few minutes, face full of tenderness. Daybreak did not lack for couples who had been or were assistants and who knew and trusted the seniors, and the seniors in turn cared about and prayed for these little families. At first, I was nervous about Roy holding babies, as he could be rambunctious and a bit unpredictable, but this was never so with babies. These tiny lives called forth a great tenderness in him. On my fridge, I have a photo of Roy holding his friend Mary Bee's firstborn, Miryam, and looking back at the camera as comfortably as if he really were the proud "Grandpa" he would have loved to have been.

Jean Vanier has spoken about the maturity and the capacity to love and thereby give life to others that resides in L'Arche members who themselves never had the opportunity to bring children into the world. What we all long for, he says, is to be able to give life, but giving life can take various forms. Far from being depressed or jealous, the seniors accepted that they had gifts of care and friendship and joy to offer – gifts that did indeed give life to these new parents and many others. The group enjoyed preparing skits, and some of their funniest were for baby showers. On one memorable occasion, big George, the least likely of all the seniors, played the baby and wore a "diaper" – a role he and everyone else found hilarious.

It was necessary sometimes to advocate for the rights of our members in the wider community. When leaders at the Town's Senior's Centre decided that our members could no longer be free like others to choose their table at bingo but must sit at the table at the edge of the room, next to the smokers' table, the five people in our group found the smoke insufferable. However, the Centre's leaders refused to consider our requests to be allowed to move. I went to the town ombudsperson, who heard us out and then met with some of us and the Centre's bingo leaders and told the leaders they could not discriminate against us. If they continued to do so, they would be removed from leadership. Like magic they changed, not only giving our group the freedom everyone else had to choose their table but also suddenly becoming very friendly towards us.

In 1996, an international conference on the "quality of life of people with developmental disabilities" was to be held in downtown Toronto. We submitted a proposal to present the life story work of members of the Seniors Club. I was already doing some reading in gerontology and had learned that "life review" was coming to be recognized as aiding the process of integration in older adults. But available literature at the time related only to people with full intellectual capacity, who could write or record their own stories. Our approach, of soliciting letters from friends and family, did not require the same degree of narrative ability or autonomy, and it brought a wide variety of perspectives and stories that revealed the richness of each person's life and the many ways she or he was valued by others.

Peggy, Thelus, Francis, and George wanted to participate in the conference. Kathy and I prepared a set of handouts on how to work with a partner to create a life story book. It included a sample letter to ask friends and family to write a letter with a special memory of the person and, if possible, one or two photos. (It was uncommon for such solicitations not to yield warm responses.) Other handouts gave suggestions for creating attractive pages incorporating the person's artwork, employing templates to shape some photos into circles or oblongs, and using acid-free paper and acid-free plastic

225

sleeves. We urged the use of a three-ringed album or binder to allow pages to be added or re-grouped.

It was decided that Thelus would formally present her book in conversation with Alan C., who knew Thelus well and was an assistant in the Seniors Club at that time, and Peggy would read a paper by herself—a single typed page that she prepared and rehearsed with help from Kathy. I made overhead projection slides (the technology of the day) to show representative pages from Peggy's and Thelus's books as they spoke. Francis and George would have table presentations of their books. Francis's was already a large book, and George's was nicely under way by then. I would give a short talk on the research behind life review work and how we adapted it in L'Arche.[6]

In those days, not many people with intellectual disabilities were to be seen at such conferences. We dressed for the conference and we all attended the opening plenary, where the keynote speaker was Sheila Hollins, a psychiatrist friend of L'Arche from the United Kingdom. She spoke about helping people who are upset to name and express their feeling through specially illustrated picture books and showed slides of the illustrations. (We later obtained a set of these books, which proved useful in grief support groups.)

On the first afternoon, we gave our workshop. My most vivid memories are of Peggy at the lectern, confident and competent in her presentation; and of Thelus, thrilled to show a page from her book with a picture of herself and the mayor in front of the cenotaph of the small town of Thelus in northeastern France. The name of the town was clearly visible on the monument. Her father, a World War I veteran, had been welcomed in this town, and he had resolved that if he survived and had a child, he would name the child after the town. (The photo was taken on a trip to Europe that Thelus had made with Alan and two other L'Arche members.)

After the conference, the regional coordinator for L'Arche in Ontario suggested that our Seniors Club might host a gathering of seniors from the other eight L'Arche communities in Ontario. This became the first of what continues as an annual three-day regional gathering, each time animated by a different community. We presented our life story work and gave a workshop in which each participant could, with a buddy or partner, prepare a couple of pages for the books they would continue when they returned home.

In 1997, the club introduced what has become another now long-standing tradition. Early that year, realizing that four of the seniors – Thelus, Francis, George, and Annie – had all come to Daybreak in 1972, Kathy and Peggy and I decided we should organize a twenty-fifth anniversary celebration for them. Since Kathy had inherited her mother's beautiful silver tea service, we decided the celebration should be a Silver Anniversary tea. I would contribute some of my mother's bone china tea cups, and we would plan the tea as a formal affair, with Peggy pouring for the first half hour. We chose the Church Street living room as the venue. There were several people who had come before 1972 and had never had such a celebration. When we prepared the invitations, we included them also. We decided the tea should be on or as close as possible to October 16, the date in 1969 that Bill V. joined the Newroths in the Big House and the community was founded.

Everyone dressed in their best. Steve and Ann Newroth and Bill V. came, and Peter R. (the pianist), and pipe-smoking David, who was the third core member to arrive, and John S. and John B. and Sue M. and a few others, including Gord, who also came in 1972, and of course the four seniors. Through Ellen's father, who knew people in the jewellery business, we arranged to have little silver pins of the L'Arche boat made. Nathan, as community leader, presented each person with a certificate and pin. Today, although some members have died, the twenty-fifth anniversary group has grown much larger. We still have a formal silver tea, Kathy still lends her silver tea service, and each new member of the group receives a silver L'Arche pin.

15. "Happy Trails": The passing of the seniors

Our lives are a mystery of growth from weakness to weakness, from the weakness of the little baby to the weakness of the aged . . . Weakness becomes a place of chaos and confusion if we are not wanted; it becomes a place of peace and joy if we are accepted, listened to, appreciated, and loved.
Jean Vanier

Made for Happiness is the title that Jean Vanier chose for the popular version of his doctoral dissertation on Aristotle, who said that the elements that lead to happiness are friendship, pleasure, and the attempt to live justly and truthfully. It seemed to me the Daybreak seniors had discovered Aristotle's formula. They were resilient and happy people who loved life with its many small and larger pleasures, were comfortable with themselves, enjoyed their friends, had suffered and learned to forgive, and were caring and compassionate.

Each of the seniors was a unique individual, with lessons to teach and inspiration to impart. Except for Lloyd and George, who were younger when they died suddenly of heart attacks – Lloyd was on the cusp of his sixty-third birthday in 1995, and George was seventy-one when he passed, in 1998 – all the seniors in the club lived well into their eighties, never developing dementia or cancer, and dying finally of old age. When I left the club in 2000, of the men only Francis was alive, but the women were still doing well. Of slight build and ever strong of will, Thelus outlived all the others.

Lloyd

I discovered Lloyd to be very well emotionally in the Seniors Club. He had become more articulate and more able to take initiative in conversations, sharing with us little stories from his early life on the family farm, to which his father had given the name Kerman and Son, recognizing Lloyd as a partner. He spoke of his father's success breeding a new, officially recognized line of Holsteins. He recounted the sale of the farm to the city of Oshawa and its having become a cemetery, and how that was good. "Better than a mall or gas station," he added. He was no longer fixed on me or on anyone else. With me, he was sensitive, loyal, and forgiving (for I am sure that he realized I was cautious in our relationship, not usually doing one-on-one activities with him). He faithfully prayed for me, and we enjoyed being together in groups, especially on visits to tea rooms. He and Carolyn got along well working on his life story book, and he was proud of his book. He responded to Carolyn's sense of humour and her teasing, and he loved Carolyn and Geoff's baby girl, Monica. He was close to his sisters and was very pleased when a small great-niece printed him a message and drew her own picture of a cow for his book.

Lloyd related comfortably to everyone in the club. He could joke with the others, but he also contributed a settled calmness. It was obvious to all of us and to Lloyd's family that L'Arche had been very good for Lloyd, gradually bringing him out of his depression after his parents died and the family farm was sold, and giving him a place where he could offer his gifts of kindness and friendship and humour, and be appreciated.

Lloyd's arthritic hip, for which he could not have surgery because of his weak heart, slowed him down increasingly. At the same time, small activities left him out of breath. Because of his heart condition, he carried nitroglycerine with him. However, nothing interfered with his ability to enjoy the group or with his hope to make a trip to England to visit his friend Dave, a previous Mill Street assistant with whom he had hit it off especially well.

A few days before Lloyd died, and a week before the actual date of his sixty-third birthday, his house threw a wonderful party for him. (They scheduled the party early to avoid its being too close to Daybreak's re-mounting of its gala, part of celebrating a visit from Jean Vanier. Lloyd was excited about his walk-on part as a Holstein cow, and no one wanted him to be too tired to perform.) The Mill

Street house rang with happiness for Lloyd as his friends packed into the small living room. We had just sung "Happy Birthday" and Lloyd had blown out the candles on his cake when a large Holstein cow lumbered up the stairs from the basement and sat in his lap. Lloyd turned as red as ever and looked like he would burst with laughter as the two assistants inside the cow costume played the moment for all it was worth – nuzzling him and trying to lick him and then lifting up a leg (more like a dog than a cow) as if to pee right in front of him.

It seemed providential that Lloyd's party was held early. By the time of his actual birthday, Lloyd was dead and we had already held his funeral.

Remarkably, I happened to be with Lloyd the day he died. He was in hospital awaiting treatment, not for his heart but for a different condition. Following Daybreak's custom when someone is hospitalized, the community had created a roster so that there was always an assistant or friend with him. In the afternoon, I relieved Steve Mosher. I was sitting close by Lloyd's bed, and he knew I was there. He was restless but sometimes dozed off. Every so often he would say just the word "Peace," and I would respond, "Thanks, Lloyd. Peace to you also." After a couple of hours, he suddenly screamed and convulsed, and I dashed for the nurses' station. The code was called immediately and the team came quickly, but his heart was too far gone and he could not be brought back, though he was kept on life support until one of his sisters, who lived out of town, could come to the hospital. Meanwhile, his closest community friends and Henri and Wendy arrived and we all stayed around him, praying and singing quietly.

More than anything, I think being known and appreciated was what mattered to Lloyd. He left a legacy of kindness to all who knew him, especially Michael and Francis, with whom he shared a friendship dating from their early days in the Green House. I was grateful to have been able to spend his final months with him in the Seniors Club, and I was deeply moved to have been the one who was with Lloyd during his final hours.

After Mary, Francis, Michael, and others were settled into the Red House, they invited Lloyd's closest friends and his sisters to join them in planting a maple tree in the back garden in memory of Lloyd, and together, we shared some of our favourite stories of Lloyd. Today, that maple is a sizable, flourishing tree. Sometimes when I am at the Red House visiting with Michael, we look at it and take time to remember our good friend Lloyd.

George

It was after Lloyd died that George decided to work on his life story. I was happy to be George's partner for this project. We sent letters to as many of his family members and former assistants as we could find addresses for, and we went together to the mall for him to choose an attractive album and other supplies. Each Tuesday afternoon George and I would head to the Richmond Hill library, where there was an area with tables and a coffee bar. We would read any new letters that had come and look over the enclosed photos. The letters from assistants expressed their respect and fondness for George and often would focus on a vacation trip or a sporting event they had enjoyed together. Joe Egan sent pictures of an early trip he and George had made to Chicago to visit Joe's family and see a Cubs game. John Guido's mother remembered his visits to her home in New Jersey and their time together at the Vanier retreat in San Diego. Matthew remembered their trip to Quebec, where they rode in a horse-drawn carriage.

I would read to George the one or two pages I had typed up from his reminiscences the previous week. He would make minor corrections and clarifications and then would continue sharing his memories. With my questions, which would get him started, he was able to give a fairly clear narrative of his early days, describing the small stores along the main street of his hometown and the Chinese café where he would stop for a coffee, the park and small lake where he and his friends had played as children, and the movie theatre where he and a cousin had seen cartoons and Westerns. He remembered attending school with his sister and taking apples to the teacher. He recalled playing hockey with Hal and other young men in the town, and he wanted me to be sure to include the story of his going to Montreal to see the Canadiens play and meeting Maurice the Rocket Richard. As he talked, he would stop sometimes and chuckle to himself. In an envelope in his book he had the tape of his friend Hal's reminiscences of their friendship, made on a visit that he and one of the assistants, Keith, had paid to his hometown.

George was proud to have been named after both of his grandfathers and had pictures of them. And he had pictures and many memories of his nieces and nephews, one of whom was named after him. All these children were married now, and he was thrilled when a great-nephew was also given his name. He was proud to include in his book letters and pictures from his sister and other family members and the family history packet sent to him by one of his nieces. He was also proud of the newspaper article about his uncle's flour mill, where he had worked, and of another newspaper clipping about the industrial league hockey team on which he had played as a young man.

Inviting Thelus to join us one day, we drove out to George's hometown to see how much of it remained unchanged, and we picked up one of his elderly cousins, took her to the local Tim Hortons, and recorded her memories of their childhood. We also visited the Richmond Hill archives to find pictures and information about the Town of Richmond Hill as it was in 1972, the year he moved to Daybreak, and about the Pickseed company, just a kilometer to the south along Yonge Street, where he had first worked.

In 1997, George's father died, and a few months later his sister followed. George handled these losses remarkably well, attending his father's funeral and, with his United Church minister and some of us in the Seniors Club, holding a small memorial service at Daybreak for his sister. In a conversation that we facilitated, he was able tell the minister and others about her and the close relationship they'd shared. I think George got through these difficult times at least partly because he was well held by both his Church Street friends and the seniors, and because he had a stronger sense of himself and the value of his life through the work we were doing. Later he asked the same minister to bless his life story book at one of the Friday evening Daybreak worship gatherings.

George's passing the next year was a shock, but I could not help thinking that at least he did not have to suffer through another long stay in hospital. The morning after he died, George's family and Daybreak members and friends were notified, and the community gathered at the Dayspring to share stories about him. Joe V. moderated, holding a framed picture of George, which he passed with the mic to each person who indicated they wanted to speak. The picture would help the individual to focus. Many core members as well as assistants had memories of living or working or vacationing with George.

At his funeral, a large Montreal Canadiens floral logo made by Steve M. and other friends rested on his casket. It was not until George's funeral that we grasped the full reach of his life. Anyone who did not make it early found standing room only in the large sanctuary of Richmond Hill United Church. Among those who came, besides former assistants, family members from out of town, and people who knew him at the church, were neighbours we didn't know, whom he was in the habit of greeting on his walks. The donut shop girls who had served George earlier on the evening he died were there. ("He always talked to us," they said.) And so was the owner of the high-end jewellery shop who allowed George to tramp through his store to use their main-floor washroom, saving him the painful descent to the basement facilities of the nearby restaurant. Other shopkeepers, the owners of the diner and waitresses from his favourite bars and restaurants, members of the softball team for whom he had been the bat man in the 1980s, several of the Mahlers hockey team, and even townspeople to whom he had delivered Daybreak's eggs more than a decade earlier were there.

If I had to choose only one word to describe George, it would be "honourable." Then there would be a list of corollary words that go with that trait: trustworthy, loyal, big-hearted, and a caring friend. When he smiled, George's sense of humour and generosity of spirit shone out from his striking blue eyes. He lived according to old-fashioned values. He felt sorrow when something had not gone right by his standards — a sports hero had disgraced himself, a marriage had fallen apart. Like many core members, George was compassionate towards those who were weaker. He suffered physically a great deal late in his life, and he suffered mentally at times as well, but he persevered, living as fully as was possible for him right to the end.

Roy

Roy had spent all his adult life in institutions until, at sixty-eight, he was able to move to Daybreak. He had made a couple of kind male friends among the staff at the second institution, just a few minutes' drive to our north, where he had spent twenty years. These friends were retired and living in Richmond Hill, and we facilitated Roy's visits with them. We would pass the institution when we drove up Yonge Street towards Aurora. In the first few years, Roy would become very agitated and let out a string of curses when he saw the building ahead of us, and he would be relieved when we had passed it. He called it the "old dump." I think that giving it this name tamed the place a bit for him.

When he arrived at Daybreak, Roy was happy about many aspects of his new home. For one thing, he had his own bedroom after sleeping for years in a dorm with twenty or more other men. For another, the refrigerator was not locked. When opportunities presented, he would stuff his pockets with tomatoes and cheese and other edibles. If he was at home, these would usually end up in his pillowcase. At the New House, where he spent most of his Daybreak years, the refrigerator was eventually locked overnight because his nighttime raids could seriously throw off his blood sugar.

During the first year or two that Roy was at Daybreak, he had no daytime program and would enjoy just sitting out on the bench by the Big House or wandering around the farm, which still had egg-laying chickens. As well, the farm raised a turkey for each house for Thanksgiving. Shortly before that weekend, Len and the farm team had to kill the turkeys. Over the years I never witnessed this unpleasant spectacle, but Roy apparently did and later vividly described the "wringing of their bloody necks." A neighbour had donated her prize pet geese to Daybreak for our pond, but they disappeared within a few days, and we thought a fox or muskrat had got them. When she came by to check on them, she asked Roy, who was sitting on the nearby bench. He probably thought she was referring to the turkeys. In any case, to her shock and dismay, he described their demise at the hands of the farm team in the same graphic terms as he had the turkeys. She drove off and did not return for some weeks.

Roy had a huge and compassionate heart and a large and strong body well into his eighties. He would joke with the women assistants and then sometimes wrap his big arm around our shoulders and pull us close for a sideways hug. In fact, he seemed to embrace nearly everyone, strangers included, in his love – except those few people he feared, particularly doctors when in their offices with needles and other instruments handy. He also feared any building that resembled an institution or a medical facility. He would never enter a hospital to visit ill friends, not even Adam, whom he lived with and loved, when Adam was dying. Roy was such a strong and caring man, and yet he could have so much fear. Certainly, this made us wonder what had happened to him during his many years in institutions.

Sometimes, if Ann P., as a nurse as well as the New House leader, was concerned about Roy, she would call his doctor and the doctor would come down to Ann's car to see Roy or would make a house call. If the doctor wore a white coat and had his stethoscope, Roy would accord him more respect and would let him check his heart, look at his eyes and in his mouth, and ask him a few questions. One day, a young woman doctor was filling in, and Ann was concerned Roy would not believe that she was a doctor, so Ann asked the doctor to put on a white coat. Exasperated, the doctor replied, "I don't have a white coat! And I am already leaving this office to meet the patient in your car. Is that not enough?" However, the doctor managed to borrow a white coat, and when she showed up at the car, Roy accepted her.

Roy was also afraid to enter a church, even for a funeral. I spent the morning of Adam's funeral driving out into the country with Roy to try to distract him in his distress. When we returned, I circled past the church, thinking we might see the pallbearers carry out Adam's casket, but Roy was very anxious. Realizing I was slowing, he let out a volley of swear words, and I quickly drove on.

Occasionally, Roy had episodes of barking like a dog, especially if he saw a dog. It was difficult to call him back to the present at such times. Perhaps he had had a bad experience with a dog. At other times he would "lose it" and scream and bang around, kicking walls and furniture, sometimes biting his hand, and maybe hitting a window with his fist. At such times, we all needed to leave the room for a few minutes. We were fairly certain these episodes were the result of his blood sugar being low. When he got tired he would collapse into a chair, and we could give him a glass of orange juice and he would become normal again.

Roy was Jewish, and, when he first came to the club, one of the things that could upset him was someone referring to his Jewish identity, even though the reference would be positive. Indeed, some of his swearing consisted of anti-Semitic epithets he would use about himself or hurl into the air. It seemed obvious that he had learned his Jewishness was a liability. But, as Carolyn remarked, he seemed also to have a kind of innocence with regard to the abusive language he used, and some of it was directed to people he liked. A rabbi and his wife, Albert and Shirley, visited Daybreak periodically. Kathy was with Roy on the lane near the New House the first time that Roy met Albert. Roy asked him, "Are you a dirty rotten Jew like me?" When Albert affirmed that he was, they both laughed, and they became friends. Shirley would spend the week with us in the Seniors Club and would have gifts for each of us. One time she brought Roy a pair of small Shabbat candleholders with a Star of David on each. He was quite shy about receiving these but was also clearly touched and pleased. Later, he was happy when a Jewish assistant doing a practicum with us would bring him some of her mother's chicken soup with matzah balls or potato latkes. After that, we made matzah ball soup for him sometimes as a lunchtime treat.

Once when I was with him, an older gentleman for whom Roy had held open a door at the mall turned and wished him "Merry Christmas." Roy was hesitant, and I hoped he would not swear. He just laughed. He did not wish people "Merry Christmas." Yet as Deiren, who lived with Roy at the New House, observed, he had a curiosity about Santa Claus, and one time when Deiren returned from taking a group to the Santa Claus parade, Roy asked in all sincerity, "Did you see Santa?"

Roy had long ago thrown away his false teeth, and he had no teeth of his own – a situation that could lead to him choking, especially as he tended to gulp down his food. We assistants had all taken CPR and first aid training. The only time I used what I learned was in performing the Heimlich manoeuvre on Roy when he was choking on a grape and turning blue. The manoeuvre worked impressively, and the grape sailed right across the room.

As he got into his eighties, Roy probably had a number of ailments that it was not possible to diagnose. Certainly, he was often tired or said he was not feeling well. On one occasion when I was not there, he collapsed while painting banners at the Seniors Club. His heart had stopped. A doctor was volunteering with the club at the time. He quickly began CPR in tandem with one of the house assistants, while Kathy called 911. Roy revived, and when the ambulance arrived he refused to let the EMR team take him to the hospital.

In November 1999, at the age of eighty-six, Roy died quietly in his bed at home – surely the way he had wanted. He had not been to the club for some days, and assistants from the club team were spending afternoons with him. He might do a little painting and then rest. By that time, I was only part-time on the Seniors Club team, and Clara, who was at the New House and close to Roy, let me and others know that we might want to visit him soon. I went to see him the evening before he died. When I entered his bedroom, his beloved Clara was sitting with him. He uttered a raspy "Hello, Beth," looking at me with his big dark eyes, and then he drifted off. On his last day, Wendy was there from the club. Roy asked her to take him for a drive. When they returned he was not interested in dinner and wanted only to go to bed. He fell asleep immediately. By this time, his doctor had been visiting Roy once a week, and this was the day for the doctor to come. When he walked in only a few minutes after Roy had gone to sleep, the doctor found Roy had passed away.

Roy's was Daybreak's first Jewish funeral. Joe V., as our lay pastor, solicited the help of a large Jewish funeral home in Toronto, and followed their instructions. We came and went through two nights, keeping vigil with his body. The funeral was in our Meeting Hall, a suitably large setting with no religious symbols or art. Roy looked strikingly dignified in his casket, wearing a blue and white tallit and with his shock of black hair neatly combed (he never went grey). He might almost have been an elderly rabbi. It was strange to see this man who was so animated and who loved so many of us with such exuberant affection so very still now. Of course, all of Daybreak and many former assistants and his caregiver friends from the institution came for his funeral, as did his sister, who used to visit and bring him warm pullovers, and a nephew and grandnephew, who remarked on the many stories that were shared and said they wished that they had known Roy better. The fact was, he could seem quite intimidating, and yet he had such an enormous, welcoming and tender heart. [1]

Annie

Annie (she preferred "Annie" to "Anne") loved to care for people. She was sensitive, tender, and compassionate, and her tears flowed readily for others – and for herself, if she perceived hurt or criticism. But her most striking gift was her sense of humour. Few things went by Annie. If she was near when there was an altercation between others, one could often hear an amusing commentary uttered under her breath. She had lots of "naughty" jokes about bloomers – the loose overpants that schoolgirls had worn when she lived with nuns in England. She enjoyed Roy's colourful language, and she and Roy were close friends. Roy was Ali Bushwah, a name he delighted in, and sometimes she was Annie Bushwah. But she might also call herself any of one hundred and ten other Annie combinations she had invented. (When he was on the club team, Doug kept a list.)

Annie loved to create special names for others as well as for herself. Some rhymed – Dougie-Wouggie, Annie Candy. Some related to a shared experience. When Phil would return on visits, he was Ginger still, and she was Fred to him. (Back in 1979, she and Phil had planned to take a ballroom dancing class, and the names were inspired by Ginger Rogers and Fred Astaire. She liked Fred, so she allocated Ginger to Phil. Though the class was cancelled, she kept the names.) She had three "Big Honeys" – Frankie, as she called Frank Sutton, and Bill Rous, both of whom had died, and David, who still worked in the Woodery. Len, the farm manager, was her Stuffed Bunny, doubtless because when not wearing his farm clothes Len often wore a vest and was a bit portly, surely reminding her of Peter Rabbit. Len liked the appellation, knowing it was a sign of Annie's fondness.

Annie shared Roy's big-heartedness and loved his unconventionality. She often chose to go on the men's outings, including fishing days with Roy and Lloyd. She also knew how to be proper, and she liked to visit her sisters, who lived in an upper-class Toronto neighbourhood, but she never embraced propriety. To many assistants who recognized her enjoyment of being British and her love for the royal family, she was Queen Anne. For her eightieth birthday, Church Street held a "Royal Garden Party," to which all the female guests were asked to wear outlandish hats. For the invitation one of the assistants drew a cartoon of her on a throne holding a sign that said, "Buckingham Palace or Bust," and two young pages standing holding a tray with a cup of tea to welcome her.

Annie died in October 2005. She had become shorter of breath as she developed congestive heart failure. She was on oxygen for a while in hospital and then in a local nursing home for her last few months.

Francis

Francis had slowed down and mellowed over the years since I had lived with him at the Green House. He was less likely to be preoccupied with his own needs and had become more peaceful. Lloyd's death was a shock for him especially, as they had lived together almost all of their years at Daybreak, but he was no longer dependent on Lloyd to follow him around and affirm him. When he moved to the Red House, he was important as a founding member and the eldest in the house. He was also happy to again receive

Michael's appreciative friendship. He saw his girlfriend Linda twice a week, when she came for dinner and when he went to Church Street, where she had come to live. His kindliness had come more to the surface. He did not need to compete with anyone either in the Club or at home in the Red House, where he sat at the head of the table and commanded the respect of the younger members of the household.

Francis had long dreamed of having his own workbench, which he had now in the garage of the Red House. There he could use the new drill that Linda's mother had given him, and he could hammer nails into boards and make crosses and trivets. He had been recognized in various ways. For instance, he had been featured twice in books by Irene Borins Ash, who was interested in portraying seniors still active in their eighties. I took him to the second book launch, where we met the jazz musician Oscar Peterson, another active octogenarian at that time.

During 2010, Francis had a bout of pneumonia and eventually went into long-term care. He knew his eighty-eightieth birthday was coming, and he seemed to be hanging on for it. He was in isolation until October 22, the day before his birthday. The next day he was able to go to the cafeteria for breakfast, and all the people there sang him "Happy Birthday." Mary Bastedo and Ann P. and I gathered at his bedside, he opened some gifts, and later he was able to go to the Mass in the nursing home. He lived just a few more days and died peacefully in his sleep, shortly after Wendy had come to anoint him.

There were some lovely tributes to Francis at his funeral, but for me the most memorable moment came as the recessional "hymn" started and several Knights of Columbus, dressed in their full ermine-trimmed regalia, rose from their seats and lined both sides of the aisle to form an honour guard, as was their custom at funerals for their members. The recessional was "Happy Trails," Francis's favourite song from the Roy Rogers movies. The procession out of the church was led by the altar servers, all Daybreak core members. At the head of the procession was a petite woman singing full throttle and a bit off-key. Then came Linda on Ann's arm weeping profusely, the pallbearers with the casket, and the celebrant. Francis would have loved it all. (As for Linda, she grieved for a while but recovered well and is happy. She says she will not have another boyfriend. "Francis was my one best boyfriend," she explains cheerfully.)

Peggy

Peggy was usually quite proper – Henri referred to her as the "grande dame of Daybreak" – but she could enjoy improper jokes and could laugh until the tears streamed down her cheeks. Peggy, like Annie, came from a privileged background. (In Toronto, their families knew each other, and it was Peggy's family who told Annie's father about Daybreak.) Peggy always chose to wear dresses – a clean one for each day of the week. She washed and took care of them herself. She had attended a private boarding school away from Toronto during World War II, and she had learned to read fairly well. She could also count out change and write her own withdrawal slips at the bank. She long subscribed to the *Globe and Mail*. She kept up to date with the Toronto sports teams, and she liked to know what was going on in the world. Not surprisingly, she voted in elections.[2]

Like Annie, Peggy was a royalist and could spend hours looking through magazines on the royals, and she rose very early to watch televised royal weddings. When Prince Andrew was studying in Canada, he stopped in at a Daybreak coffee house one evening. Peggy helped to welcome him, and she never forgot that special moment.

Peggy loved to swim and went regularly to the local pool with Julia. As she aged, Peggy could not walk well, but swimming probably helped her stay healthy. Towards the end of her life, she relied on a wheelchair and was clearly failing. In early September 2013, she was in hospital for a few days. There was a Tim Hortons on the main floor of the hospital, and the last times I visited her in hospital, she asked for a Tim Hortons cappuccino with lots of whipped cream and, before I left, another one. I would need to hold the cup and spoon for her. Then she moved to a nursing home, where she passed away in her sleep after only a couple of days. When

I visited her there the day before she passed on, she was very quiet. Peggy was a practical person, and I suspect that, once she realized the end of her life was near, she did not want to linger. She died just a few days before her eighty-eighth birthday. Her funeral was in the best Anglican tradition, with hymns she loved and a bagpiper piping the procession into and out of the sanctuary. She had always been proud of her Scottish roots and would have been thrilled.

Thelus

Thelus and Peggy and Wendy lived together with others first at Centre Street and then at the Brookwood house. They were all fond of Wendy's black lab – Kate, it was called. It was the same dog that caught Roy's loaf of bread. In many ways, Kate helped create their sense of family and home. Thelus and Peggy would giggle when the dog got into some food she should not have found, but when the dog ate an entire box of chocolates including the wrappers and became very ill, they were deeply concerned and prayed fervently for her recovery. Each evening Thelus would take Kate upstairs on the elevator, give her a dog biscuit, and tell her to go to bed in Wendy's room.

Thelus had a well-developed sense of occasion and of ceremony and the importance of special roles. My earliest strong memory of Thelus is driving her to Joanne and Allan's wedding, in 1982. Clearly proud to be the maid of honour, Thelus was looking radiant, wearing a beautiful dress and pearls and white gloves. When Henri invited Thelus and Wendy to accompany him to a Quaker college in the United States where he was being given an honorary degree, Thelus was happy to support him by sitting on the stage with other dignitaries.

She was delighted when asked to be godmother for Joe and Stephanie's first child and, later, for Alan and Judy's little daughter, and she was careful to remember the children's birthdays. She developed a strong bond with Rabbi Albert and his wife, Shirley, and, with Wendy, attended their daughter's wedding in Michigan. She loved to celebrate people and to welcome guests. One day when my birthday fell at a time when many Daybreak people were on vacation and I was alone, she and Wendy invited me for dinner at Brookwood, and Thelus proudly presented me with a gift – one of her mugs, decorated with her readily recognizable red, orange, yellow and blue "sunflowers" and with her name signed in her characteristic script. I still prize the mug.[3]

At the club, Thelus always looked neat. Like Peggy and Annie, she regularly had her hair done by a caring hairdresser whose salon was just a short walk along Centre Street. She wanted to have her nails done as well and would ask an assistant to do them for her. Thelus liked to create a homey atmosphere, and her favourite activity, baking, contributed to this. Although she always needed a baking partner, she often claimed she had taught herself how to make whatever it was – cookies or pies most often. Perhaps because she had grown up with younger brothers, she especially liked to look after the young male assistants – Chris, Lorenzo, Alan C., Patrick or whichever young man was on her house team at the time. She would set aside extra cookies for them.

Chris played the guitar and had written a song about another Daybreak member. Thelus asked him to write a song about her. After some thought, Chris decided that the song should be in Thelus' own words and should be about Thelus's weekly routine, which she would recite at house meetings. The song's title and refrain was, "Thursdays, I do my laundry." She was delighted with the song – *her* song. He sang it often at her request and, for the last time, at her funeral.

Thelus was short and slight – factors that no doubt contributed to her developing osteoporosis and her spine becoming very bent. After she broke her hip badly she was no longer able to walk. She spent her last years in a nursing home that was just a stone's throw from Daybreak. There, Thelus continued to bake weekly for some time with her faithful friend Marion, using the small kitchenette, and she continued to touch hearts with her smile and her "thank you, doll.")

For her first years in the nursing home, someone on the Brookwood House team would pick her up in the wheelchair van to attend community events and for Sunday dinner at the house, but eventually her bones became too brittle for her to be transported. She kept hoping she could go home for her ninetieth birthday, but it was not to be. Nevertheless, she celebrated this birthday in the nursing home lounge, surrounded by her nephew and her closest friends.

Thelus weighed less than sixty pounds when she passed on quietly one night a few months later, Warren (another Daybreak member) at her bedside. While her physical body got smaller her spirit continued to shine brightly. She always found energy to smile brightly and connect with others, whether a Daybreak visitor or her new handsome male nurse.

As with each of the seniors' visitations and funerals, at Thelus's, many stories were shared, memories of humorous and touching moments and ways that Thelus had blessed our lives with her friendship and care, and inspired us with her determination, her pride, and her appreciation of beauty. Thelus is buried near Henri and Bill V. and Rose and some of the other Daybreak "saints." As is our custom, after her gravestone was in place, a number of us who were close to Thelus gathered in the cemetery to bless her grave.

16. Drawing the Threads Together

None of us knows what to do with the deep brokenness of our world. Maybe that realization can bring us back to community. We can do nothing on our own. We need somewhere to be together. Jean Vanier

In 1981, when I first came to L'Arche, I was searching for a place to put down roots, make a contribution, and live a meaningful life. I was deeply touched and changed by coming to know people in my home as friends, and I had a growing sense of the meaning in what we were doing as assistants.

This sense was nourished for me and others by the trustful sharing at Tuesday Morning Meetings. We were all being transformed by our life together. And we could see that our community was indeed a sign of hope to families and many others, even to government representatives who came to inspect our kitchens and paperwork.

The people who were less strong in their intellect – people who often had suffered in ways that we who did not have such disabilities were unlikely ever to suffer – had gifts of acceptance and of welcome that were unique. They brought us out of ourselves to engage and to laugh together, to celebrate, and to empathize with one another. Thus, they created the sense of community that is particular to L'Arche. But they could bring these gifts only if there were others to support them and to recognize and receive their gifts. There was – and still is today – a spirit of fun in the community. It is dependent not on sophisticated jokes but on simple things – Lloyd chasing Phil with a bucket of water, Peter flicking his tea towel in jest at Annette or whoever was washing up the pots after dinner. (He knew well that he was supposed to be drying, but he invariably managed to delay or avoid this task.)

I was initially attracted to L'Arche because it was a faith-based community engaged in a work of social justice. At Saint-Malachie,

I was humbled and redirected inward by my personal experience of emptiness. This and many other experiences have borne out the truth to which Phil alluded early on, that L'Arche is a mixture of comfort and challenge. To find myself, in the language of the Beatitudes, "poor in spirit" was unfamiliar but freeing. Over the years, I have indeed found this state to be a source of blessing, a door to greater inner freedom. As Jean Vanier has often remarked, L'Arche is founded on the Beatitudes.

I went to L'Arche Le Printemps intending to spend a year and perhaps much longer, but in fact, in the grand scheme of things, it seemed I went so that I could discover that I *belonged* at Daybreak. I loved the people and the simplicity of life at Le Printemps, but it was at Daybreak that I could put down roots and be fruitful. Being called to responsibility for the community by serving on the Daybreak Council and later on the administrative team deepened my sense of belonging. An added gift of my time in Saint-Malachie was the friendship across cultural and linguistic differences that our two communities came to share.

I discovered my vocation in L'Arche – not right away but gradually. I came a rather shy person. Community life lightened me up. I grew in willingness to lead. I enjoyed the fun, and I shed some of my reserve, becoming a little more outgoing and even able to create moments of levity. My sense of belonging grew through such moments. In a truly welcoming setting, people can experience inner healing, discover their gifts, and grow into their full humanity. I came to understand this as the essence of the therapy of L'Arche, and that it is a therapy not only for the core members. Many assistants who have passed through L'Arche would say they also have experienced the healing and transformation that can come from being welcomed and valued simply for who they are and not for what they know or can do.

The spirituality of L'Arche suited me well. Rooted in daily life and without creedal emphasis, it is simple, non-judgmental, broad, and flexible. The life of an assistant in a L'Arche home lends itself to the teaching of Saint Thérèse of Lisieux – to do small things well and with love. In my early years in a L'Arche house, I found meaning in this spirituality. I was also drawn to the writings of the monk Thomas Merton, because of his interest in Eastern meditation. I would take a little time each day simply to sit before an icon and try to be present to God. Friends gave me subscriptions to *Continuum,* a liberal Catholic magazine, and to the *New Oxford Review,* a conservative one, and accompanying Ellen to the synagogue led me into interfaith friendships and increased my knowledge of modern Judaism.

Gradually, I became hungry for more intellectual nourishment, and I found this in conversations with Henri and some others and in studying theology. As for my childhood trust in the Twenty-third Psalm, I have spent good amounts of time in "green pastures" and have often experienced my soul being restored, usually by an interaction with a core member, when I was tired or discouraged. I did approach "want" briefly when, in late 1996, my three-year house-sitting arrangement ended and I discovered my assistant's pay was not enough for even a grubby welfare apartment. I thought I might need to quickly find a teaching job, but Paula, then acting community leader, raised my salary so that I was able to rent a small but quite acceptable walk-out basement apartment. (Eventually, L'Arche Canada put in place a standard salary grid that raised the salaries of all assistants.)

ॐ

To make his point that forgiveness and celebration are essential to any community, Jean Vanier uses the model of a triangle with forgiveness the base and celebration the apex. It is not possible to truly celebrate even a nice meal if people around the table are holding grudges against one another. In day-to-day life in a L'Arche home, there can be constant irritants – someone leaves dirty dishes in the sink yet again, someone neglects to pass on a message, someone is late or noisy. Clear, direct, respectful communication is essential if difficulties are to be worked through. Once they are, a new lightness can be felt throughout a household, or a community. This is why accompaniment and house and team meetings are so important. If disagreements are not well addressed and people complain behind an individual's back, or if people feel they are not listened to, situations can fester. Sometimes people leave upset, and the whole body feels the wound and loss.

I am thankful that this has not happened very often in my experience. However, I think of the meeting in which some of us spoke up defending Ellen's place in the community. If Ellen had nevertheless been pushed out of the community, would I have lost my trust in the community and left? I don't know. For sure, I would have raised as much fuss as I could. That would have been my duty, given the knowledge of Ellen that I had. As it turned out, with good support Ellen got her bearings and we could all celebrate her staying.

There were odd occasions when I myself did not feel well supported. In such situations I usually found it was best, after speaking about it, to give the other person the benefit of the doubt. There were also at least a couple of situations when assistants felt I expected too much or was not supportive enough. When they spoke up, it helped me to see my expectation from their perspective. We could then resolve the tension and move on.

∽◦∾

As the huge institutions began to close, people with disabilities became more visible and a new understanding of them as contributing citizens was beginning to emerge. While previously not wanting to attract the attention of those who might see some L'Arche members as curiosities, in this new climate and encouraged by Henri Nouwen, L'Arche was eager to share the stories of its members or to help others do this wherever possible. My work with young assistants who were touched by the people with whom they lived increased my passion to spread the message of Jean Vanier and L'Arche.

When, in 2001, I began to work with Nathan on the newly created L'Arche Canada Foundation, this outwardly directed work amounted to my finding a second, deeply satisfying vocation within L'Arche – one which resonated with my desire to write but which I could not have pursued without the many years I had spent immersed in the daily life of L'Arche Daybreak and without my ongoing contact with Red House friends and a few others, including Ellen and Mel. My focus continued to be on making the vision and values of L'Arche better known, especially to educators and to young people. Still today, the metal horn player I was given in 1984, with the call to recruit and care for assistants, occupies a place of honour in my apartment.

One of our first initiatives was a small, free e-quarterly, which we called *A Human Future: A Thought Sheet for Canadians*. In it, we sought to put the values and vision of L'Arche in dialogue with some of Canada's best thinkers on what makes for a healthy society. The time was soon after the 9/11 attacks, and our first issue was titled "Welcoming the 'Other'." Philip Coulter of CBC Radio's *Ideas* program, who had produced Jean Vanier's Massey Lectures and other programs on L'Arche, kindly helped me hone interview questions for the likes of physicist and social justice advocate Ursula Franklin, writer Margaret Atwood, Mayor Naheed Nenshi of Calgary, and Truth and Reconciliation Commissioner Marie Wilson. The thought sheet developed a wide readership over its seventeen years.

As the foundation shifted to focus solely on fundraising, my work moved under the umbrella of L'Arche Canada. Besides performing some communications tasks, I collaborated with Toronto educator and student leadership head Greg Rogers on writing educational materials that related L'Arche best practices to high school social studies and college social services programs. Our resources, which address the Inclusion, Diversity and Equity agendas of provincial ministries of education and were often bilingual, have proved popular with educators. What was important to me was that they broke through stereotypes and revealed that in many ways people with and without disabilities are very similar. In most of our video content, people with disabilities speak for themselves.

Government of Canada grants helped me carry out two major projects. One, a best practices book of stories about the contributions of people in L'Arche communities across Canada, allowed me to visit many of the then twenty-six Canadian communities. The second was our interactive website to help people with disabilities form lasting friendships. Amanda and Robin from Daybreak are among those who contributed stories or videos for it. Two years later, a series of donated magazine and bus ads complemented this project. Conceived by John O'Donnell, each showed two people, one with a disability, enjoying some activity together – biking, cooking, dining out, shopping. Under each picture was the word *With* in a bold font. The ads conveyed that doing something with a person who might seem very different can be enjoyable, and the brief text suggested this can also help change our world for the better. Daybreak photographers Warren Pot and Tomek Sewilski took most of the pictures for the ads.

For senior secondary dance students, in collaboration with Partners for Planning we wrote study guides for videos on learning to dance with a young woman dancer who uses a wheelchair and communicates only by facial gestures. My final educational project, *Pareil pas pareil* (Alike, yet not alike), was a collaboration with L'Arche in Quebec, a multi-level, bilingual resource based on a video in which several core members speak candidly about their lives, their limitations, their abilities and their interests. I think our work on these resources has helped students and teachers shed some of their stereotypes and contributed to integration. [1]

~∞~

Personal and societal transformation happen mainly in the nitty-gritty of daily life. In a way, this is a humbling experience. When I look back over the years, I see how my life has been shaped by the people I came to know well – Michael, with whom I have shared a friendship from my earliest days; Gord, who prayed for all of us; Helen, of whose fierce love I was occasionally the recipient; Anne Marie, who challenged me to see that she had the right to make her own decisions; Ellen, who claimed her spiritual identity, and all of the seniors, especially Roy and Annie, who lived with such delight, and Lloyd and George, who cared deeply for me. In particular, I realize how formative has been Michael's influence to my understanding of L'Arche. He can have dreams, yet somehow, he manages to hold the dream and the reality in balance, and most days he finds something to be enthusiastic about. I came to L'Arche with dreams of contributing to a better world, and I have never lost these, yet the day-to-day may consist of helping someone with laundry or with a phone call, shopping together, celebrating a birthday, and grieving when someone leaves or dies.

Of course, like others, I have needed to find a balance in my personal life. I have made some good friends over the years. I take time to meditate, and one of my great pleasures is spending time in nature. When Kathy and Joe came to Daybreak, they introduced several of us assistants to kayaking. For twenty summers now, I have participated in kayaking retreats and trips on Georgian Bay.

Many young assistants have passed through the community, and many core members have died. Often it was as though their lives flared forth most brightly with their deaths, like stars at their end, streaking across the sky. So many people come to Daybreak funerals — family and church and community members, friends and volunteers, townspeople, and people even from across the seas. Very often, former assistants return for funerals of people they lived with or came to know well. They come because their lives were set on a new course by their sharing life with this particular member, whose gift of friendship, or whose embracing of life and living it creatively within the given limitations, gave the assistants pause to reflect. Those who come and those who are still here tell stories and look at old photo albums and keepsakes and express their gratitude for knowing the individual and for the ways they were blessed or transformed through the friendship they shared. They speak about feeling loved unreservedly, going on a trip together, gaining self-confidence, learning practical skills, discovering their gifts, and becoming caring spouses and parents. They speak of finding joy and learning to keep their hearts open, as Gord so often prayed. While some found their vocation or career direction through L'Arche, I think all would say their hearts grew larger and more tender.

Epilogue: Change and Continuation

Over the years, there have been changes to our structures and ways of doing things in L'Arche, but little change in the community spirit in which we share our lives. Recent government legislation concerning the amount of time that assistants can be "working" in their homes led us to name the essential elements of our community life. We identified three – eating together, praying together, and celebrating together. At Daybreak, Carl has retired after leading the community for thirteen years, and we have a new community leader – Trish Glennon, who came from Marquette University some years ago – and a new mandate, the same mandate that L'Arche around the world has adopted. It focuses on claiming more deeply the fundamental principles and values of L'Arche, getting more involved in the wider society, and strengthening the International Federation of L'Arche. Today there are thirty-one L'Arche communities in Canada and more than 150 around the world.

Of course, change has characterized our individual lives. Of the core members I lived with at the Green House, only Michael is still alive. I now see him a couple of times a week at the Red House, but he has not been able to visit me since he was hospitalized with a serious bout of pneumonia this past August of 2018. He is not bouncing back, and he has new limitations to his mobility and even in eating, as he has difficulty swallowing. Nevertheless, his interests and his personality have not changed.

Of those I lived with at Church Street, Gord has developed Alzheimer's disease and has some significant medical needs. He is living at the nursing home near Daybreak where Thelus lived. Anne Marie continues to live at Church Street and to work at ARC. Recently, Anne Marie had cancer surgery and, as I write, she is going through treatments. Despite her anxiety, she has been coping well day by day. She and I try to go out for tea every couple of weeks.

Ellen and David and John B., all now retired, spend some time at the club each week. Ellen still comes for dinner at my apartment. She is completing her life story book with the help of Toni. Linda, Francis's girlfriend, works part-time in the Woodery and in the Daybreak office, helping Khalida, and she also spends time at the club. If she is in the office when I drop in, I am often blessed with her loud and cheery cry, *"There's my lovey-dovey girl, Beth!"* She offers the same greeting to several other women. Men get *"There's my wonderful good man!"*

Every Friday noon, the present Woodery crew still eat at the local hamburger and falafel place, and former workers and a few others of us come along: Kathy, Joe, Jim, Mary Bastedo, and sometimes, Warren and Carl. Periodically, Joe and Mary Egan bring David. It is a great time to re-connect. Rob and Rhona and Philippe, of the group that used to accompany Peter to the pub, sometimes still gather there after Friday worship, now with other younger core members.

I and others in my age group have seen a whole generation of assistants marry and raise their children in L'Arche, and now a new generation is beginning families. Of those who left Daybreak, many entered the fields of health care and pastoral care or the social services. They work for affordable housing for those who are most marginal, they direct the United Way in their city, they care for the dying, they are chaplains and pastors or priests, nurses and occupational therapists, teachers and social workers and social service administrators.

Some stayed in L'Arche but went to other communities. Among those who figure prominently in certain chapters of this book, Gus and Debbie Leuschner and family moved to Nova Scotia, where Gus was community leader of L'Arche Antigonish for many years. Nathan Ball and Paula Kilcoyne and their family moved to the United States, where Paula is community leader of L'Arche St. Louis and Nathan works with L'Arche USA. The Wiebe family moved to L'Arche Lethbridge, where Doug was community leader for three terms. John Guido is working with L'Arche Canada. Joe Egan is organizing the L'Arche Canada archives.

The beautiful, still new-seeming Dayspring chapel building is well used. Clara leads the student retreat days with Amanda and other core members. Liska, also a former house assistant, became an Anglican priest and is our pastor, with Wendy, who is retired, sometimes filling in. There is a strong music group for Friday evening worship. We continue to alternate Anglican, Roman Catholic, Protestant (United Church of Canada) services and Taizé prayer.

As I write this, Jean Vanier has recently celebrated his ninetieth birthday and the publication of his latest book, *A Cry is Heard*. He has received many awards and honorary degrees. In 2015, he was awarded the Templeton Prize "for his innovative discovery of the central role of vulnerable people in the creation of a more just, inclusive and humane society." Always he receives these awards and honours in the name of the people of L'Arche. Since having a heart attack in the autumn of 2017, Jean has had to slow down. Two or three times a year, he continues to write a quite lovely letter to all the communities of L'Arche and Faith and Light. Jean's recent letters can be found on the website, http://www.jean-vanier.org/en. In 2007, his letters from 1964 to May 2007 were published as *Jean Vanier: Our Life Together – A Memoir in Letters*. The year 2019 marks the fifty-fifth anniversary of the founding of the first L'Arche community, by Jean in France, and the fiftieth anniversary of L'Arche Daybreak, and thus, of the founding of L'Arche in Canada.

Notes

Introduction
The epigraph is from Jean Vanier, *Made for Happiness* (Darton, Longman and Todd and House of Anansi Press, 2001).
[1] Adapted from Steve Mosher's eulogy at George's funeral (October 27, 1998).
[2] For more information on communities, see the website of the international Fellowship for Intentional Community: https://www.ic.org. Religious communities have their own websites. The website of L'Arche Canada is https://www.larche.ca. In the USA, it is https://www.larcheusa.org; in the United Kingdom it is https://www.larche.org.uk; and internationally, https://www.larche.org.

1. Labour Day[1] 1980
The epigraph is from Jean Vanier, *Becoming Human*, [the 1998 CBC Massey Lectures] (Darton, Longman and Todd, and House of Anansi Press, 1998).
Thank you to Ann and Steve Newroth, Joe Egan, Jo Cork, and Hope Montess for certain details or suggestions related to this chapter.
[1] In North America, Labour Day is the first Monday in September.
[2] Our Lady's Missionaries, the nuns who gave the property for a L'Arche community to be established, are based in Toronto. They are concerned with social justice and reach out to the poor locally and abroad. The Basilian Fathers, who had at one time owned the entire property, leased their 120 acres of farmland to Daybreak. The land on which L'Arche Daybreak and Richmond Hill itself are located is the traditional territory of the Huron-Wendat, the Anishnaabeg, Haudenosaunee, Métis, and the Mississaugas of the New Credit First Nation. This territory is covered by the Dish with One Spoon Treaty and the Toronto Purchase. L'Arche Daybreak recognizes the enduring presence of Indigenous peoples connected to this land.

2. The Crash Pad
The epigraph is from Jean Vanier, *Becoming Human* (Darton, Longman and Todd, and House of Anansi Press, 1998).
Thank you to Ann and Steve Newroth, Joe Egan, David, Greg, Jane Powell, and Marilyn Logan for some details or suggestions related to this chapter.
[1] Steve was able to obtain some provincial government funding from the beginning, but L'Arche in Canada and elsewhere has always needed also to raise funds. This is largely because it provides a higher ratio of assistants to core members and more opportunities for core members than the government pays for.
[2] Alberta was the last province to abandon such a policy. The Sexual Sterilization Act of Alberta was repealed in 1972.

[3] The experiences of people who lived in institutions, some of whom now live in L'Arche, led L'Arche Toronto's *Sol Express* arts and drama group to create a play about the plight of people who were institutionalized. The play, titled *Birds make me think about Freedom*, won a Patrons' Pick Award at Toronto's 2018 Fringe Festival.

3. "You and your husband can come in"

The epigraph is from Jean Vanier, *Community and Growth*, rev. ed. (Darton, Longman and Todd, and Paulist Press, 1989).

Thank you to Carlene Danes and Joe Egan for current information on orientation and membership, and to Annette Chisholm and Sue Mosteller for some details or suggestions related to this chapter.

[1] New assistants were given time to get to know the core members, before learning their medical histories. The intention was to avoid creating a medical or psychiatric lens through which the assistant would always then tend to view the core member. Still today, L'Arche tries to follow this policy, though essential training is given immediately, during an orientation week.

[2] Jean Vanier mentions the challenge of trying to welcome such people in the first edition of *Community and Growth*, and in the revised edition, he writes more explicitly about the sense of failure and guilt a community can feel when they are unable to keep someone: "Marginal people in a community have very particular needs…. They can be buffeted by terrible anguish, which drives them to attack others or themselves in ways that even they cannot understand…. Sometimes a community feels guilty when it is not able to keep the person. They feel they have failed. But there is no community that can save everybody." (pp. 275, 278).

[3] Bill Clarke, SJ, wrote an early book, *Enough Room for Joy*, (Novalis, rev. ed., 2007), about the nearly three years he spent living in L'Arche in France when he was a newly-ordained Jesuit. Likely the informality of not often using religious titles such as "Father" or "Sister" is an effect of having priests and sisters live with us as assistants in our homes, and maybe also it is a legacy of the somewhat hippie roots of L'Arche. In any case, priests who come to L'Arche often ask us to drop their title.

[4] Still today, after three months, and then annually for several years, assistants are invited to a review designed to help them decide whether they want to stay. Principles of servant leadership guide these reviews. Membership in the community has four phases, stretched over a number of years. Orientation and "formation" – another French word – are provided for both assistants and core members. Orientation themes are similar: helping with house chores, coming together for a well-prepared dinnertime and prayer, communicating as clearly as possible… Formation has to do with understanding the values and vision of L'Arche. In addition, some core members and assistants may seek spiritual accompaniment. It is often noted that in any given L'Arche house or program there will be someone whom we love spending time with and someone who is the last person on earth we would choose to be with, and it is from the latter person that we stand to learn the most. However, it can be difficult to see what that precious learning might be. Talking to a wise guide outside the situation

can help. I have long been grateful for Bill Clarke's counsel through the ups and downs and occasional crises of my life in L'Arche.

4. "Nice day, eh?"
The epigraph is from Jean Vanier, *Becoming Human* (Darton, Longman and Todd, and House of Anansi Press, 1989).
Thank you to Jim Russell, Jo Cork, Carmen Ellis, Joe Egan, and Jane and Tom Sagar for certain details or suggestions related to this chapter.
[1] "There must never be talk, either open or hidden, against a brother or a sister, against their individual characteristics – under no circumstances behind their back. Without the commandment of silence there is no faithfulness and thus no community. The only possible way is direct address … [It] brings a deepening of friendship and it is not resented." (From a 1925 document by Eberhard Arnold, quoted in a book by him, and in a blog by Dori Moody on the contemporary Bruderhof website: https://www.bruderhof.com/en/voices-blog/life-in-community/shelve-the-gossip.)
[2] Two years later, when they had had their first child, Joan and Robin began welcoming an "Agape" group of a few Green House people for periodic dinners in their Toronto apartment. These intimate groups of present and former community members helped maintain friendships and broaden our social circle. Peter would be beside himself with excitement to see Joan again, and everyone, myself included, would enjoy the evening.
[3] While there have been many marriages of L'Arche assistants over the years, Joanne and Allan's was the only marriage of Daybreak core members. This is probably because L'Arche wants to offer a home for life and has tended to welcome people who need more support rather than those who could readily master skills of independent living. While L'Arche teaches skills of independence, it values interdependence. Also, especially in earlier days, most families who placed their members at L'Arche probably did not want them to have serious romantic relationships or become sexually active.

5. "Je m'abandonne à toi"
The epigraph is from Jean Vanier, *Becoming Human* (Darton, Longman and Todd, and House of Anansi Press, 1998).
Thank you to Geneviève Montquin for reading this chapter, to Kevin Burns for information about Saint Malachy and to Kevin and Tom Sagar for corrections to the French in this chapter.
[1] *Le Printemps* is French for the season of spring.
[2] Saint Malachy (the English spelling) was an early Cistercian monk. He was eulogized by St. Bernard of Clairvaux as "a mirror and example, [giving] as it were, a relish to the life of men on earth" (from Saint Bernard of Clairvaux, *Life of Saint Malachy of Armagh*, trans., H. J. Lawler [Macmillan, 1920]).
[3] In 2016, when talking with the present community leader, Geneviève Montquin, I learned that, for a recent regional celebration, the Saint-Malachie parishioners had chosen the L'Arche boat logo as one of three symbols to represent the parish's roots and development, the others being the shamrock, representing the Irish, and the fleur-de-lis, representing the French.

[4] Dr. Thérèse Vanier wrote an English version of the Prayer of L'Arche, addressing God the Father instead of Mary, and in the mid-1970s, Brian Halferty, a Canadian who was in L'Arche in Trosly in 1966, and who later lived with his wife, Mary Lou, and infant son in the New House, wrote the music for this version. Other versions are used in L'Arche in India and Africa. Recently a shorter version simply addressing God, has appeared.

[5] Michael Lerner, *Jewish Renewal* (Putnam, 1994), pp. 418–422.

[6] The story of the modular shelving is in L'Arche Canada's best practices book *More than Inclusion: Honouring the Contributions of People with Developmental Disabilities* (pp. 45–47), published in 2005. The book can be accessed on the Resources page of www.larche.ca. In French, the book was published as *L'Envers du monde: Contributions méconnues des personnes ayant une déficience intellectuelle*.

6. "Pzatt!"

The epigraph is from Jean Vanier, *Community and Growth*, rev. ed. (Darton, Longman and Todd, and Paulist Press, 1989).

Thank you to Phil Nazar, Steve Mosher, Kathy Kelly, Clara Fraschetti, Deiren Masterson, Ann Pavilonis, Carl MacMillan, Rob Ens, and Steffen Müller for certain details in this chapter.

7. A Decade of Change and Growth

Thank you to Julie Gittins, Joe Vorstermans, Joe Child, Joe Egan, Mary Bastedo, Ann Pavilonis, Zenia Kushpeta, Sue Mosteller, and Caroline Hughey (neé Lomas) for providing certain details in this chapter.

[1] A Snoezlen room blocks out noise and bright lighting and provides a multisensory experience that is soothing and stimulating and promotes a feeling of well-being. It can be a helpful therapy for people who have intellectual disabilities, autism, post-traumatic stress, and dementia.

[2] Henri Nouwen's book *Adam: God's Beloved* (Darton, Longman and Todd, and Orbis, 1997) was completed by Sue Mosteller and published posthumously. Of being Adam's student, Henri wrote, "Was he some special angel? Not at all. Adam was one person among many others. But I had a relationship with Adam, and he became special to me. I loved him and our relationship was one of the most significant of my life. Adam's death touched me deeply because for me he was the one who more than any book or professor led me to the person of Jesus" (p. 16).

[3] Faith and Light, co-founded in 1971 by Jean Vanier and Marie-Hélène Mathieu, is an international support network of non-residential communities of families and friends of people who have an intellectual disability. Its website is https://www.faithandlight.org.

[4] Of course, "being with" is exactly what L'Arche is about. Sue Mosteller recounts this story about David and Joe in her book *Body Broken, Body Blessed* (Novalis, 1996); later published as *A Place to Hold My Shaky Heart* (Crossroad, 1998).

8. "Tell me, which one is which"

The epigraph is from Jean Vanier, *Becoming Human* (Darton, Longman and Todd, and House of Anansi Press, 1998).

Thank you to Anne Marie, Carmen Ellis, Colleen O'Loan O'Neill, John O'Donnell, Julie Gittins, Joe Egan, Sue Mosteller, Steve Mosher, Carl MacMillan, John Guido, Sharon Mayne, Marysia Tarlowska, Lola Pickard, Kathy Kelly, and Kathy Baroody for contributing stories or clarifying details in this chapter.

¹ Refrain of the song "I Come Like a Beggar" (Sydney Carter, 1915–2004), © 1974 Stainer & Bell Ltd, 23 Gruneissen Road, London N3 1DZ, England, www.stainer.co.uk is used by permission. All rights reserved.

² Jean Vanier passed the international leadership of L'Arche to Sue Mosteller in 1975. She worked with two francophone coordinators, Alain Saint Macaray and Hubert Allier. During Sue's ten-year tenure, the number of L'Arche communities around the world nearly doubled, to sixty-two. Joe Egan worked with Claire de Mirabel. During their tenure L'Arche continued to grow, and it developed stronger structures.

³ A few years later, the slogan "One Heart at a Time" was chosen as the title of Daybreak's twenty-fifth anniversary theatre gala, written and produced by Robert Morgan and David Craig of Roseneath Theatre. The theme song was "You can change the world with love, one heart at a time."

⁴ Gord visited the Bromhead family, who had come to know him when they lived for a time in the Big House in the 1970s. They carried L'Arche back to Australia, founding the first community there. Their son Michael returned to Daybreak as an assistant in the mid-eighties.

⁵ One of the challenges of living the busy life of a L'Arche home was to stay up-to-date with what is going on in the rest of the world. I would try to read George's *Toronto Star*.

⁶ L'Arche Bethany did have to close. Two years later, Kathy Baroody, a member of L'Arche Toronto who had been one of the initial Bethany assistants, returned in order to maintain the relationship between the International Federation of L'Arche and the members who had been in L'Arche Bethany and to support the founding of a new community in Bethlehem. It is led by Mahera Nassar Ghareeb, a Palestinian woman. Its workshop creates felted nativity scenes and other items from the wool of local sheep.

⁷ When I later worked with L'Arche Canada, we built an interactive bilingual website (www.ibelong.ca or www.jai-des-amis.ca) to help young adults with intellectual disabilities learn the skills of friendship.

9. "Just gig-nore him"

The epigraph is from Jean Vanier, *Community and Growth* (Darton, Longman and Todd, and Griffin House, 1979).

Thank you to Ann and Steve Newroth, Sue Mosteller, Lillian Lowens, Carmen Ellis, Julie Gittins, Joanne Shaughnessy, Carl MacMillan, John Guido, and Joe Egan for contributing stories or clarifying details in this chapter.

¹Jean Vanier, *I Meet Jesus: He Tells Me "I love you"* (Paulist Press, reissued 2014). Helen's favourite reading was on page 6. Quoted with permission.

² People who have Down syndrome sometimes have difficulty with depth perception. Looking down from heights and descending stairs can be challenging for them.

10. "Hey! Hello!"

The epigraph is from Jean Vanier, *Community and Growth*, rev. ed. (Darton, Longman and Todd, and Paulist Press, 1989).

Thank you to John Guido, Carl MacMillan, Steve Mosher, Joe Vorstermans, Joe Child, Jeff Gilbreath, Anjali Joseph, and George's nephew, John, for contributing stories or confirming details in this chapter, and to Jim McCall and Susan S.M. Brown, who made suggestions for an earlier version of this chapter.

[1] Steve Mosher provided text about George's importance at the Mahlers hockey games. The Gustav Mahlers team was formed by a group of students at the Royal Conservatory of Music in Toronto in 1974. Gradually, the team members moved or their lives changed. When they disbanded, only three of the team were working as musicians.

[2] This brief story was one of the weekly short vignettes–L'Arche e-stories, we called them– that Carl MacMillan contributed during the years that L'Arche Canada offered these.

[3] Dr. Ralph Pohlman's column, titled "Big George," appeared in the November 13, 1998, *Toronto Sun*.

11. "Mistah Henri"

The epigraph is from Jean Vanier, *The Heart of L'Arche* (Novalis, 2012).

Thank you to Kevin Burns, Sue Mosteller, Joe Egan, John O'Donnell, Mary Bastedo, Wendy Lywood, and Carl MacMillan for suggestions and some details in this chapter.

[1] *The Return of the Prodigal Son: A Meditation on Fathers, Brothers and Sons* (Darton, Longman and Todd, and Doubleday, 1992). Besides maintaining an extensive ministry, Henri wrote more than forty books, several of them during his years at Daybreak. Most have been translated into a number of languages. Sue Mosteller found herself unexpectedly the literary executor of his estate when he died. With others, she formed the Henri Nouwen Society, and later the Henri Nouwen Trust. Still today, new books about Henri are published every year. The Henri Nouwen Society is the best resource for all films and publications by or about Henri (https://henrinouwen.org). The Henri Nouwen Archive is located in the Kelly Library, University of St. Michael's College, Toronto. Now retired, Sue continues to travel and speak about L'Arche and the spirituality of Henri Nouwen.

[2] Henri J. M. Nouwen, *Love in a Fearful Land* (Orbis, 1987).

[3] Nathan Ball was Daybreak's community leader through most of the 1990s. He was somewhat of a mentor to me in the later 1990s and 2000s. In 1999, he arranged that I be given time away from the Seniors Club to respond to a request from Sue Mosteller and the Henri Nouwen Society to work on an anthology of essays about Henri for the fifth anniversary of his death. (The resulting book, *Befriending Life: Encounters with Henri Nouwen*, eds. Beth Porter, Susan M. S. Brown, and Philip Coulter, was published by Darton, Longman and Todd, and Doubleday, in 2001.)

[4] We replaced "ransom captive Israel" with "...ransom *all* (or *us*) *who on the earth do dwell.*" And in the refrain, we replaced, "Rejoice! Rejoice! O Israel," with "Rejoice! Rejoice! *Good news the prophets tell.*"

[5] After the opening of the new Dayspring in 1999, the bungalow became the Cedars retreat house. It was renovated to be fully accessible and to offer more bedrooms and a small prayer room. The library containing many of Henri's books is still there. Henri's bedroom is now one of the retreatant bedrooms. On its wall is a small picture of Henri and a quotation from one of his books exhorting the reader to "Love Deeply." Visitors who have been helped by his writings come from around the world to visit Henri's grave and to see where he lived, and sometimes they ask to stay in his room.

12. "Mazel Tov!"

Portions of this chapter originally appeared in my 1998 *Journal of Pastoral Care* article, "L'Arche Daybreak: An Example of Interfaith Ministry among People with Developmental Disabilities" 52, no. 2 (Summer 1998): 157 – 165.

Thank you to Joe Child, Toni Urbanski, Claire Weinstein, Julie Malichen-Snyder, John Guido, Steve Mosher, Rhona and Ben Carniol, Otto Baruch Rand, Robert Morgan, and Jennifer Day for corrections and some details in this chapter.

[1] During my studies I discovered that in 1987 the Canadian bishops had published a special edition of "The Passion Narratives for Holy Week." In accord with Vatican documents issued after Vatican II, the bishops recommended changing "the Jews" to "the Jewish authorities" when such texts are read during worship. At Daybreak, we have long followed this practice, substituting also "the crowd" or "the people" for "the Jews." (The texts are still problematic, of course, having been written long after Jesus' death and almost certainly shaped in a manner not to alienate the Roman rulers of the day.)

[2] The *Torah* scroll contains the first five books of the Bible, known as the Books of Moses.

[3] Daybreak held the large pre-Passover Seders for several years. More recently, as everyone has become older, Ellen's mother or Toni have led smaller Seders. At Rosh Hashanah and Hanukkah, if Ellen is up to coming, she lights the Shabbat candles before the start of our Friday community worship, and one of us assistants helps Ellen speak about the meaning of the festival. At *Rosh Hashanah*, assistants in Ellen's house prepare trays of apple wedges and honey which are offered to all with the wish for a sweet new year. On Friday nights in her home, she lights the Shabbat candles.

[4] When I read this chapter to Ellen, I realized that I had never in the intervening years revisited with her the troubled period of her assessment. Ellen listened carefully and was eager to hear the whole chapter. I think that hearing it together, albeit years later, further deepened our friendship.

[5] Robert first heard this song sung by Dave Van Ronk. It is a variation of a song by George Martin Lane called "The Lone Fishball" (circa 1868). In 1944, Hy Zaret & Lou Singer wrote the version Mel and Robert sang. From: https://genius.com/Dave-van-ronk-one-meatball-lyrics. Helene Blue Musique Ltd has granted permission to reprint the refrain of "One Meatball."

13. My House of Belonging

The epigraph is from Jean Vanier, *The Heart of L'Arche* (Novalis, 2012).

Thank you to Mary Bastedo, Michael Arnett, Rex Arnett, Amanda, John McLean, Steve Knezevic, Trish Glennon, Tanya Brethour, Sharon Karney, Dan Cook, and Anna Maclean for some stories or details in this chapter.

[1] Earlier, when Julie got married, John Guido and Gord travelled to England, and Gord gave a wedding toast. Julie has had a career in social services. In recent years she served on the founding board of L'Arche Manchester. She has returned to visit us every few years.

[2] Often, the shorter-term assistants come from a variety of countries. As I write, in the Red House are assistants from Germany, Korea, Morocco, and the Philippines as well as a long-term assistant from the United States and the three of us long-term Canadian assistants who support the house weekly.

[3] Deuteronomy 30:19.

14. *"How's That, Kathy Kelly?"*

The epigraph is from Jean Vanier's "Transforming our Hearts," statement on winning the Templeton Prize, March 11, 2015, http://www.templetonprize.org/pdfs/2015/20150311-vanier-news-statement.pdf.

Thank you to Carolyn Whitney-Brown, Doug Wiebe, Kathy Kelly, Mary and Joe Egan, for some details in this chapter.

[1] The words and music for the song "Daisy, Daisy," also known as "A Bicycle Built for Two," were written by Henry Dacre in 1892.

[2] L'Arche Daybreak set up some apartments in the early 1990s, all on one floor of a building in Richmond Hill. Kathy headed this project. However, some core members developed significant medical needs and after three years the model proved no longer viable.

[3] Still at that time, leaders were not paid differently from other assistants, though years of service were recognized. This fact allowed for a helpful flexibility in the teams.

[4] When Marcie left at the end of 1995, Paula and then Siobhan led the Spirit Movers for a year or so, after which Kathy took the leadership for several years.

[5] The Daybreak homes in Toronto began to function as a separate community in 1996, when population growth was making commuting to Richmond Hill more and more difficult. John Guido was the first community leader. L'Arche Toronto was officially established in 2005.

[6] After our presentation, I wrote an article about our life story process and the rationale for such life review. It was published in *Journal on Developmental Disabilities* 6, no. 1 (August 1998): 44–59. I said in part, "Literature on healthy aging indicated that life review assists seniors to integrate past positive and negative experiences, and to gain a sense of meaning and ownership for their life journey.... Gero-transcendence, the capacity of older people to move into renewal and transformation, seems to have been achieved to a considerable extent by the seniors at Daybreak through involving themselves in life story work. Peggy's review of her health and personal history led her to decide to have orthopedic surgery, which has greatly increased her mobility and her enjoyment of life. ... At seventy-five, Francis's world is not contracting but expanding" (quoted with permission).

15. "Happy Trails"
The epigraph is from Jean Vanier, *Becoming Human* (Darton, Longman and Todd, and House of Anansi Press, 1998).
Thank you to Wendy Lywood for stories about Thelus, and to Carolyn Whitney-Brown, Kathy Kelly, Phil Nazar, and Warren Pot for other details in this chapter.

[1] Roy was buried in the Jewish cemetery in Richmond Hill – the same cemetery where other friends (Ellen's father, and Baruch's wife, and Lieba Lesk) are buried. A few weeks earlier a Toronto teen had been brutally murdered by a gang of older boys who had demanded his cigarettes. We noticed that his grave was near Roy's. Nathan remarked to me that maybe I could write something about the contrasting lives of Roy and the boy, Matti. Roy had faced many limitations but had lived a long and, at least in recent years, very full and fruitful life. Matti's young life was so brutally cut off. Violent incidents in Toronto had become increasingly common in the preceding months. I wrote, "For the culture of violence [of which Matti's murder was just one manifestation] to change will need a pervasive re-birth of hope…The culture of peace exists – fragile but growing as individual people discover that it allows space to be truly human and to nurture the humanness of others…" The article appeared as an op-ed in the *Toronto Star* (February 7, 2000) with a photo of Roy proudly holding a fish he had just caught, and the title, "What kind of a society do we want?" The subtext was my conviction that people with disabilities can have a humanizing influence on our society. As it happened, it was seeing this article that led Toronto photographer Irene Borins Ash to contact us about photographing active seniors with intellectual disabilities.

[2] Lloyd and George also voted. George kept his political opinions to himself, but Lloyd let it be known that he was a staunch Conservative. As the party had been led for a time by Robert Stanfield, whose Nova Scotian family had founded Stanfield's Underwear, Lloyd was often teased by the assistants: "Was he wearing his Standfield's today?" He seemed to enjoy this very much.

[3] As a Woodery project, Joe C. had decals made with the characteristic designs of three or four core members and imposed them on plain white mugs and tiles. For the latter, they made wood frames so that the tiles could be used as trivets.

16. Drawing the Threads Together
The epigraph is from Jean Vanier, *Living Gently in a Violent World*, quoted in *Jean Vanier: Essential Writings*, ed. Carolyn Whitney-Brown (Darton, Longman and Todd, and Novalis, 2008).

[1] Some of the educational resources are described on the Resources page of L'Arche Canada's website.

Acknowledgements

It is a pleasure to be able to thank the many people who contributed to my writing this book. Its genesis is two-fold: When I edited L'Arche Canada's Weekly e-stories, short vignettes submitted by L'Arche people, I enjoyed occasionally writing something from my own daily experience when no submission came. Besides some of these pieces I have incorporated a few of the vignettes of others in this book. I hope I have properly acknowledged you. The book's other genesis lies in the urging of David Lesk, who met Mel and others at dinner parties I hosted in order to bring together a few Daybreak friends and friends from the small synagogue with which we had formed a connection. Ever since, David has commented to me periodically, "These are very interesting people. You should write about them!" And so I did.

I thank Jean Vanier who believed in this book from the time I first mentioned my ideas for it to him, and who graciously provided the Foreword.

Knowing I would need help to keep myself on track, I registered for a full-time graduate correspondence course at the Humber College School for Writers. As the tuition was expensive, I reached out to friends and family members to support me, partly through a Go-Fund-Me campaign. I was heartened by their generosity and confidence in me. You know who you are. I am deeply grateful to every one of you.

The well-known Canadian writer Helen Humphreys was my advisor for the course, faithfully commenting on and sending back chapters that I submitted every couple of weeks. I thank Helen also for suggesting the title of this book.

In the midst of some doubt about the value of the manuscript, I consulted Kevin Burns, a writer and editor who is familiar with L'Arche and Henri Nouwen. His advice, encouragement and confidence in me were of great help. I am deeply thankful to him.

Given the length of the book and the many people I mention, I turned to my friend Susan M.S. Brown, with whom I had worked on an anthology about Henri Nouwen. Besides making other suggestions, Susan did a copy edit and was meticulous, developing a detailed style sheet and list of names to assist with the publisher's final editing.

Especially, I thank the members of L'Arche and their families for allowing me to tell their stories and for their interest and encouragement. Many friends supplied details or read and commented on parts of the manuscript. I am grateful to each one. I have tried to acknowledge those who contributed to particular chapters in the chapter notes. If I missed mentioning you, I ask your forgiveness.

I thank architect Joe Lobko who sent me some maps of the Daybreak property, Jo Cork for allowing me to use her early napkin map, and Matt Rawlins for drawing the contemporary one in a similarly informal vein.

My long-time L'Arche mentor and friend Joe Egan faithfully read every chapter of every draft. I thank him and his wife Mary, who gave an especially close read of the final draft. Kathy Kelly and Joe Child and my teacher friends Jane and Tom Sagar were enthusiastic about this book in a way that gave me impetus to continue. Kathy and Joe read early drafts, unfailingly encouraging me in this project over many pots of tea. I thank Jane for suggesting the sequence for some material and Tom for his meticulous reading of the entire manuscript. Ben Carniol has helped me anticipate some of the decisions that come with publishing. Brian Cohen helped me with some legal considerations. Trish Glennon read early chapters and pointed out that some stories could be adapted for educational purposes – perhaps a task for the future.

For their encouragement, I thank Georgia and Gerry Helleiner, the Shabbat Study Group of which I am privileged to be a member, and the L'Arche friends who attend the Heliconian literary lectures, especially Mary Jane Kelley, who wanted me to write about Michael, and Sharon Walters, who corrected early chapters.

I am grateful for Warren Pot's patient support and his photographic and technical expertise in scanning more than a hundred photos. I thank those who helped me find photos and identify photographers, including Simon Rogers of The Henri Nouwen archives, and I thank Jacquie Boughner, for her artistic advice.

As I approached publishing, the professional advice of Karen Pascal of the Henri Nouwen Society, and of Sally Keefe Cohen and Kate Henderson was very helpful.

I also thank those who so kindly contributed commendations.

I was drawn to submit the manuscript to Darton, Longman and Todd because their website said that they publish "books with heart." I was thrilled when publisher David Moloney accepted the manuscript immediately. Working with DLT has been a pleasure. I am grateful to David for his publishing expertise and his unfailing courtesy, patience, and attention to detail, to Helen Porter (no relation), Managing Editor, for her care with the manuscript; to Will Parkes, Marketing Director; and to Ken Ruskin, Production Director.

I am pleased that the international presence of L'Arche is recognized in the simultaneous publication of this book in the United Kingdom, Canada and the United States. It seems appropriate that a Canadian-based company, Novalis, will have the North American rights to the book, a book that in its own way celebrates the legacy of a great Canadian, Jean Vanier. At Novalis, I thank Joe Sinasac, Simon Appolloni, and Anne Louise Mahoney.

Picture credits

The numbered photos below are courtesy of the people whose names are shown. All photos for which I do not give a credit are courtesy of L'Arche Daybreak.

1. Taken on Steve Newroth's camera
2. Steve Newroth
3. Taken on Phil Nazar's camera
4. Taken by Beth Porter or Julie Gittins
5. Beth Porter
6. Taken by one of the men in the breakfast group
7. Mary Bastedo
8. Leo Cameron, OSA
9. Steve Newroth
10. Beth Porter
11. Julie Gittins
12. Jeff Gilbreath
13. Warren Pot
14. Regina Spinola
15. Todd Rothrock
16. Carl MacMillan
17. Wendy Lywood
18. Beth Porter
19. Henri Nouwen Archives
20. Beth Porter
21. Beth Porter
22. Warren Pot
23. Warren Pot
24. Taken on Julie Gittins' camera
25. Rory Skelly

26. Mary Bee Baroody
27. Irene Borins Ash
28. Doug Wiebe
29. Beth Porter
30. Warren Pot
31. Beth Porter
32. Bill Wittman

Identity & Mission statements of L'Arche International

Our identity

We are people with and without intellectual disabilities, sharing life in communities belonging to an International Federation.

Mutual relationships and trust in God are at the heart of our journey together.

We celebrate the unique value of every person and recognize our need for one another.

Our mission is to...

Make known the gifts of people with intellectual disabilities, revealed through mutually transforming relationships.

Foster an environment in community that responds to the changing needs of our members, while being faithful to the core values of our founding story.

Engage in our diverse cultures, working together toward a more human society.

Approved March, 2007